D0378896

SELECTIVE ADMISSIONS IN HIGHER EDUCATION

Comment and Recommendations and Two Reports

A REPORT OF THE CARNEGIE COUNCIL
ON POLICY STUDIES IN HIGHER EDUCATION

*Comment and recommendations
by the Carnegie Council
on Policy Studies in Higher Education*

A report by Winton H. Manning

*A report by Warren W. Willingham and
Hunter M. Breland and Associates*

SELECTIVE ADMISSIONS IN HIGHER EDUCATION

Public Policy and Academic Policy

The Pursuit of Fairness in Admissions to Higher Education

The Status of Selective Admissions

Jossey-Bass Publishers

San Francisco • Washington • London • 1977

SELECTIVE ADMISSIONS IN HIGHER EDUCATION
The Carnegie Council on Policy Studies in Higher
Education, Winton H. Manning, Warren W. Willingham
& Hunter M. Breland & Associates

Copyright © 1977 by: The Carnegie Foundation
for the Advancement of Teaching

Jossey-Bass, Inc., Publishers
615 Montgomery Street
San Francisco, California 94111

Jossey-Bass Limited
28 Banner Street
London EC1Y 8QE

Copyright under International, Pan American, and Universal
Copyright Conventions. All rights reserved. No part of this
book may be reproduced in any form—except for brief quotation
(not to exceed 1,000 words) in a review or professional
work—without permission in writing from The Carnegie Foundation
for the Advancement of Teaching and the publishers.

*This report is issued by the Carnegie Council on Policy Studies
in Higher Education with headquarters at 2150 Shattuck Avenue,
Berkeley, California 94704.*

*Copies are available from Jossey-Bass, San Francisco,
for the United States, Canada, and Possessions.
Copies for the rest of the world are available from
Jossey-Bass, London.*

Library of Congress Catalogue Card Number LC 77-88501

International Standard Book Number ISBN 0-87589-361-9

Manufactured in the United States of America

DESIGN BY WILLI BAUM

FIRST EDITION

Code 7756

The Carnegie Council Series

82482

Contents

Preface

Admissions policy for selective schools has long been a concern within higher education. Recently, it has become an issue for public policy as well at the legislative, the administrative, and the judicial levels. Policy and procedures in this area are now (fall 1977) before the Supreme Court of the United States in the case of The Regents of the University of California v. Allan Bakke.

The Carnegie Council and the Carnegie Commission on Higher Education before it had been continuously interested in this issue and related matters.[1] It is out of this background of concern by the Commission and the Council that the Carnegie Council approaches the current issue.

To assist it in its deliberations, but much more importantly to provide bases for thoughtful consideration by others, the Council asked the Educational Testing Service (ETS), through the good offices of its president, William W. Turnbull, to address the problem from two standpoints—one, *how to think* about admissions to selective schools and the other, *what to know* about admissions policies and practices. The two resulting reports are included in this volume and form part of the review of the issues by the Council. The Council considers each report to be of great value—the first as a careful and sophisticated analysis of the issues, and the second as the best summary of the known facts. Each is an indispensable document for an examination of the problems and possible solutions to it.

The Council is deeply appreciative of the efforts of Mr.

---

[1] See, in particular, Carnegie Commission on Higher Education, *A Chance to Learn: An Action Agenda for Equal Opportunity in Higher Education* (1970), *The Purposes and the Performance of Higher Education in the United States: Approaching the Year 2000*, (1973a), *Priorities for Action: Final Report of the Carnegie Commission on Higher Education*, (1973b); and Carnegie Council on Policy Studies in Higher Education, *Making Affirmative Action Work in Higher Education: An Analysis of Institutional and Federal Policies with Recommendations* (1975).

Turnbull and of the three principal authors: Winton H. Manning is senior vice-president for development and research, ETS; Warren W. Willingham is executive director of program research, ETS; and Hunter M. Breland is research psychologist, ETS. In the course of preparation, a number of people generously reviewed and offered helpful advice regarding all or parts of the two papers. The ETS authors express appreciation to the following individuals for their useful contributions and constructive suggestions, though they share no responsibility for any shortcomings in the final content of the reports: Myrna C. Adams, director of alternative learning program, State University of New York College at Old Westbury; Bernard Anderson, The Wharton School of Business, University of Pennsylvania; Carlos H. Arce, Institute for Social Research, University of Michigan; Lawrence V. Barclay, College Entrance Examination Board; Derrick A. Bell, Harvard Law School; Theodore L. Bracken, assistant director, Consortium on Financing Higher Education; Lloyd C. Elam, president, Meharry Medical College; Sanford S. Elberg, dean of the graduate division, University of California at Berkeley; Margaret S. Gordon, associate director, Carnegie Council on Policy Studies in Higher Education; Fred A. Hargadon, dean of administration, Stanford University; Arturo Madrid, director, Spanish and Portuguese department, University of Minnesota; Thomas H. Meikle, Jr., dean, Graduate School of Medical Science, Cornell University Medical College; James Rosser, acting chancellor, New Jersey State Board of Higher Education; Albert G. Sims, vice-president, College Entrance Examination Board; Arthur L. Singer, Jr., vice-president, Alfred P. Sloan Foundation; James A. Thomas, associate dean, Law School, Yale University; W. Loren Williams, director of educational planning and development program, Medical College of Virginia; E. Belvin Williams, senior vice-president, Educational Testing Service.

August 1977

Members of the Carnegie Council on Policy Studies in Higher Education

Nolen M. Ellison
President
Cuyahoga Community College

E. K. Fretwell, Jr.
President
State University of New York College at Buffalo

Philip R. Lee, M.D.
Professor of Social Medicine
  and Director, Health Policy Program
University of California, San Francisco

Margaret L. A. MacVicar
Associate Professor of Physics
Massachusetts Institute of Technology

Rosemary Park
Professor of Education Emeritus
University of California, Los Angeles

James A. Perkins
Chairman of the Board
International Council for Educational Development

Alan Pifer
President
The Carnegie Foundation for the Advancement of Teaching

Joseph B. Platt
President
Claremont University Center

Lois D. Rice
Vice-President
College Entrance Examination Board

William M. Roth
Trustee of the Carnegie Institute
  of Washington, D.C.

Stephen H. Spurr
Professor
LBJ School of Public Affairs
University of Texas, Austin

Clark Kerr
Chairperson
Carnegie Council on Policy Studies in Higher Education

SELECTIVE ADMISSIONS IN HIGHER EDUCATION

Comment and Recommendations and Two Reports

A REPORT OF THE CARNEGIE COUNCIL
ON POLICY STUDIES IN HIGHER EDUCATION

All of us do not have equal talent, but all of us
should have an equal opportunity to develop our talents.

John F. Kennedy

Part One

Public Policy and Academic Policy

Comment and Recommendations

by the Carnegie Council
on Policy Studies
in Higher Education

Comment and Recommendations

We note, by way of introduction, that a number of admirable American ideals are involved in setting policies for admission to selective schools but that they are not fully compatible with each other. As a consequence, difficult choices must be made.

We place great emphasis on equality of opportunity, which means a strong concern for finding and developing potential talent, and thus a lesser emphasis upon simply rewarding already developed talent.

We stress consideration for the contributions a student can make to the education of his or her fellow students and prospectively to society after graduation rather than consideration alone for the preexisting academic merit of the student as measured by grades and test scores.

We emphasize consideration for the individual rather than for groups in their entirety, while considering special characteristics which have derived from the group and home and social environment from which the individual comes—specifically, from experience with educational disadvantage or with social discrimination, and knowledge of a minority culture, or direct acquaintance with and inclination to help correct important deficiencies in community services.

We accent institutional autonomy, limited by government control only when it is clearly necessary in the public interest.

We believe that following these several choices, rather than their opposites, will best serve both public and academic policy.

We recognize that many other persons, facing these same choices, have come to many different conclusions along the extended spectrum which reaches from adherence to a carefully calibrated totally meritocratic approach at one end to a precisely measured equality-of-result egalitarianism at the other.

We have sought, instead, a "golden mean" balance of considerations that draws on several American ideals rather than on any one alone; that rejects no basic American ideal in its entirety in the name of some other.

Few issues before the American people today place so many cherished aspirations in such uncertain balance or call as insistently for a blending and harmonizing of such divergent principles. It is in its actual choices among conflicting ideals that a nation defines its inner spirit; in its reconciliation of warring ideals within one body politic that it shows its internal strength.

In essence, our recommended approach to selective admissions, in the midst of many dilemmas and perplexities, is as follows:

- A fairer chance for all young Americans, offsetting, to the extent reasonably possible, the consequences of prior educational disadvantage and social discrimination, with preferment based on individual characteristics, effort, performance, and promise.
- Consideration for the contributions that students prospectively may make, not only to their own advancement, but also to their fellow students in college and their fellow men afterwards.

An institution of higher education with selective admissions is choosing a student body and not just judging a footrace based upon "objective" credentials when it makes its selections.

We distinguish three different situations. First, at the undergraduate level:

1. *Nonselective admissions.* These include admissions to most community colleges, which accept all high school graduates and sometimes persons over 18 without a high school diploma; and to a substantial number of liberal arts colleges and comprehensive colleges and universities.

2. *Selective admissions.* These policies cover a wide range of possibilities that vary from the highly selective to the moderately selective at all levels of higher education.

3. *Selective admissions at the graduate and professional schools that, in addition to (2), control or strongly influence entrance to a profession.* Illustrations are entrance to medicine and law through attendance at accredited medical and law schools,[1] but such admissions are also found in other professions or parts of professions, including veterinary medicine, dentistry, some university-level teaching, parts of engineering, and so forth.

We are concerned here with selective admissions (2) and particularly with selective admissions that influence entrance to a profession (3). The issues relating to the latter are especially important both because of the "gatekeeper" role of schools with such admissions policies in controlling entrance to the related professions and also because these schools have a great surplus of applicants over places. Both circumstances lead to intense public interest.

We estimate very roughly that actual admissions are distributed among these three categories about as follows:

    (1) nonselective admissions—40 percent

    (2) selective admissions—50 percent

    (3) selective admissions that control entrance to a profession—
       10 percent

There are, of course, variations in selectivity within each of these categories, and particularly within (2) and (3).

The question before us is: What approach to admissions should be followed by schools with selective admission policies and particularly by schools that serve as the nearly sole point of entrance to their professions? More specifically, we are concerned with what is good public policy and what is good academic policy governing such

---

[1] Most states require that persons attend an accredited school in the United States before taking the state licensing examination in medicine and law. About two percent (1.7) of Americans who become medical doctors attend foreign schools and then pass state tests to receive their licenses in the United States. (Noncitizens also do this in much more substantial numbers.) About 5 percent of Americans who become lawyers do so after attending an unaccredited law school or serving as an apprentice in a law office or taking a correspondence course (one state), depending upon state laws which vary, and then passing the bar exam.

admissions, and how the two may best be reconciled if their requirements diverge.

Public Policy

The public has a clear interest in access to higher education.

This interest begins with the creation of places for students. Most of the original colonial colleges, including Harvard, were established with public help. All private colleges have had indirect public aid, through tax exemptions, in their supply of student places throughout our national history, and many now have direct aid as well through the federal government and 40 of the states. The land-grant movement was initiated by the federal government in order, in large part, to create places in college for farmers and mechanics. All of the states have established and supported public institutions of higher education.

Many of the resulting places (we have estimated 40 percent of them) are open on a nonselective basis (for persons with a high school diploma but sometimes not that). Society thus has a special interest in the criteria used in filling the selective places (60 percent of the total); in particular, in assuring that they be filled on the basis of fair and reasonable institutional policies and procedures, and that no one is subject to discrimination on the basis of race or sex or religion or ethnic origin.

The federal government has established a policy of "affirmative action" applied on behalf of persons subject in their employment to practices of discrimination, particularly women and minorities. The principles of affirmative action translated from employment to educational practice may be said to imply:

1. That no policies or practices may continue to lead to discrimination against members of such groups,
2. That special efforts should be made to recruit members of these groups,
3. That compensatory education should be available to such persons when deemed helpful,
4. That special financial assistance and counseling should be provided when needed, and
5. That goals may be set against which progress can be measured.

These rules for action are based on the accepted principles of equality of treatment and of equality of opportunity.

The public, we believe, has additional interests in the case of admission to the gatekeeper schools which largely determine the composition of the professions and thus affect the professional services available to society. These schools should not knowingly admit, and should never confer degrees upon persons who they believe will be incompetent in practicing the profession; otherwise the consumers of the services provided by such persons may be unnecessarily injured. These schools should also make every effort to admit, and to graduate, persons who will meet the needs of the public for service, and these needs are both quite diverse and subject to change.[2] No geographical community of reasonable size and no substantial group of people, however composed, should be deprived of access to essential services because these schools deliberately did not admit and graduate persons with the ability and the interest to provide these services.[3]

Society has other concerns that apply to all of higher education. We are a pluralistic society, yet we are one nation. Individuals within each identifiable group should have a fair chance to rise to positions of leadership, including persons within those groups where such a possibility has not normally existed in the past. "The object is to bring into action that mass of talents which lies buried in poverty in every country."[4] In more modern times, the concept of poverty might be broadened to include other forms of deprivation, including those resulting from racism and sexism. Models they may emulate are important to the young; and mentors out of similar backgrounds who can provide special understanding are important along the way. These leaders and these models of advancement and these under-

[2] Medical schools, for example, train persons to teach, to conduct research, to practice a specialty, to carry on a general practice, to serve as a member of the staff in a community hospital in an urban center or as a single individual in a rural community, or to serve in other ways. Many different kinds of people with many different kinds of training serve in many different ways.

[3] Throughout American history there has been an interest in having enough trained teachers at first the elementary and later at the secondary level, and properly distributed geographically; thus service to the public is an old element in American educational performance.

[4] Thomas Jefferson, letter to M. Correa, November 25, 1817 in Honeywell (1931), p. 148.

standing mentors drawn from throughout the many strands of our society are of importance to the overall quality of a college community as a place of education, of a profession as a means of service, of a church as an effective source of ethical teaching and moral inspiration, of a political entity as an expression of concern for and fair play toward all its citizens, of the nation as a whole as a means to serve the general welfare.

Potential talent must be able to rise from all sources in society and thus must be seen as actually rising in the form of qualified individuals, not in the form of rigid numbers assigned in advance. It is individual talent that should be recognized and given a chance to advance in accordance with the effort that accompanies it. This is the way to encourage motivation, to draw forth energies, to inspire the desire to compete and excel. Members of all groups must know that advancement is possible but not guaranteed. Able persons from all groups must be given opportunities to contribute to the progress of society and thus also to its "domestic tranquility" and its "general welfare." When groups that have suffered discrimination are heavily underrepresented in the privileged roles resulting from selectivity in higher education, there are grounds for making special efforts to find, prepare, and admit qualified individuals from such groups.

Higher education, as one of the great sorting devices of society, has an opportunity and a responsibility, and particularly so in all of its institutions with selective admissions, to identify and to advance talent wherever it may and can be found. This is very much in the public interest of a democratic and pluralistic nation. Higher education has a great affirmative responsibility to advance this dimension of the general welfare. Nowhere is the responsibility more grave than in the gatekeeper schools that lead to the most visible and the most prestigious of all the professions—professions that yield many of our community, regional, and national leaders. These schools stand in a very special position today to make effective in practice the most fundamental principles of the American nation while at the same time meeting the individual's claims to equal protection.

Academic Policy

The admissions policies of institutions of higher education are varied and complex.

For institutions with selective admissions, the composition of their student bodies is of great, sometimes dominating, importance. This composition is determined, first of all, by those who apply to them (and many have strong programs of recruitment) and, second, by those among them who are admitted and then actually enroll. The student body reflects and expresses the special identity of the college, serves as an attraction for future applicants, affects the hiring and retention of individual faculty members who have preferences for the type of students with whom they wish to work, determines the composition of the alumni body and thus influences support of the college. For nearly all colleges, the student body is the major reason for existence; for most colleges, it is also the major source of contributions to society. Admissions policies, as a consequence, variously reflect academic, economic, and political considerations.

The United States prides itself on the great diversity of its colleges; on the lack of conformity among them. This diversity offers prospective students a wide range of choices, provides society with graduates with a broad range of types of training and academic experiences, gives wide latitude for experimentation among colleges to see what works best, affords the individual college a special sense of concern for the students it selected on its own, attracts the attachments of alumni and friends, gives the communities in which the colleges are located special flavors, and reflects the pluralism of American society. One college may tend to concentrate on the all-around student, another on rural youth, another on persons with high scientific capability, and so on.

Consequently, since the diversity of colleges depends so substantially on the diversity of the composition of their student bodies, and since this diversity is a national asset, colleges should have, and historically have had, very substantial autonomy in setting their own admissions policies. The exercise of this prerogative of autonomy has not excluded responsiveness by colleges to public need as demonstrated most recently by substantial expansion of programs to meet changed social, economic, and demographic requirements. This is not to suggest that no restraints should be placed upon colleges but rather that such restraints upon institutional autonomy should only be imposed when there exists a substantial public interest that cannot be served in other ways. The importance of preserving institutional diversity argues strongly for restraint by state and national governments in attempting to control admissions procedures and policies.

Institutions with selective admissions policies may be very selective—taking, for example, only one applicant in ten; or only slightly selective—taking, for example, nine applicants out of ten. They vary even more in the considerations they take into account and the weights they give to these factors. Combining the degree of selectivity and choice of the weighting of considerations, the possible admissions policies are almost infinite in number.

We set out below, in outline form, some of the considerations variously taken into account, whether one agrees with them or not:

Prior scholastic grades and rank in class

Test scores—both aptitude and achievement

Special academic interests and abilities—for example, in some branch of science

Special abilities—for example, ability to play in the band or the orchestra, skill in the performing arts, adeptness in competitive sports, talent for peer group leadership

Special interests—for example, in community service

Special identities—for example, by religion or by alumni percentage

Special personal characteristics—for example, proven ability to rise above obstacles including language barriers, poor prior schooling, inadequate home environment, social prejudice, physical handicaps; or, as another example, successful past work experience

Contributions to diversity of the student community—for example, by state or nation of origin, by occupations and incomes of parents, by cultural backgrounds

Potential contributions to a profession—for example, by interest in serving in a neglected area or in a neglected specialty

Contributions to a campus tradition—for example, by taking students from a particular locality or ethnic group or stratum of society

Contributions to the political or economic or community needs of the institution—for example, by taking children or friends of a political leader, or a trustee, or a leading donor, or a member of the profession served, or a faculty member.

What may be a positive consideration for one institution may be a negative one for another—for example, an out-of-state student may be viewed as a special asset by a private college attempting to build a national image but as a potential embarrassment to a public college sensitive to legislative preferences for service to citizens of the state.

We should like to comment on several of these considerations:

1. Grades and tests looked at together are more predictive of subsequent academic performance than grades alone or tests alone.[5]

2. Grades are less helpful than they once were because of the all-pervasive grade inflation; so also are letters of personal recommendation because they are no longer so confidential.

3. Traditional measures like grades and test scores are useful but are usually not sufficient as a sole basis for action. They are best at determining at one end those applicants who are likely to distinguish themselves academically, and at the other end those likely to fail—and failure is costly to the student and to the institution. They are not suited for fine tuning in between—a 525 score is not clearly better than a 500 score; and the same student may make these two different scores when taking equivalent tests. Yet tests are often used for making fine distinctions. Reasons for this include: it is easier to make policy on what are seemingly precise and objective grounds; such policies are easier to explain (although not easy to justify if challenged); such policies tell potential applicants in advance whether they should apply or not; such policies are easy to administer—they can be applied by clerks or by a computer; such policies give admission officials and others a score card that they can display to trustees, alumni and other competitive admissions officers —"This year we did better than last year" and "My school did better than your school." Fine tuning with test scores can look attractive, but it is also a misuse of tests. Used properly, test scores are of

---

[5] More generally, Torsten Husen (1976) has noted that: "Extensive empirical research tells us that at most half of individual differences in educational attainments are attributable to purely intellectual factors. The rest may be attributed to motivation, interest, perseverance, health, and, of course, home background" p. 413). Some of these other factors, however, have proven difficult to assess prior to admission. These other factors also, of course, affect earlier grades and entrance test scores.

enormous value. Used improperly, they are a bureaucratic curse.

4. Colleges often choose to build academic and social communities through their admissions policies. These communities are themselves educational mechanisms, for students learn from each other.[6] Achieving diversity in student bodies is not only a legitimate but can also be a highly important aspect of the admissions process. Getting to know persons of different backgrounds and cultures is advantageous to citizenship training; it can also provide a helpful background for working with others with understanding and sensitivity in later life. The presence of persons who, because of their origins and experiences, have different perspectives on society and different viewpoints about it can add, under proper circumstances, to the quality of class discussion in many courses—particularly in the social sciences and the humanities. Such persons can help educate their classmates about American society by bringing to bear minority experiences and minority cultures.

5. Professional schools often in the past have been too little concerned with providing professionals who will offer a balanced set of services to society. In medicine, for example, there have been too many surgeons and too few general practitioners, and too many doctors located in wealthy suburbs and too few in rural areas and inner cities. Federal policy has consequently sought to intervene to redress these imbalances. In the profession of education, as another example, too few graduates have been trained to participate in remedial education, in dual language instruction, or in special techniques to aid the handicapped.

6. Too many favors have been given by too many institutions, including professional schools, to those with special influence. Such actions do not meet the test of fairness, however realistic they may be as specific political actions.

7. Admission is often different at the graduate level than at the undergraduate. There is more of an academic record to review and the academic standards to be met are usually at a higher level, particularly for the Ph.D. degree. Consequently, it is reasonable that past

[6] "The two most powerful determinants producing change in the undergraduate and alumni samples were their roommates and the intellectual atmosphere and traditions of the college." Douglas H. Heath (1968, p. 197), Feldman and Newcome (1969, Chap. 8), Chickering (1969, Chaps. 11, 13).

academic performance should be weighed more heavily. Admission to a science program is often different from that to a creative arts program, particularly at the graduate level. Ability to pursue science is much more precisely measurable than ability to follow the creative arts, and academic prerequisites are more specifically important—for example, one particular course may be absolutely essential to science students in a way that no particular course may be essential for the creative arts. This variation by field is one reason why admission to graduate programs is often made essentially at the departmental level. Another reason is that faculty members often like to choose personally the graduate students with whom they wish to work.

8. The gatekeeper schools are distinctive in at least three major respects: (a) they must be much more careful not to admit students who lack the ability to practice the profession with competency and integrity; (b) they must be much more conscious of the desirability to supply graduates who will meet the varied needs of the public; and (c) their graduates face uniform tests after graduation (bar exams, National Board of Medicine exams, and so forth), and the results of these tests are added up as a way of rating the individual schools—thus these uniform standards erected on top of the degree programs reflect back on admissions policies and practices. These schools may have a quite legitimate interest in special persons with special characteristics, for example, those who have shown a strong interest in community service, or those who have shown they can face adversity and conquer it through the force of their own personalities —for these characteristics relate directly to potential service within a profession. Different professional schools, of course, look for different things. A medical school, for example, that specializes in preparing research specialists and instructors of medicine will look for a different type of student than one concentrating on preparing doctors for family practice. The gatekeeper schools must be particularly careful to be fair among applicants given their influence over entry to a profession and to be considerate of the needs of the public for the same reason.

Public and academic policy will diverge if, for example, public policy were to lead to a reduction of academic standards, or if it interfered too greatly with professional judgments; or if academic policy obstructed affirmative action, or was not otherwise fair and reasonable. But they need not diverge. The challenges are to apply public policy without undue interference with academic judgments and concerns, and for institutions to satisfy public policy without loss of academic standards. Meeting these challenges calls for the most careful consideration, and full attention to complexities and differences and even fine distinctions. There are no universal, mechanical solutions.

Recommendations for Public Policy and Academic Policy

We now turn to our specific suggestions for policy affecting admissions to selective schools at both the undergraduate and graduate levels:

1. These schools should adhere to a policy of affirmative action in educational practices, as outlined earlier:
   a. That no policies or practices may discriminate against members of groups subject to discrimination,
   b. That special efforts should be made to recruit members of these groups,
   c. That compensatory education should be available to such persons when there is reason to believe that undeveloped potential can be realized by providing it,
   d. That special financial assistance and counseling should be provided when needed, and
   e. That goals may be set against which progress can be measured.
2. Race or background in a non-English language home should be considered in individual cases where it (a) reflects prior adverse social discrimination, or (b) contributes to prior educational disadvantage, or (c) involves direct knowledge of special cultural patterns and experiences, or (d) indicates, along with other evidence, the probability of subsequent provision of specially needed services to society.[7] The first and second considerations (a

---

[7] Students from lower-income families are more likely to enter general practice than those from higher-income families, who tend to enter specialities. (Gough and Ducker, 1977, pp. 31-43). We are dealing here, of course, with probabilities. There is no way to be certain in advance what a student will do after graduation, let alone any way to guarantee it.

and b) are based on the principles of equality of treatment and equality of opportunity, the third (c) on institutional interest in diversity in the student community, and the fourth (d) on the needs of society for service.

We emphasize racial experience, not race per se; and experience in a non-English language home, not "heritage" or "surname" per se. Thus we say *in individual cases*. Most persons with a minority racial background or raised in a non-English language home now have one or more of the four special characteristics which we believe warrant consideration, but not all do—some have not experienced prior adverse social discrimination, have not been educationally disadvantaged, have had little or no contact with a minority culture, and have no interest in special services to society.

We note, also, that persons without a racial or other minority identification may have one or more of these same four characteristics, particularly (b), (c), and (d). These characteristics are not dependent only on race or other minority status, although they are often associated with it.

Race or other minority status should be only one of several dimensions considered as aspects of prior disadvantage or adverse discrimination, as one of several indicators of prospective contributions to the diversity and quality of the academic experience for other students, and as one of several intimations of intention to serve society in neglected areas.[8] Thus individuals from the majority group may also warrant special consideration depending upon their background circumstances.

3. No student should be admitted who cannot meet the general academic standards set for all students. These standards should be set, through assessment of prior grades and test scores and personal qualifications, at the minimum level at which there is a reasonable chance of success in completing the course work without reduction in academic or professional standards. Race, other minority status, or sex is clearly not a consideration here. One source of help

---

[8] We recognize that these categories of factors for consideration make an already very complex process of admissions much more complex; but many colleges and schools long have taken them into account.

in determining this level is to look at the level of, say, 10 years ago when competition for admissions was less intense but competent graduates and practitioners were being trained. When there are very large numbers of applicants for a limited number of student places, the cut-off point in many gatekeeper professional schools exceeds such a reasonable minimum level as a device to eliminate substantial numbers of applicants. The pool of applicants from which specific selections can be made is almost certainly larger than the pool now receiving individual consideration by many schools.

4. No numerical quota for any component should be set, but rather goals should be established that may change over time as conditions change and may be exceeded or remain unmet depending on the composition of the body of applicants in any one year.[9]

5. Financial aid should be provided to students from low-income families to attract them in sufficient numbers into the "pool" of applicants within which choices will be made.

6. All applicants should be processed through the same set of procedures to assure that they are looked at together and not separately, that an effective student body is being assembled and not separate quotas being met, and each person is being evaluated on his or her own merits.

7. Procedures should apply everywhere which already apply in a number of schools, namely, that members of the faculty, particularly in the case of gatekeeper schools, themselves participate actively in the admissions processes and take responsibility for the decisions, with reasonable delegation of authority to review and

---

[9] We distinguish a quota and a goal as follows:

Quota	*Goal*
An assigned share	An intention
A proportional result	An aim
A fixed division of numbers	A purpose
Must be met	Try to meet
Precise—no variation below or above	Subject to variation depending on circumstances
Rigid	Subject to change over time
Permanent	Can be abandoned when no longer needed

We believe it is important to note and to maintain these differences.

classify individual applications. Substantial additional funds may be necessary to supplement the faculty (and the as isting staff) to make this possible in some schools. In the absence of fully objective criteria, application of professional judgment is the best available approach.

8. Schools should be given maximum latitude in exercising their judgments about the admission of individual students with respect for the professional expertise involved in the judgments, for the complexity of the characteristics desired in the students, for the detailed and changing needs for graduates of the varying programs in different localities served, and in consideration of the wisdom of encouraging diversity among the schools.

Autonomy for higher education is a basic principle, but we note that its acceptance in practice can be reinforced by colleges and schools through careful concern for their professional integrity and thoughtful attention to the needs of society. We suggest the following:

a. The public trust, in both publicly and privately supported institutions, is given primarily and most obviously to the governing board. The governing board itself, with faculty, student, and administrative advice, should set general admissions policies related to institutional missions and to public policy, and should review admissions procedures and the results of admissions policies.

b. Statements of policies and procedures should be made available to the public.

9. The judgment of courts, legislatures, or government officials should not replace professional judgment except when clearly required by the public interest. Rigid and simplistic formulas externally imposed should, in any event, be avoided. Student bodies should be chosen on a multidimensional basis and not as the result of a unidimensional contest to be won or lost on the basis of a single (and imprecise) measure. Also, the nation changes, each profession changes, the needs of society change. Policies and practices which may be desirable in this period of transition may be less desirable or take on new forms in later periods.

Conclusion

We hope that race and other minority status will be much less of a distinguishing feature of American society in the future as we overcome the consequences of past discrimination in education and elsewhere. Race or other minority status would thus become less germane to achieving diversity in student bodies and to ensuring prospective service to the public. We hope that the current period of transition will not last longer than until the end of the current century—less than one generation. Changes will be taking place in the schools and colleges and society in the meantime, and policies should be adjusted as these changes occur. Significant progress has already been made within higher education;[10] but there is still a substantial way to go. Race or background in a non-English language home will, over time, become less important considerations to the extent that American society becomes more just and more integrated. In the meantime, in making selective admissions to institutions of higher education, consideration of special characteristics that often derive from such backgrounds is a major means for American society in its efforts to become more just and more integrated.

References

Carnegie Commission on Higher Education. *A Chance to Learn: An Action Agenda for Equal Opportunity in Higher Education.* New York: McGraw-Hill, 1970.

Carnegie Commission on Higher Education. *The Purposes and Performance of Higher Education in the United States: Approaching the Year 2000.* New York: McGraw-Hill, 1973a.

Carnegie Commission on Higher Education. *Priorities for Action: Final Report of the Carnegie Commission on Higher Education.* New York: McGraw-Hill, 1973b.

Carnegie Council on Policy Studies in Higher Education. *Making Affirmative Action Work in Higher Education: An Analysis of Institutional and Federal Policies with Recommendations.* San Francisco: Jossey-Bass, 1975.

[10] College enrollment among those aged 16–21 is now 52 percent female, as compared with 51 percent of the civilian population in this age group; blacks account for 10.5 percent of enrollment, compared with 13 percent of the civilian population in this age group. (U.S. Bureau of the Census, "School Enrollment—Social and Economic Characteristics of Students: October 1976 (Advance Report)," Series P-20, No. 309, Washington, D.C., July 1977, p. 2 and Table 6).

Chickering, A. W. *Education and Identity.* San Francisco: Jossey-Bass, 1969.

Feldman, K.A., and Newcomb, T. M. *The Impact of College on Students.* Vol. 1. San Francisco: Jossey-Bass, 1969.

Gough, H. G., and Ducker, D. G. "Social Class in Relation to Medical School Performance and Choice of Specialty." *Journal of Psychology,* May 1977, *96,* 31–43.

Heath, D. H. *Growing Up in College.* San Francisco: Jossey-Bass, 1968.

Honeywell, R. J. *The Educational Work of Thomas Jefferson.* Cambridge, Mass.: Harvard University Press, 1931.

Husen, T. "Problems of Securing Equal Access to Higher Education: The Dilemma Between Equality and Excellence," *Higher Education,* November 1976, 5 (4), 413.

U.S. Bureau of the Census. "School Enrollment—Social and Economic Characteristics of Students: October 1976," *Current Population Reports,* ser. P-20, no. 309 (Advance Report). Washington, D.C.: July 1977.

Part Two

The Pursuit of Fairness
in Admissions
to Higher Education

Winton H. Manning
*Senior Vice-President for
Development and Research,
Educational Testing Service*

1

The Points at Issue

A brief word concerning the case of *Bakke* v. *The Regents of the University of California* may be useful, despite the wide attention given to it in the press and other media. So much has been written about *Bakke,* that skeletal facts of the case may have become obscured.

The plaintiff, Allan Bakke, a Caucasian, applied for admission to the Medical School of the University of California at Davis in both 1973 and 1974.

There were 2,644 applicants for the 1973 entering class and 3,737 for the 1974 class. There were only 100 places available each year, of which 16 were filled under the special admission program. In the latter program, separate standards of admission were applied, resulting in the acceptance of minority applicants who, Bakke claimed, were less qualified for the study of medicine than he.

Allan Bakke was denied admission to the University of California Medical School at Davis in both years and was not admitted to any other medical school. He brought suit against the University, alleging that he was a victim of invidious discrimination because of his race, in violation of the equal protection clause of the Fourteenth Amendment of the United States Constitution.

The trial court held that the special admissions program used by the University's medical school discriminated against Bakke on the basis of race and was, therefore, unconstitutional under the Fourteenth Amendment. The California Supreme Court affirmed that portion of the trial court's decision holding the special admissions program unconstitutional. The United States Supreme

Court granted the University's petition for *certiorari* and is expected to hear the case in the fall of 1977.

The major issues facing the U.S. Supreme Court are:

1. Should all discrimination on the basis of race be treated the same way under the Fourteenth Amendment;

2. If discrimination against a majority group or discrimination in favor of a minority group is to be treated in some different way, what test should be applied to determine whether the discrimination contravenes the Fourteenth Amendment; and

3. If the traditional "strict scrutiny" test is applied, can the Board of Regents demonstrate the existence of a "compelling state interest"—one that is more than a merely "legitimate" or "lawful" state interest—and prove that the admissions process that excluded Bakke was the least restrictive alternative available to meet that compelling state interest?

In the weeks that followed the decision by the U.S. Supreme Court to hear the case, an increasing torrent of articles, conferences, scholarly papers, and legal briefs have begun to appear. The importance of the case for society in general—especially including constitutional law, affirmative action programs in employment, and the operations of colleges and universities—can scarcely be overestimated. At the level of practical affairs in the administration of a university the matter is captured well by the following excerpt from a release by the Stanford University News Service describing the dilemma facing colleges and universities:

> Stanford may file an amicus brief with the U.S. Supreme Court on the impact which upholding the California Supreme Court's decision in the *Bakke* case could have on minority admissions, President Richard W. Lyman disclosed Monday, Feb. 14.
>
> Clad in shirtsleeves, he spoke through a bullhorn to about 250 minority students and their supporters on the Inner Quadrangle in front of his office.
>
> "The *Bakke* case, if simply sustained on the same basis that the California Supreme Court used, will put us all in deep trouble," he declared. "I devoutly hope that will not happen.

"I don't know what the (U.S.) Supreme Court ought to decide. I'm not a lawyer, I'm not a Supreme Court justice, and these are not easy issues. And anybody who tells you they are is misleading you.

"But I do know that they ought to take into account the effects of simply confirming what the California State Supreme Court said. I hope that if they feel they must decide in favor of the plaintiff (Bakke) as an individual, that they will find the narrowest possible grounds, and enable us to continue what has been one of the most important educational efforts of my lifetime, certainly, and I guess that means of yours."

After reading both opinions Lyman said, "It's not an easy matter" to decide but "the majority ... makes a fundamental mistake in arguing that there are many ways other than those pursued by UC-Davis by which one could achieve a satisfactory or a constructive representation ... of minority students.

"We don't have much evidence on that, but what little evidence we have leads me to believe that there are not many ways by which we can do that and live with the rest of the majority opinion."

Referring to the *Bakke* decision, Lyman said the California Supreme Court decision "speaks only to the admissions practices of public institutions in the State of California. That decision does not control our admissions practices, as is evidenced by our behavior since that decision was announced, and we have not taken any steps to change our admissions practices in response to it."

While it is difficult to predict the outcome of any U.S. Supreme Court review of the *Bakke* decision Lyman said, "We will, to the extent that we can, " continue to pursue our policies and practices meant to satisfy the aspirations which we have set for ourselves in this most important and sensitive area."

This paper examines the policy issues that are at the root of the *Bakke* case, from the standpoint of education rather than the law.

The central issue is whether racial or ethnic minority status may be explicitly considered in the process of admitting students to higher education.

The main argument of the paper is that *race is relevant* within the admissions process, because important educational and professional objectives will not be attainable unless consideration is given to the minority status of applicants as college and universities go about the task of making admission decisions. Nevertheless, an appreciation of the nature of the admissions process itself also suggests that *how* "race" is considered may be very important in creating a fair admissions policy. Admission to college or graduate school, it is argued, is not a "contest" but rather a complex system of "sponsored" admission, in which responsible educators seek to advance the objectives of the professions and of scholarly research through admissions policies aiming at optimal uses of human talent. Important distinctions, as between determinations of *admissibility* and *selection* among minimally qualified applicants bear a relationship to the question of how *race* may be fairly considered. Moreover, it is also clear that there are ways in which the consideration of *race*— indeed of nearly any human characteristic—could defeat the aims of responsible admissions policy. What is argued here is that race can be a relevant consideration in admissions decisions, when sensitively used within a complex, sequentially ordered decision process, whose *fairness* must be judged in terms of the operation and objectives of the entire admissions system, rather than as an abstract issue.

2

The Central Role of Values in Pursuing Fairness in Admissions

The issues raised in *DeFunis* v. *Odegaard* and now joined in *Bakke* are basic questions, whose roots extend downward into the bedrock of our moral and social philosophy, and outward into the economic and technological foundations of American society. At the center of these issues stands the painful question: Should universities adopt explicit policies that grant preferential treatment to racial and ethnic minorities? Pursuing preferential admissions policies would seem to be inconsistent with our deeply held convictions regarding individuality, merit, and personal responsibility. Failing to pursue such policies seems to reveal moral and ethnic blindness on the part of the majority to the historic and contemporary condition of racial minorities in American society, and is therefore perceived to be contrary to humanitarian and egalitarian themes within our national experience.

Questions about the fairness of their policies are especially poignant ones for colleges and universities which, rightly or wrongly, have long been seen by Americans as a primary force for constructing a more just and wholesome society. Richard Wynn (1962, p. 211) has observed that "Schools are the self-corrective mechanism of a democracy; in fitting the young to the culture the converse question of the fitness of the culture for youth is forever implied." Questions about the fairness of policies pursued by higher educational institutions, no less than the schools of which Wynn was speaking, have particular salience. It is to education that youth first turns to be instructed in the meaning of our constitutional guarantees of due process and equal protection. In the eyes of youth, the fitness of our institutions is bound up with the question of the fitness of university admission policies in securing and maintaining these constitutional rights. How the issue of fairness in admissions is resolved will have important consequences for the ability of colleges and universities to serve as instruments of social change and as agents for opening opportunity for minorities and others who have long suffered from discrimination in education and employment.

Kingsley Davis (1962) succinctly states that "there are two conditions that produce class mobility: inequality of rewards and equality of opportunity." The aim of securing the larger, more satisfying rewards attendant upon completing graduate or professional study is obvious. But it is precisely the question of determining the means by which "equality of opportunity" is pursued that lies at the heart of the problem. Is "equality of opportunity" to be defined in terms of individual merit, in which rewards are attained only by those who earn them through their individual efforts? Or, does "equality of opportunity" require taking into account the effects of poverty, prejudice and discrimination with which racial and ethnic minorities have for generations been burdened? This is an issue of group versus individual equity, raised by *Bakke*, but which, far from being new, has been with us from the beginning of our efforts to insure that the constitutional guarantees of "equal protection of the laws" are realities for all citizens.

Under the law, it is generally understood that equal protection does not mean that all must be treated identically, or even similarly, but that all must be treated similarly who are *similarly situated*, in the sense that they constitute a defined class or group. But, it is also clear that how one determines whether two persons are similarly situated is not always, or even usually, self-evident. Indeed, in the last analysis, all of us are different persons, bound up in our individual histories and current problems. "What is required, in other words, is a material or substantive principle, a standard by which to determine when the differences between individuals justify treating them

differently.... But the material principles which determine whether
individuals are similarly or differently situated necessarily rest upon
value choices" (italics added; Sandalow, 1975). The search for a
solution to this problem—the principle by which individual and
group equity is synthesized—in the long run depends upon how one
resolves the issue of choice among competing values.

These value choices will be addressed by the United States
Supreme Court within the framework of the Constitution and the
laws of the nation. Except incidentally, it is not the purpose of this
discussion to examine the constitutionality of special minority
admissions programs; rather the aim is to examine these value choices
from the perspective of educational policy and experience, particularly as reflected in the functioning of the nation's graduate and
professional schools.

The usefulness of approaching these value dilemmas from the
standpoint of education arises in part from the observation of Justice
Holmes that the "life of the law has not been logic; it has been
experience." Admission to college or university is an integral part of
the educational process, and the courts should intrude no further into
that process than is necessary in order to safeguard essential human
rights and legal principles. Correspondingly, the experience of
education in wrestling with the perplexing value choices implicit in
the issue of individual versus group equity are relevant to the court's
deliberations, as well as to the illumination of the problem among
the interested public.

3

Institutions and Individuals in the Admissions Process

Admission to graduate and professional schools clearly represents access to the functional rather than the symbolic values of education; that is, the benefits of education in a medical school, law school, or other graduate program are most often directly used in accomplishing a *purpose*, rather than primarily as a symbol of *status*. The student who is admitted and successfully completes the educational program and other requirements functionally uses the specific knowledge and skills he or she has acquired in the practice of a profession: in teaching, in research, or in some other comparable professional employment. Such a career naturally brings with it rewards of prestige, status, and substantial earnings, and hence entering it is a highly desired objective. In many fields the number of persons aspiring to enter such careers greatly exceeds the *aggregate* number of places in graduate and professional schools. This problem is complicated by the unequal distribution of applicants among institutions, in which some programs of real or presumed superiority attract 10, 20, or even 50 times the number of applicants that the institution can accept.[1]

It is not altogether artificial, therefore, to draw a parallel between the admissions process and a game in which many compete, but few win. Although the immediate reward for the applicant may

[1] Primary attention in this paper is given to the problems of admission to graduate and professional schools, but the observations, analyses, and recommendations are, in most instances, also applicable to selective undergraduate institutions.

be admission to a program, the ultimate goal is entry into a desired profession with all that this implies.

Furthermore, for both majority and minority youth, graduate and professional education is increasingly regarded as a means for gaining the upward social mobility that undergraduate study once more reliably conferred. In a survey a few years ago, Baird (1973) reported that in 1961, 76 percent of seniors had plans to continue their education but in 1971, 93 percent said they had such plans. Furthermore, evidence from several studies suggests that black students have higher degree aspirations than whites (Baird, 1974). With intensification of these aspirations for postbaccalaureate study, concern about the admissions process itself has grown apace. Increasingly, students have questioned the procedures and the admissions decisions made by graduate and professional schools, and they have demanded greater accountability and disclosure on the part of all institutions and agencies connected with the admission process. On the whole, institutions have responded to these concerns, albeit slowly, and most institutions are sincerely endeavoring to maintain a reasonable balance between the applicants' desires and the institution's responsibilities.

Nevertheless, at a more fundamental level, one can distinguish between two different norms or idealized modes of admission. These may be described as "contest admission" and "sponsored admission"—concepts which are parallel to the framework developed by Ralph Turner (1961) in analyzing the modes of social ascent through education.

Contest admission is conceived as a system in which admission to the college or university is a prize attained by the applicant's own efforts. It is, to use Turner's (1961) description, "like a sporting event in which many compete for a few prizes. The contest is judged to be fair only if all players compete on an equal footing. Victory must be won solely by one's efforts. Enterprise, initiative, perseverance and craft are admirable qualities if they allow a person, initially at a disadvantage, to triumph."

By contrast sponsored admission rejects the pattern of the contest and substitutes a controlled selection process. "In this process ... (those) who are best qualified to judge merit, *call* those individuals ... who have the appropriate qualities" (Turner, 1961). In sponsored admission, individuals do not *win* matriculation, but rather are *inducted* into an educational program that leads to a professional career, following *selection* by competent sponsors or judges.

In practice, these ideal types—contest and sponsored admission—probably never occur naturally, and elements of both are discernible both in the rhetoric and the diverse practices of higher education institutions. It is nevertheless clear that at the graduate and professional level the predominant mode is that of sponsored admission, which has as its objective that of making the optimal use of the human resources of talent that are available to the institution. In a sense, the adoption of a philosophy of sponsored admission is inevitable, given the apprentice-master relationship that is implicit in the postgraduate educational enterprise itself. At its most fundamental level education is concerned with the transmission of a cultural heritage of knowledge, and with the development of inner resources of the individual to use this knowledge in satisfying and productive ways. At the center of this process is the relationship between student and teacher, and in the choice of which students to educate the judgment of the faculty is critical. Consequently, the institution usually views the admissions process as one in which applicants judged to have the desired attributes are "called" or selected, according to rational principles developed out of long experience with this task of education by faculty and professional admissions officers.

By contrast, most students (and some faculty) often see the admission process as a contest, in which "the most satisfactory outcome is not necessarily a victory of the most able, but of the most deserving, ... (and) victory by a person of moderate intelligence accomplished through the use of common sense, craft, enterprise, daring and successful risk-taking is more appreciated than the victory of the most intelligent or the best-educated" (Turner, 1961, p. 123). Those who view admissions as a contest err in a number of ways, not the least of which is that of transplanting the norm of the marketplace to the realm of education. Opposition to sponsored admission beguiles some persons because they confuse the exercise of responsible judgment by those experienced in educational selection with notions of privilege, secrecy, and arbitrariness, which are as much an enemy of sponsored admission as of contest admission.

Sponsored admission, it can be argued, assures even greater attention to elements of fairness in educational due process than does contest admission, precisely because the former emphasizes a systematic evaluation of applicants rather than a mere "contest," which may be governed by some rules of fair play, but in which the "contestants" have wide latitude in the strategies they may employ.

If one accepts sponsored admission as a more adequate model of the process of admission to graduate study, are there no restraints that operate to curb the preferences of the institution with respect to their choices among applicants? Of course there are. At the very minimum there are the restraints of law, which although applying to all institutions may have particular force with respect to publicly supported and governed universities. Beyond this, there are ethical and moral considerations in the treatment of applicants which operate to reduce the discretionary latitude available to institutions. Even so, proceeding from the starting point of a sponsored admissions model leads to a different perspective on the problems presented by *Bakke* than is the case if one assumes a model of contest admissions. If a contest admissions model were to be accepted it might require that law schools follow the advice of Wigmore (as quoted by Justice Douglas in his dissenting opinion in the *DeFunis* case) that "the way to find out whether a boy has the makings of a competent lawyer is to see what he can do in the first year of law studies," a suggestion similar to the one offered a few years ago by the then president-elect of the American Bar Association.[2] Or, contest admission might require that an institution adhere to the position of DeFunis, who argued that an admissions committee may not use *any* subjective criteria whatever, but rather must rely on a more or less automatic ordering of candidates based upon one or two wholly "objective criteria" such as tests scores and grades. Wigmore's advice is impractical because of the numbers of applicants (and in fact does not dispose of the problem of exercising responsible faculty judgment but merely postpones it) and DeFunis' argument is irresponsible in view of its consequences—the virtual abandonment of any effort to appraise human qualities or activities other than those that

---

[2] Address to the Annual Meeting of the Law School Admission Council by Chesterfield Smith, June 5, 1973.

can be readily quantified.

In summary, the choice of students that can best profit from a graduate education program is a complex and difficult one, requiring experience and a clear understanding of the talents needed, and is of necessity administered by those trained to assess whether the candidate has the qualities the faculty believes are important for society to see represented in the profession or discipline for which the student is to be prepared.

Bakke understandably evokes a concern as to the limits on discretionary choice. How are personal attributes such as persistence in the face of overcoming the obstacles of disadvantaged and impoverished origins to be weighed? How are these personal qualities to be judged in relation to the student's academic record? To what extent may race or ethnicity be considered in searching for qualities that are desired by a profession? The answers to these questions must be sought be setting the boundaries of institutional discretion, within a sponsored admission framework, not by prescribing a new, untried, and wholly inappropriate model of admissions that is based on conceiving it as a contest.

4

Arguments for Consideration of Race in Admissions Policies

Sponsored admission places a heavy responsibility on faculties and adminstrative officers of graduate and professional schools to make admission decisions wisely, recognizing their obligation to ensure the vitality of their professions through the continual infusion of trained scholars, researchers, and practitioners, and their obligations to the larger society that their professions serve. Ultimately, all universities—public and private—are accountable for their actions to the larger society. The *Bakke* case seriously calls into question the collective wisdom of American graduate schools which, in their commitment to admissions policies designed to increase minority enrollments, have also given particular attention to the task of integrating racial and ethnic minorities within higher education.

Recently the *New York Times* reported the results of a Gallup poll which asked the question: "Some people say that to make up for past discrimination, women and members of minority groups should be given preferential treatment in getting jobs and places in college. Others say that ability, as determined by test scores, should be the main consideration. Which point of view comes closest to how you feel on this matter?"

The article goes on to say that "Seldom before have the American people been in such agreement on a controversial issue.

Over all, of the 1550 adults interviewed in the survey 83 percent said that preferential treatment should not be given to women and minority groups, 10 percent said it should be given and 7 percent had no opinion. ... However, 64 percent of non-white participants say they back the idea of making ability alone as determined by tests the basis for hiring and college entrance; 27 percent favored preferential treatment for women and minorities and 7 percent had no opinion" (*New York Times*, 1977).

This unanimity of opinion is impressive, particularly in view of what appears to be a superficial contradiction between the practices of graduate and professional schools and the prevailing attitudes of the general public. How is it possible that the widespread concern in higher education with enrollment of larger numbers of minority students is so much at variance with the views of majority and minority citizens?

Two factors may account for the apparent results of the Gallup poll. The first is that the term "preferential" admissions may suggest that *unqualified* minority persons are being given preference over *qualified* majority applicants. As noted in the earlier discussion, such a practice is not necessarily implied by the mere consideration of race as one of the many factors relevant in the admissions decision.

A second reason for the lopsided results of the poll may be more subtle, and that is that the Gallup question links a particular justification—compensation for past injustice—to the policy of "preferential" treatment. A number of justifications have been offered for giving some weight to "race" in the admissions process. Compensation for injustice is one of them, but from an educational policy standpoint it may not be the most important. Others of these arguments that have been offered in support of affirmative action in admissions are discussed below, and it may very well be the case that if the pollsters had led into their question with a different argument for "preferential" treatment, somewhat different results in the poll might have been obtained.

In any case it is of some interest to review, even briefly, the major arguments for special consideration of minority applicants for the reason that opponents of such a policy often cite only one or two such arguments and then, having demolished these, conclude that the issue is settled.

Without necessarily implying the author's agreement with each of the following, the principle arguments offered in support of considering race as a factor in admissions decisions are:

1. *Diversity.* Teachers have long observed that students—all students—can benefit educationally from a learning community in which students are culturally diverse, creating thereby an enhanced potential for a lively intellectual environment that will contribute materially to the students' development. At a fundamental level, all knowledge is shared experience and its acquisition is an overwhelmingly social act. Admissions policies that assure the selection of an entering class that is heterogeneous in background, interests, cultural experience, and objectives have long been pursued by many of the nation's leading institutions. Furthermore, in professional schools such as law and medicine, a very important aspect of the educational program is the process of socialization into the profession—its norms, traditions, ethics and controversies. One can scarcely doubt that the quality of such an education is not enhanced by diversity in viewpoints and experience. Inclusion of students from the rural farm and the urban ghetto, the plains of Texas and the brick canyons of Chicago or New York can contribute enormously to the vitality of the educational experience. Moreover, a central problem of our society—the key issue of our lifetime many would say—is the effort to build a society in which the infection of racism is eliminated from the tissues of our national life. For these reasons participation of racial and ethnic minority students in graduate and professional education is an essential ingredient in fashioning excellence in educational programs. Diversity is an ingredient because it cannot, alone, do more than permit the educational process to be improved. Actual improvements must occur as a consequence of the institution's commitment to the objective of fostering in students an increased respect for the value of cultural diversity. Thus the contribution of diversity per se cannot be realized unless the educational program links the potential of diversity to a new breadth of vision, an openness to

ideas from unfamiliar sources, and an increased awareness of the "pulls and tugs" in a society that often appears to have no uniform aspirations. Efforts to assure diversity in admissions, particularly racial and ethnic diversity, are properly conceived as a foundation upon which institutions may build in their effort to provide excellence in educational programs and to fulfill the function of the institution as an instrument for elevating our national experience.

2. *Professional Service.* Ethnic and racial minorities constitute a large and growing segment of the population of the United States. Furthermore they are overrepresented among the poor, for whom more ready availability of quality professional services is a national objective.

The numbers of blacks and other historically oppressed minorities who are members of the professions, however, are woefully small. Medicine, law, and other professions requiring advanced training do not contain within their ranks significant numbers of minority practitioners and researchers, despite very recent gains. However, it should not be assumed that the needs of low income minority citizens for professional services will be met by minority professionals—such an assumption is not only unsupported by facts, but unwarranted by reasonable appraisals of social or human aspirations in a free society.

But, if professional schools such as law and medicine are to serve all citizens well, including those who have been poorly served in the past, changes in the perspectives of the profession on how best to deliver its services are needed.

All professionals need to have a keener sense of the perspectives and problems of the various elements of the community in which he or she serves—to gain an intimate understanding of the ways of thought and the modes of feeling that he or she will encounter in all walks of life. To achieve this end, it is necessary to assure participation of minority students and faculty in professional education because this participation becomes the instrument for enriching and strengthening the individual resources of *all* persons who aspire to the provision of professional services within our diverse society.

These two arguments for improving quality—the needs for
diversity in education and professional service—are generally regarded as the most persuasive justifications for regarding race as
relevant to the admissions policies of graduate and professional
schools. Others that also possess merit include:

3. *Leadership.* Special efforts are needed not only to expand the
    numbers of minority persons available to assume positions of
    leadership in business, government, education, and public life
    but also to serve as role models for minority youth. Access to
    graduate and professional education is a primary avenue to
    such positions, and consideration of race in admissions in this
    context is directly analogous to programs of affirmative action
    in employment.

4. *Remediation.* Colleges and universities, including graduate
    and professional schools have an obligation to deal with the
    continuing effects of unequal and often inadequate educational
    experiences that too often characterize urban or rural minority
    schools and colleges. Remedial programs designed to amelio-
    rate the effects of disadvantaged education are a reasonable
    means for higher education to compensate for the consequences
    of the educational system's failure to educate all students
    thoroughly and effectively.
        It is no doubt correct that the burden of this problem falls
    more heavily on the undergraduate colleges, but it would be
    blind to overlook the fact that many minority students have
    been "undereducated" throughout their schooling, including
    through the baccalaureate level. Efforts to deal with this
    problem should not encourage graduate schools to undertake
    more than they can effectively do; nevertheless, sound and
    sensitive admission programs can often distinguish between
    the able but undereducated student and the student who despite
    strong motivation and interest is unqualified to pursue graduate
    study. It is important that future policy guidelines emanating
    from a decision in the *Bakke* case not constrict the latitude of

admissions officers and committees to encompass remedial programs within their admission policies.

Two arguments cometimes used to support special admission programs for minority students spring mainly from technical questions arising from the use of tests. More detailed consideration of these issues is provided by Willingham, Breland, and associates (1977), and in Linn (1974) and Manning (1968, 1976). These two arguments are:

5.   *Bias.* It is argued by some that traditional standards for admission, particularly aptitude and achievement tests, are culturally biased. Tests such as the Law School Aptitude Test, the Medical College Admissions Test, the Graduate Record Examinations, the Graduate Management Admissions Test, and the Scholastic Aptitude Test and Achievement Tests of the College Board have been widely used, and many studies have been completed by investigators who have examined the question of their alleged bias against racial and ethnic minorities. The preponderance of this evidence is that these tests are useful predictors of a wide range of relevant measures of educational outcomes, and are equally well related to success in college or graduate school for minority and majority students (Linn, 1974). Nevertheless, the average performance on tests (and grades) for most minority groups usually is lower than for majority students. (Oriental Americans typically score about as well as the majority students.) The argument of cultural bias for special admission of minorities assumes that such differences in average performance are artifacts of the tests themselves, and consequently in evaluating minority candidates the results of the tests should be discounted or adjusted to compensate for such "bias."

There is little support within the research literature for such a belief or for such a practice. On the other hand, the research literature and sound professional practice argue against defining "merit" on the basis of test scores and grades alone. Other factors need also to be considered in the admissions process.

6.   *Insufficiency.* It is sometimes argued that objective standards
      for admission are insufficient bases for evaluating applicants.
      Consequently, the appearance of an unambiguous order of
      merit based upon test scores and grades—the "predicted first
      year average" much discussed in both the *Bakke* and *Defunis*
      cases—is deceptive. The "order of merit" might change signi-
      ficantly if other less readily quantifiable factors were included,
      or if other criteria than tests and grades were used in calculating
      a composite index.

            In statistical theory, the concept of the "sufficiency" of a
      statistic is sometimes of interest. Thus the range of scores in an
      array would be less "sufficient" as a measure of their variability
      than would the standard deviation, because the former depends
      upon only two scores (high and low) whereas the latter reflects
      the degree of dispersion of *all* the scores around the average.
      The metaphor is obvious: Admissions data should be *sufficient,*
      in the sense that evaluations of applicants will be fairer if they
      arise from many diverse assessments of talent rather than only
      one or two.

            This argument does not imply that tests are insufficient in
      the sense that they lack validity, but that they are insufficient
      because they do not reflect a broad enough spectrum of the
      talents for graduate study that are important in reaching
      admissions decisions. To the extent that institutions rely
      exclusively on tests and grades as sole criteria, the argument
      that some students should be evaluated along other dimensions
      than these alone has some merit. More properly, however, *all
      students* deserve to be evaluated as a tapestry of talents rather
      than as a pen and ink drawing, despite the fact that the latter
      may be a faithful rendition of the essential outlines of the
      portrait.

      Two other arguments are sometimes offered in support of
giving particular attention to "race" in the admissions process.
These arguments are essentially rooted in social or political philosophy, rather than in education, per se.

7.   *Reparations.* Not widely different from the implied justifi-

cation contained within the Gallup poll question is the argument of reparations: that two centuries of injustice and cruelty of the majority white society toward racial and ethnic minorities requires reparation through deliberately extending preferential treatment. The "collective guilt" of white society, despite the innocence of particular persons, requires adoption of policies of entitlement to preferential treatment, at least for a period of time during which progress toward parity in educational opportunity is being attained.

Closely related to this is another argument:

8. *Accommodation to Political Stress.* Lack of trust by minorities in the motivation of traditionally white graduate and professional schools requires a publicly visible, readily accountable means for assuring that genuine efforts to open access to education for minorities do occur. Special admissions programs for minority students are one means of providing such accountability, and these programs fulfill a necessary role, in order to resolve or contain the potentially destructive political tensions within the institution, and between the institution and its various constituencies.

Both of these last arguments are essentially political in nature. As a consequence, these arguments pervade educational policies, but go far beyond them, affecting the way in which all of our public and private institutions—not just higher education—function. Colleges and universities are, however, human institutions, whose vitality depends in important ways upon the gaining and maintaining of a consensus. Consequently, there is little doubt that admissions policies have been influenced to a degree by political and ideological considerations such as these.

By far the most important justifications for treating race as a relevant factor in admissions are the first two arguments—diversity and professional service.

In this respect, programs designed to help assure access of minorities to graduate and professional education—including special admissions programs—are analogous to a scaffolding erected for the purpose of constructing a building. Without that scaffolding, efforts of educators to build a new structure that is large enough to accommodate *all* of our citizens regardless of race will be seriously, perhaps fatally, impeded. Critics of this effort to rebuild the edifice of higher education and the professions confuse the shape of the scaffolding, which consciously pays attention to race, with the design of the construction itself—a new structure of education and the professions—that is free of the legacy of racial discrimination. To force the abandonment of the principal tools of such an effort, at an early stage in the task of rebuilding, would be a tragic decision for us all. Educational institutions should be granted the widest possible latitude, consistent with the constitutional requirements of equal protection and due process, in the creation and implementation of their educational programs. The make-up of the class of students, who together with the faculty constitute a "community of learners," is not a process that lies outside the doors of the classroom or the laboratory. It is a process that undergirds the act of teaching and learning, and permeates it in a multitude of ways. The preservation of the essential freedom of the college to create the learning environment that in its judgment most effectively embodies its philosophy and objectives is inseparable from preserving the freedom of the college to select its students.

5

Educational Due Process in Admissions

Earlier, we discussed the distinction between "contest" and "sponsored" admissions, arguing that this process should not be considered a mere contest, in which the winners are more or less automatically determined. Rather, "sponsored" admission is a process in which the institution chooses, based upon carefully devised assessments, those applicants who demonstrate the qualities the institution is seeking.

Despite the broad discretion legitimately accorded to the institution in its choice among applicants, there are nevertheless limits to that freedom, and both the *Bakke* and *Defunis* cases have beneficially illuminated some practices in higher education that need to be strengthened or abandoned. A primary consideration that ought to govern the admissions policies of colleges and universities is the development and application of the concept of "educational due process" to admissions. The lack of systematic, demonstrable, clearly documented guidelines for making judgments about applicants is a valid issue, which may in some circumstances demand resolution by the courts.

Beyond the legal framework for evaluating admission policies there is the question of institutional accountability to society. *Bakke* has cast a cold and relentless beam of light upon an area of institutional policy making—admissions—that has for too long lingered in the shadows. It is not merely for the benefit of applicants that admissions policies and procedures need illumination. Rather, the gatekeeping function of higher education requires that connections between stated institutional missions and goals on the one hand, and admissions policies and procedures on the other, be understood by all the various constituencies the institution serves. Some process akin to that employed in accreditation may be needed, in which an institution's admissions policies, procedures and practices are documented, carefully assessed, and publicly evaluated by independent authorities. If the pursuit of fairness in admission to higher education is to have lasting, practical significance, and if standards of "educational due process" are to be publicly accountable, admissions—no less than other areas of educational policy— should demonstrably express the values of the larger society, not only at the level of broad generalizations, but at a level of specific working principles.

Addressing this issue of due process in admissions (to law school) Gellhorn and Hornby (1974, pp. 1002–1010) present an analysis that may be summarized as follows:

1. At a minimum, state-supported graduate and professional schools should articulate "ascertainable" standards or criteria for admissions. Once developed they should be disseminated to the field of applicants and then applied in a uniform and impartial manner.
2. The standards or criteria for use in selecting matriculants must be validated—that is, reliably shown to measure qualities relevant to legitimate educational objectives of the graduate or professional program.
3. Whatever criteria are used, universities should routinely allow applicants the procedural opportunity to demonstrate that those particular criteria are inappropriate for assessing their attributes.
4. Upon request, a rejected applicant should be given a statement of the reason(s) for his rejection.
5. Where rejection relies on information not submitted by the applicant, he should be given access to this information and opportunity to explain or contradict it.

To these recommendations it would seem to be reasonable to add two others, aimed at providing *educational* due process:

6. Standards or criteria for use in selecting matriculants should

represent a reasonably broad array of those qualities shown to be relevant; that is, assuring "sufficiency" in standards employed rather than relying on one or two attributes, such as academic competence as reflected in test scores and grades alone.

As discussed in somewhat greater detail later in this paper, the process of admissions should provide for consideration of all students who are *admissible* (that is, minimally qualified to do the work), with *selection* based upon "sufficiency" of standards. Bearing this in mind:

7. An institution may employ different or overlapping standards in two or more phases; that is, the institution may choose to identify first a pool of minimally qualified candidates, relying primarily upon assessments of academic competence to determine *admissibility;* and then utilize in a second stage assessments of other characteristics, including personal attributes, life experience, and other traits that commend themselves for consideration in the *selection* process.

Implementation of these recommendations would not prove onerous for the leading graduate and professional schools, but it would require a substantially larger investment of resources in the admissions process of most universities. For some institutions it would require a major overhaul of their policies and practices, entailing a larger financial outlay. Nevertheless, not only legal considerations but also ethical responsibilities of colleges and universities to their applicants and to the public recommend serious consideration of these policies.

Graduate education in the United States operates today something like a public trust that requires a mutual appreciation by institutions and governments of the special relationship between the public interest and graduate and professional study and research. For the graduate and professional schools, the adoption of these recommendations would go far to dispel the suspicion of capricious actions and veiled motives—suspicions that too often seem to characterize attitudes toward admissions practices that are widely held by both applicants and their families. Further, one of the most arbitrary barriers to the more effective use of human resources of talent is simply the lack of reliable information about graduate programs and their admissions requirements and such information should be made more widely available to undergraduate students and their counselors, to say nothing about secondary schools.[1] Ideally these "educational due process" recommendations should operate so as to encourage formation of an informed pool of applicants for graduate and professional study who, when distributed among the varying institutions, will experience less confusion, dissatisfaction, and failure in the admissions process.

Logically there are two major ways to improve the quality of students entering graduate study. One is to find better ways of selecting applicants from the existing applicant population. Another is to increase the general quality of the pool of applicants and to improve their distribution across institutions. Information to dispel ignorance and mistaken beliefs about the admissions policies of institutions could be reasonably expected to help improve the quality of the pool and its distribution, and such policies would therefore not only be in the service of better fulfilling the ethical obligations of graduate and professional schools to their applicants, but also would be in the self-interest of the schools themselves (Manning, 1970).

Implementation of due process policies in admissions, coupled with broader dissemination of information about programs and admission requirements would be of particular help to minority students, who are often enrolled in undergraduate schools and colleges that are comparatively lacking in information about graduate and professional education. Minority recruitment efforts have always been hampered to a degree by the dearth of reliable information about graduate school admission policies, and the key role that such programs as NSSFNS, CLEO, and various foundation fellowship programs have played in encouraging and identifying talented minority youth can hardly be stressed too strongly.

---

[1] Another very significant barrier is the relative lack of financial aid, particularly at the graduate and professional level, which is probably the most important deterrent to access to higher education for many students.

6

A Two-Stage Model of the Admissions Process

Selective graduate and professional schools, like many selective colleges, not only have many more applicants than they can admit, but they have many more *qualified* applicants than they can enroll. Accordingly, many selective institutions make an effort, first, to eliminate from consideration those applicants who do not meet some minimal standard of admissibility, and then, secondly, to focus attention and efforts on the difficult task of selecting a class from the still large pool of qualified applicants. Although there are many variations in procedures, timing, and other refinements, the distinction between these two decisions—*admissibility* and *selection*—is an important one, especially in considering the issues raised by *Bakke*.

A decision about the *admissibility* of an applicant is concerned with the question: *Does the applicant possess the requisite prior education and minimum intellectual abilities and aptitudes necessary to pursue a sustained program of academic study offered by the institution?*

The justification for establishing a "floor" with regard to expected academic competency is widely understood but not always accepted. At the undergraduate level, some institutions have adopted policies of "open admissions," which purport to give every student an equivalent opportunity to try to succeed in a program. Even in these instances, however, "open" is usually a relative term, in the sense that very few colleges (other than "open door" community colleges) admit students who have not completed secondary school, and many have other more restrictive requirements than this one. At the graduate and professional school level, the establishment of some minimal levels of competency in academic preparation and skills is required, either explicitly or implicitly, and "open admissions" policies are rarely practiced.

Establishing minimal standards of admissibility should not be a casual or arbitrary process. Minimal standards must bear a rational relationship to the demands of the curriculum, and empirical data showing the validity of the standards must be compiled. It should also be recognized that decisions regarding admissibility can never be infallible—some students falling below the minimal standard adopted might succeed, and others above the minimal standard may do poorly or fail. Such outcomes are, in practice, unavoidable, so that the implementation of a minimal standard policy assumes a model in which a probability is attached to the decision and acceptable risks are defined.

Decisions concerning admissibility, as distinct from selection decisions, ordinarily focus on academic competencies rather than on personal attributes and accomplishments of a nonacademic character. Ordinarily, graduate-level institutions would set minimal requirements with respect to such factors as:

1. *Curricular preparation.* Has the student taken the essential prerequisite courses, if this is relevant?
2. *Grades.* Does the student's undergraduate record indicate the requisite capability to handle academic work, particularly in fields deemed relevant to graduate or professional study?
3. *Test scores.* Is there evidence that the student can write effectively, read with comprehension, analyze problems by identifying issues, understand and use quantitative methods, and possibly (depending on the field) demonstrate mastery of one subject in considerable depth?

Of course these dimensions are also relevant to selection decisions, but it is important to remember that at this point in the two-stage process, the task for the institution is that of setting *minimal standards* of admissibility in each of these areas, and such assessments of academic competence take precedence.

In recent years, graduate and professional schools have often been caught up in an "inflationary" spiral, in which minimal standards have been successively inflated, in response to a variety of pressures. Undergraduate grades, formerly a primary basis for establishing minimal standards of competency have lately become so inflated at some undergraduate institutions as to be virtually useless, as in the case when a majority of students graduate with "honors." This has resulted in an increasing escalation of expectations by graduate schools with regard to grades, and an excessive reliance upon tests. The aspirations of students for advanced degrees have also inflated the size of applicant pools, so that some schools, notably in medicine and law, have simply raised minimal standards as a means of coping with their burgeoning applicant populations, thus removing by a procrustean thrust much of the clerical burden of dealing with larger and larger numbers of applicants. On the other side of the equation, the inflation of institutional ambitions sometimes has led institutions to set *minimal standards* at a very high level, more for purposes of public relations and enhancement of prestige than as a consequence of careful, rational analysis of the intellectual demands that their own programs genuinely require.

The inflation of minimal standards has a particularly unfortunate effect upon the educationally disadvantaged student, who is often poor and also a member of an ethnic or racial minority. "Minimal" standards that are set at artificially high levels have the effect of screening out very high proportions of these students, and consequently can be perceived by them as arbitrary and unreasonable barriers. Likewise the faculty, having created an artificial "floor" that is too high by far, is tempted then to waive or alter such standards on the basis of race or disadvantaged status—creating thereby potential dissension, and sometimes causing understandable resentment on the part of minority students for the paternalism that such actions may imply, as well as accusations of unfairness voiced by majority students.

Our contention is that minimal standards should be set *no higher* than is necessary to make decisions concerning *admissibility*. If such levels are reasonably arrived at, there is no reason why all applicants cannot then be judged uniformly by them for purposes of admissibility decisions. Indeed, minority educators and students are nearly unanimous in their opinion on this subject; stated eloquently and succinctly by Kenneth Clark (1971), who said: "For blacks to be held to lower standards, or in some cases no standards at all is a most contemptible form of racism."

In summary, a series of avoidable problems have arisen in part because of the arbitrary inflation of minimal standards of admissibility by many graduate and professional schools. By inflating the currency of academic competence the standards of admissibility became indistinguishable from the standards employed in selection decisions. It is productive in the long run to maintain this distinction between admissibility and selection, because important consequences can flow from it, including the following:

1. Standards used in admissibility focus on *academic* competency, whereas selection standards should usually be more inclusive, taking into account other factors that also relate to the objectives of the institution and the needs of the profession.
2. Decisions on *admissibility* of a student can be made without respect to considerations of minority status or other background factors, thus assuring to all—and especially to minority applicants themselves—that those applicants who are deemed *admissible* do indeed possess the requisite minimum aptitudes and abilities to undertake the program of study.
3. Applicants generally would benefit from a clearer understanding of standards of admissibility; indeed, considerations of due process, as noted above, suggest that students have a right to such information. Although it may, in practice, be cold comfort for an applicant to learn that he or she is "admissible" and then not be "selected," it is nevertheless an important distinction to many students who find the prevailing confusion of these two processes to be a source of frustration and discouragement.
4. Decisions concerning "admissibility" could be made in many cases at a much earlier point in a student's education, thus giving both the student and the institution greater flexibility and more realistic expectations.

As suggested earlier, once a decision on admissibility has been reached, the second stage of the admissions process—that of *selection*

—can begin. At this point, the task of the institution is to select those whom it believes would make up the best available entering class. This decision is concerned with the question: *Given that these applicants are admissible, what subgroup of them will best advance the educational philosophy and objectives of the institution, the profession, and society?*

At the selection stage in the admissions process, the full range of the value preferences of the institution come into play. Whereas decisions regarding admissibility were based on minimum standards designed to assure academic competence to pursue a graduate program, decisions regarding the selection of a student can and should reflect a much broader range of objectives. To be sure, an institution may wish to seek out applicants with superlative intellectual abilities, and in this respect some or all of the same dimensions considered at the point of admissibility may continue to be relevant, but at a different level. On the other hand, the most selective professional and graduate schools have always given considerable attention to nonacademic criteria. Personal attributes such as evidence of resourcefulness or of persistence in the face of obstacles; unusual personal experience or independent accomplishments; academic and nonacademic interests; career goals; evaluations of teachers, peers, and others who have known the applicant well—all of these are pertinent to the process of deciding whether, among the pool of admissable applicants, a particular applicant is desirable as a student.

The hard question is whether at this point in the two-stage model—selection—racial or ethnic group membership may also be considered. A more detailed examination of this issue is given below, but responsible admissions committees do ask questions concerning what kinds of people should make up the entering class in order to fulfill the educational objectives of the graduate or professional school programs, or what kinds of people should be sought out as potential members of a particular profession or discipline in order to fulfill its objectives for society or scholarship. In considering the many factors—academic and nonacademic—that enter into the selection decision, the question raised by *Bakke* is whether race of the applicant is relevant. *From the standpoint of education and professions the answer to that question should be yes.* Race *is* relevant because it represents not mere skin color, but the consequences of the minority racial experience in America. It is that experience—that perception of what it means to be locked in a life struggle—that is valuable not only to the educational process, but to the effective and responsive functioning of professions like medicine, law, clinical psychology, social work, economics, and a host of others.

Of course, there must be restraints on the use of constitutionally suspect classifications, such as "race," within the selection process. However, within the two-stage model that has been described, the balance of reasoned judgment tips in the direction of recognizing the relevance of racial or ethnic minority status as one of many factors that may be considered in selecting students from among admissible applicants.

Critics of this position would argue that giving any explicit consideration to race in selection decisions will automatically lead to the patronizing of minorities and is itself a subtle, but insidious form of racism. Cohen (1977), in the pages of the *Chronicle of Higher Education,* recently argued that:

> Above all, racial preference clouds the accomplishments and undermines the reputation of those superbly qualified minority group professionals who neither need nor get special favor. When, in the minds of everyone, black and white, a physician's dark skin is automatically linked to charity and payoff, who among members of minority groups is served? It is a cruel result.

The policies against which Cohen is inveighing are not the policies we are advocating. If the institution has first assured itself that the pool of *admissible* students all *do meet* minimal standards for admission, there can be no suggestion that at the stage of selection the subsequent consideration of race, among many other academic and nonacademic factors, would reek of "charity" or "payoff." On the contrary, to deny the possibility of an institution's attaching some positive weight to the race of a candidate, as a means, for example, of enriching the intellectual life of the school assuring diversity in the backgrounds of its students, is to react to race defensively. Admittedly there are ways in which the use of race—

indeed of nearly any human characteristic—could defeat the aims of responsible admissions policy; what we are arguing for here is the relevance of race to selection decisions within a complex, sequentially ordered process, *whose fairness must be judged in terms of the impact of the entire system rather than dealt with as an abstract component.*

7

Special Programs

In selecting students, many universities have recognized that, even though all admissible students are minimally qualified to pursue the regular academic course, there may nevertheless be a fairly wide range of competence represented in the class selected. In order to compete with students whose academic preparation has been a relatively superior one, some students may need additional assistance in the form of tutoring, remedial work, counseling, and access to related resources. This may be true even though the students in need of such assistance *are*, in fact, minimally qualified. It is understandable that many students in need of academic assistance of this kind are disadvantaged students whose previous preparation has been hampered by lack of educational opportunity and resources, sometimes extending over many years. The development of special programs to assist such students after matriculation is not incompatible with adherence to a minimal standards model, if the institution carefully evaluates the progress of such students, and assures that uniform standards of admissibility and performance are expected of *all* students.

Furthermore, the adoption of special programs of admissions and tutoring in no way should compromise the uniformity and objectivity of output standards. The objective of the special program is to break an otherwise vicious educational cycle by providing additional assistance to some students so that they can meet the common standards to which all will be held in their courses and degree requirements. So long as minimal standards of admissibility are maintained, the introduction of special admissions programs at the selection stage is no more then a reasoned anticipation of the need to provide special assistance to some students, even though minimally qualified, if they are to compete with other, better-prepared classmates.

The California Supreme Court in rendering its decision in the *Bakke* case called attention to the desirability of recruiting and admitting disadvantaged students, but objected to the explicit consideration of the applicant's race in selecting students to participate in special programs.

There are two issues intertwined, namely, the objective of the institution to recruit and admit qualified minority applicants, and the recognition that many minority students (who are frequently also disadvantaged) will also need special assistance, if they are to compete in the academic programs with more educationally advantaged majority students.

The argument has been made that disadvantaged status may be taken into account in selecting a student for admission and for programs providing special assistance, but that *race* may not, under the Constitution, be considered. Leaving aside for the moment the legal aspect of this question, a policy of limiting institutions to consideration of disadvantaged status *alone* in selecting students for special programs will have the effect, as Evans (1977) and others have shown, of drastically reducing the number of minority applicants who might otherwise be admitted. Furthermore, it is important to understand that ethnic or racial group membership often reflects a broader deprivation of educational opportunity than low social and economic status implies.[1]

This can be illustrated by recourse to an example drawn from actual data, compiled for the purposes of examining this question. It may be recalled that Justice Douglas (Douglas, 1974) in his *DeFunis* dissent offered an observation suggesting that the degree to which a student had overcome disadvantaged origins and obtained test scores,

---

[1] This point has been made by a number of authors. For example Kardiner and Ovesey (1951) pointed out that "we are in no position to say how far the findings of the lower class Negro apply to lower class whites. . . . The situation cannot possibly be as bad in these latter groups, because they do not have the caste situation to contend with, and among the disastrous effects that register their impact on Negro life, that of caste is the worst." (p. 386).

say, of a moderate level, may be a more impressive credential than high test scores obtained by an applicant from an affluent background.[2] This idea has considerable merit, and has certainly influenced the behavior of admissions committees for many years, who would agree that perseverance in the face of obstacles of birth and poverty should somehow be recognized in the admissions process.

One way of defining this issue more sharply is to construct a quantitative measure of this effect—the degree to which a candidate obtains test scores higher (or lower) than that predicted on the basis of his socioeconomic background. The details of the statistical operations need not concern us here. Suffice it to say that the method is illustrated by comparing two applicants with identical scores—one from an applicant with low family income, whose parents have had little formal education, and where another language than English is spoken; the other is an applicant (with the same test scores) whose family has a high income, high parental education, and for whom English is the native language. Although a somewhat crude measure, the first we would regard as a socially disadvantaged applicant, the second not. Surely the scores of the first student (though identical numerically) represent an academic accomplishment that is in some sense superior to that of the second student?

In a forthcoming paper (Manning and Wild, in progress) an index (Residual Selection Index: RSI) has been constructed that represents the extent to which a student has exceeded or fallen below his expected score, where the expectation is calculated from information about family socioeconomic status and the primary language used.

[2] Justice Douglas did not precisely propose the analysis we have undertaken, but his observations regarding the relative value of equivalent demonstrations of observed academic competence seems entirely consistent with the model we have used for examining the question. In his dissenting opinion Justice Douglas said, "A Black applicant who pulled himself out of the ghetto into a junior college may thereby demonstrate a level of motivation, perseverance and ability that would lead a fair minded admissions committee to conclude that he shows more promise for law study than the son of a rich alumnus who achieved better grades at Harvard. That applicant would not be offered admission because he is Black, but because as an individual he has shown he has the potential, while the Harvard man may have taken less advantage of the vastly superior opportunities offered him." The statistically derived example we have offered illustrates the effect that would obtain were test scores to be adjusted to reflect, as it were, an indication of the motivation and perseverance of students in overcoming obstacles to their educational attainment.

In Table 1 are displayed some of the results of the Manning and Wild study that are pertinent to what happens when students are selected upon the basis of (1) a test score composite alone and (2) the residual selection index (RSI) taking into account income, education, and language spoken.

The data in Table 1 are based upon eight samples of approximately 2,000 cases each, drawn from ETS files, for a total of 16,000 cases.

Table 1. Effects of disadvantaged status and race on proportions of candidates selected within racial or ethnic groups: an illustration

Proportion selected (percent within group)[a]

	Male				Female			
	Black	White	Hispanic	Oriental	Black	White	Hispanic	Oriental
Test[b]	3.3	19.6	6.2	16.6	2.5	13.4	4.2	12.7
RSI[c]	4.7	16.3	8.7	17.4	3.0	11.4	6.5	11.9

[a] Statistics are based on 16,000 cases, equally divided between male and female, and equally divided among the eight groups (N=2,000).

[b] *Test variable:* A composite test score obtained by combining the candidates SAT-verbal and SAT-mathematics scores by the formula $(2V + M)/3$.

[c] *Residual Selection Index (RSI):* The extent to which a candidate's composite test score is above or below the score predicted on the basis of family income, parental education, and whether the student's primary language is other than English.

When the test score composite was used to select the upper 10 percent of the distribution for all 16,000 cases, the proportion of the black male applicants selected (from among that group) was 3.3 percent; of whites 19.6 percent; of Hispanic applicants 6.2 percent[3]; and of Oriental applicants 16.6 percent. Similar results were obtained for females.

When disadvantaged status (as reflected by income, education, and language) is taken into account, and the upper 10 percent of the combined group is selected using the Residual Selection Index, there is some *increase* in the proportion of the minority group samples that are selected, and a modest *decrease* in the proportion of the white majority applicants selected. *But the change is not marked.*

[3] Problems of sample sizes in the initial analyses made it difficult to break down this group into different constituencies, which would have been desirable.

As we have said earlier, this result could have been anticipated, because there are a great many more whites in the poverty population than there are racial or ethnic minority persons. The impact of selecting students with an eye toward disadvantaged status alone (taking no account of race) cannot therefore be expected to alter the proportions selected within any racial or ethnic group in any substantial degree from the proportions that would have been selected if no account were taken of disadvantaged status.

The meaning of all this for special admissions programs at graduate and professional schools is that (1) There no doubt are many good reasons for taking into account obstacles of social and economic background in selecting students; (2) if that is the sole basis for selecting students into special programs, the proportions selected will include a few more minority students, but not many;[4] and (3) if race is also considered *even indirectly* in identifying students whose test scores signify that they have overcome obstacles of family origin and experience, then the proportions of minority students selected will of necessity increase.

Colleges and universities should consider *race* as a factor in selection from among a pool of minimally qualified applicants. Furthermore, special programs for disadvantaged students that seek out students who have overcome obstacles to their educational growth should also consider, among other factors, the *race of the applicant.* This can be done without the explicit reservation of places for various racial and ethnic groups. The Court should, we believe, permit the use of *race* as one of many factors to be considered in selection of students, especially, it seems, for special programs designed to assist admissible students in overcoming relative deficiencies in their academic preparation.

[4] This point is also made by Evans (1977) in an analysis of data for applicants to law school. Evans states, based upon an empirical study of applicants, that "the method of using low-income background as a way to add minority persons to the law school population would not result in the desired increases" (p. 62).

8

Decision Strategies

Much of the concern aroused by the *Bakke* case arises from the procedures pursued by the University of California, Davis Medical School (and the University of Washington Law School in *DeFunis*), which, if not employing racial quotas, seem to most people to be nearly indistinguishable from such a strategy.

A quota arises when an applicant is not permitted to compete for all the places in an entering class. Typically the applicant pool is separated into two or more groups (for example, minority or majority), with admissions for each group limited to an assigned number or proportion. The effect of this is that one group is not considered in competition for the places allotted in the other groups.

In special admissions programs giving preference to ethnic and racial minorities, the adoption of a quota strategy is compounded further when different admissions committees, using inevitably different standards—both qualitative and quantitative—are employed. In such a case it could be argued that except for a single faculty and a common geographical location, the result is uncomfortably similar to operating two segregated schools.

Bickel and Kurland (1973) have argued with considerable eloquence that racial quotas are not only unconstitutional but odious to a democratic society. In their words, "A racial quota is derogatory to those it is intended to benefit and depriving of those from whom is taken what is 'given' to the minority. A beneficent quota is invidious as it is patronizing."

The issue of the constitutionality of racial quotas in admissions will be decided eventually in the courts. More to the point of this paper is their evaluation from the perspective of sound educational policy, and we agree that the use of *predetermined quotas are undesirable*. Moreover, they serve no useful purpose, save a beguiling administrative simplicity; better strategies for organizing the admissions process are available.

At the first stage of the admissions process, at which point *admissibility* should be the question, we have already argued that decisions should rest upon ascertaining whether the applicant exceeds the minimal levels of academic competence prescribed by the institutions. Several different areas of competence may be judged separately in a noncompensatory way. For example, excellent reading performance may not compensate for poor mathematical ability, particularly if the student plans to study engineering or the natural sciences. In other fields it may make sense to follow a compensatory model, which allows deficiencies in one area to be offset by strengths in another.

At the stage when selection decisions are to be made it is most probable that some kind of compensatory weighting system can be usefully employed. Such a system usually requires the quantification of each variable, including, for example, subjective ratings and various personal evaluations (recommendations, interview appraisals, and so on) and the assigning of a weight to each factor proportional to the importance that each is judged to contribute to an overall assessment of the applicant's "desirability." Such formal models can handle very elaborate and complex arrays of factors. The fact that weighting systems are not used more widely stems more from the difficulty admissions committees have in making the bases of their judgments explicit and in forging agreement on the relative importance of each factor than on any technical inadequacies of the model.

Several leading institutions do in fact proceed on a basis not unlike this—see, for example, the description of Harvard's admissions procedures in their *DeFunis* amicus brief (Cox, 1973)—although each institution obviously differs in its particular procedures. Using a factor-weighting strategy requires that the contribution of no one factor to an overall index be so large as to negate the effects of the other factors. Were that to happen, the entire procedure could degenerate into a pseudo-quota system.

What usually happens when a weighting model is employed is that wherever the selection cut-off might be drawn, there are inevitably large numbers of candidates whose combined selection indices differ only slightly or not at all from one another. Hence, final consideration of the pool of candidates suggests that an additional step be taken, namely the detailed assembly of the selected class according to certain *targets* or *goals*. These targets might include consideration of geographic distribution, career aspirations, ethnic or racial status, and so forth. Pursued in this way, the selection process first identifies a number of persons who are clearly extraordinarily well qualified (who are ordinarily selected without question) and then, in the vicinity of the proposed selection cut-off, a larger group of qualified candidates whose overall evaluations are very similar. These records are then examined very carefully with an eye toward the consideration of securing diversity in the class, and other objectives. Rather than simply ranking these latter persons to the requisite number of decimal points, drawing a line, and then letting the selection chips fall where they may, some institutions at this point give particular attention to the "mix" of the class, balancing various objectives so as to reflect in the selected class a mosaic of those education and professional aims they seek to realize through the admissions process (Manning, 1971).

It is at this point in a complex sequence of decisions that some applicants of a minority group may well be given "preference" over some majority candidates. Similarly, some majority candidates will be given preference over other majority applicants in the effort to assure a desirable "mix" of students. Following the sequence outlined above would assure that such a policy: (1) would apply only to persons who are qualified candidates, (2) does not permit race or any other single factor to prevent consideration of other factors that are also sought, and (3) permits institutions to exercise reponsible judgment regarding the qualities in applicants that are regarded as desirable for the institutions, for the professions, and for the society they serve.

It would be a significant loss to education and society if those institutions which have developed sensitive, suitably complex, and functionally sound admissions systems that incorporate considerations of race into the process, were to be barred from continuing their policy because the particular practices presented to the courts in some cases invite a blanket proscription. The remedy for bad practices should not be fashioned so as to burden or destroy responsible programs. Admittedly, the type of admission model we have described requires a much greater effort than many institutions now seem willing to invest, but "so long as the alternatives have the virtue of constitutionality, however, the Equal Protection Clause commands their use rather than the unconstitutional means that may be quicker, or less difficult, or less expensive" (Bickel and Kurland, 1973).

9

Summary and
Conclusions

In the foregoing sections of this report, we have attempted to outline the education policy considerations relevant to the *Bakke* decision. It may be useful to review briefly the major points of this overview.

- The central issue of the *Bakke* case is the problem of balancing considerations of individual and group equity—a problem which turns upon difficult value choices.
- Admission to higher education should not be conceived as a contest in which the winners are more or less automatically made evident in the process of playing the game. Rather, the process can be more accurately described as sponsored admission, in which the institutions choose, based on a controlled process of assessment, those persons who in the institutions' judgment have the appropriate qualities they are seeking.
- Race is relevant to the process of choice because it is connected to important educational and professional objectives—particularly the benefits to the intellectual environment flowing from *diversity* in a student body, and the educational requirements necessary if excellence in *professional service* programs is to be attained.
- Consideration of the implications of due process in admissions suggest the need for reform in certain of the practices typically employed by colleges and universities—notably the articulation by institutions to the public of ascertainable standards for admissions, the validation of these standards, and the avoidance of

the practice of relying on only one or two readily quantifiable attributes.

● Quotas represent an educationally undesirable decision strategy; the use of racial quotas is potentially iniquitous and demeaning. On the other hand, incorporation of race as one factor in a weighting system in which it is considered at the final stage of selection with respect to balancing the mix of a class has been a technique usefully pursued by numbers of institutions for many years. It would be a serious handicap to higher education if institutions were precluded from taking account of the race of applicants in this way.

● The courts should intrude no further into the educational process, of which admissions is an integral part, than is absolutely necessary in order to assure that constitutional principles are guaranteed. From an educational policy standpoint, ethnic and racial status *is* relevant to the fulfillment of the educational objectives of graduate and professional schools. Sensitive, responsive, and fair admissions policies can be devised and implemented that do take special factors such as race into account, and do so in ways that are conducive to the attainment of important educational goals.

Writing several years ago, Alice Rivlin observed that "the graduate schools of the United States encompass a predominant portion of the intellectual forces that can assure the Nation of continuing capability to insure knowledge, to extend the basis for technological progress, to influence the social, cultural, and economic quality of national life, and to exert intelligent and effective leadership in world affairs" (1969, pp. 18-19).

The capacity of universities to continue to fulfill this critically important role requires the development and implementation of educational policies that are wise and just—no less so for admissions than for other parts of the educational process. Where error exists, critics should root it out; where it persists the courts should eradicate it, but always with an eye toward preserving to the maximum degree an essential ingredient of education—freedom from unnecessary restraint. For higher education, no less than for the community of learners generally, "simply as education, freedom is indispensable" (Goodman, 1962, p. 310).

References

Baird, L. *Careers and Curricula*. Princeton, N.J.: Educational Testing Service, April 1974, pp. 1–233.

Baird, L., Hartnett, R., and Clark, M.J. *The Graduates*. Princeton, N.J.: Educational Testing Service, March 1973, pp. 1–210.

Bickel, A., and Kurland, P.B. *Brief of the Anti-Defamation League of the B'nai B'rith, Amicus Curiae, DeFunis v. Odegaard*, October, 1973.

Clark, K.B., as quoted in an article entitled "Compassion, Minorities, and Subtle Racism," *The Chicago Tribune*, June 29, 1971.

Cohen, C. "Racial Preference is Dynamite." *Chronicle of Higher Education*, May 2, 1977.

Cox, A. *Brief of the President and Fellows of Harvard College, Amicus Curiae, DeFunis v. Odegaard*, October 1973.

Davis, K., "The Role of Class Mobility in Economic Development," *Population Review*, 1962, *6*, 67–73.

Douglas, W.O. Dissent, in the Opinion of the U.S. Supreme Court, *DeFunis v. Odegaard*, April 23, 1974.

Evans, F.R. *Applications and Admissions to ABA Accredited Law Schools: An Analysis of National Data for the Class Entering in the Fall of 1976*. Report No. LSAC 77-1. Princeton, N.J.: Educational Testing Service, 1977, pp. 1–108.

Gellhorn, E., and Hornby, D.B. "Constitutional Limitations on Admissions Procedures and Standards—Beyond Affirmative Action." *Virginia Law Review*, 1974, *60*, 975–1011.

Goodman, P. *Compulsory Mis-Education and the Community of Scholars*. New York: Vantage Books, 1962.

Kardiner, A., and Ovesey, L. *The Mark of Oppression*. Cleveland: World, 1951.

Linn, R. "Test Bias and the Prediction of Grades in Law School." Prepared for Conference on the Future of Law School Admissions Council Research. Urbana, Ill., September 27-28, 1974.

Manning, W.H. "The Measurement of Intellectual Capacity and Performance." *Journal of Negro Education*, Summer 1968, p. 251–267.

Manning, W.H. *The Research Program of the GRE Board*. Princeton, N.J.: Educational Testing Service, 1970, pp. 1–28.

Manning, W.H. "Personal and Institutional Assessment: Alternatives to Tests of Scholastic Aptitude and Achievement in the Admissions Process." In *Barriers to Higher Education*. Princeton, N.J.: College Entrance Examination Board, 1971, pp. 81–99.

Manning, W.H. *Current Controversies in Education*. Princeton, N.J.: Educational Testing Service, 1976, pp. 1–47.

New York Times. "83% in Poll Oppose Reverse Bias Plans." Sunday, May 1, 1977.

Rivilin, A. "Toward a Long Range Plan for Federal Financial Support for Higher Education." U.S. Department of Health, Education and Welfare. Washington, D.C.: Government Printing Office, 1969.

Sandalow, T. "Racial Preferences in Higher Education: Political Responsibility and the Judicial Role." *University of Chicago Law Review*, 1975, *42*, 653-704.

Turner, R.H. "Modes of Social Ascent Through Education: Sponsored and Contest Mobility." In A.H. Halsey, J. Floud, and C.A. Anderson *Education, Economy, and Society.* New York: Free Press, 1961.

Willingham, W., Breland, H., and associates. "The Status of Selective Admissions." In *Selective Admissions in Higher Education.* San Francisco: Jossey-Bass, 1977.

Wynn, R. "Administrative Behavior in Education." In Goodman, P. *Compulsory Mis-Education and the Community of Scholars.* New York: Random (Vintage), 1962.

Part Three

The Status of
Selective Admissions

Warren W. Willingham
and Hunter M. Breland

In association with
  Richard I. Ferrin and Mary Fruen

Preface to Part Three

The essential issue in the *Bakke* case is whether, and under what circumstances, race can be used as a basis for selecting applicants to an educational institution. The potential implications are obvious for affirmative action programs in hiring as well as college admissions. There are also far-reaching implications with respect to the general conduct of college admissions; for example, what types of selection measures can be used, what procedures are necessary to insure equity, and on what grounds is the process validated and justified? These are complex issues concerning individual rights, group equity, and the proper social role of educational instituions. As a natural result, the *Bakke* case has attracted a great deal of attention and stimulated a very substantial amount of writing in the popular as well as the scholarly press.

Concerning this widespread attention, it is likely that many persons interested in issues raised by the case may not be familiar with basic facts concerning admissions to selective institutions. Furthermore, it may prove useful even to those well versed in college admissions to have available a current report on relevant research literature and the status of admissions to different types of selective institutions. Thus, the purpose of this report is not to argue aspects of the *Bakke* case, discuss the value issues it raises, or to suggest alternate solutions. It is rather to describe briefly the nature of selective admissions and special admissions programs, to summarize recent enrollment data, and to discuss evidence concerning the strengths and weaknesses of various measures typically used in selection.

With respect to the enrollment data cited in this report, it is important to provide a few caveats. The enrollment analyses are limited by the availability of data and by the quality of those data that were available. Caution is necessary in their interpretation and readers are advised to rate general trends rather than rely too much on particular details of data that may be inaccurate. Inaccuracies in the enrollment data result, first, from sampling errors. Collecting data on an entire population of students is frequently difficult, but samples are not always representative. Other inaccuracies enter into surveys because of definitional difficulties. Some stem from the fact that different surveys focus on the problem differently or use different definitions of minority groups. And, at times, individuals or institutions are unable or even unwilling to provide the information requested. Notwithstanding these many sources of error, concerns regarding possible inaccuracies in interpretation may be somewhat assuaged by the notable consistency in some kinds of statistics. For example, the enumeration of Chicanos and Puerto Ricans has been especially plagued by the lack of proper identifying labels—but the percentage representation of these two groups combined is highly consistent across studies and within different subpopulations.

Several highlights of this report warrant special attention:

- Selective admissions to higher education occurs in thousands of schools and departments, and limitations in available information about the process seriously restrict conclusions one can safely draw. There is little published information concerning actual selection procedures, and national summary data are often imprecise.

- During the past decade there have been significant changes in admissions. Declining enrollment and limitations in financial aid have affected many undergraduate institutions and some graduate schools and may continue or worsen over the next decade. Professional schools, on the other hand, have become more attractive to students and more selective.

- Extensive efforts to increase representation of minority students and women have succeeded to some extent over the past decade. The proportion of women has increased from about 10 to 25 percent. In the case of minority students affirmative action in those schools has often taken the form of higher probability of acceptance in relation to quality of traditional credentials.

- Whereas the proportion of black, Spanish-surname, and native American college-age individuals in the population is on the order of 17 percent, the proportion of those groups represented in first-time enrollments in 1976 was approximately as follows: under-graduate, 12 percent; graduate, 8 percent; law, 8 percent; medicine, 9 percent; and management, 5 percent.

● It is evident that the process of selecting students is complex except from among the most obviously outstanding or unqualified applicants. Institutions pursue a variety of educational objectives in selective admissions, and many different types of student qualifications are weighed, though typically not in any formal or set procedure. Student self-selection according to interests, job market conditions, and so on, also has a major bearing on the admissions process.

● A substantial amount of research does not support the contention that admissions tests are biased against minority students. While both tests and grades have important shortcomings, the evidence indicates that these traditional measures, taken together, provide the best available estimate of future academic success of majority as well as minority students.

● This overview of current practice and research evidence reinforces the often stated view that institutions should not place undue reliance on traditional selection criteria and should seek additional evidence of talent and competence that is related to the students' intended academic program. There is also recognized a heightened need for institutions to define more clearly their purposes in selection and to develop improved procedures for achieving those purposes in a fair and effective manner.

The authors express appreciation to the reviewers and contributors mentioned in the preface to this volume and to many ETS colleagues who offered helpful advice. We are also especially grateful for the collaboration of Richard Ferrin and Mary Fruen who are largely responsible for Chapters 2 and 5, respectively. We also appreciate the research assistance of Jane Stutz and Ann Jungeblut for their valuable assistance.

Warren W. Willingham
Hunter M. Breland

1

Introduction

In the 1960s both national and individual aspirations for economic and social development became closely linked in the public mind with the issue of educational opportunity. Expanding educational opportunity was accorded a high priority throughout the world as many nations sought to improve the quality of life and place themselves in a more competitive position within the modern society. Harbison and Myers (1964) were among the influential economists who described this movement as resource development. Bowles (1969), on the other hand, spoke of it as an educational revolution—a democratization that "seeks to eliminate all restrictions upon educational opportunity, whether based on class, economic status, race, or on a quota system imposed by the professions" (p.11). He asserted that its idealized goal was the full development of the talents of each individual.

In the United States there is intense interest not only in minority enrollment and in the admissions process generally, but also in the closely related services of student guidance and student financial aid. Furthermore, Americans increasingly recognize that educational opportunity is intimately connected with such complicated issues as educational assessment, curriculum design, and effective connections between education and work. All of these services and processes are related in one way or another to an overall conception of effective access to higher education (Willingham, 1973a).

Acknowledging that true educational opportunity depends upon much more than gaining entry, admissions policy is, nonetheless, a pivotal issue. In national discussions concerning admissions policy, two broadly contrasting orientations stand out—open admissions and meritocratic admissions. The case for open admissions is argued on both social and educational grounds. For example, Astin (1969) has urged that rigid adherence to strictly academic credentials results in serious underrepresentation of minority students, and that it is more appropriate for institutions of higher education to admit students that they can help than to concentrate on those who have already achieved. The meritocratic philosophy of admissions is well stated by Glazer (1970), who emphasizes the fairness of rewarding those who have worked hard and the value of a social strategy that places a premium on effective training and maximum utilization of rare talent.

Both orientations are found at the undergraduate level, but in graduate and professional schools the meritocratic philosophy tends to prevail. At both levels many, if not most, of the highly selective institutions, have special admissions programs designed to increase enrollment of minority students. At both levels it is fair to say there is a stratification of institutions, some being much more selective than others. There are, however, important differences among undergraduate, graduate, and professional schools with respect to admissions policy and practice.

Large segments of undergraduate education are purposely or de facto nonselective, but in virtually all universities and even many community colleges, admission to some individual programs is highly selective. Many undergraduate colleges stress diversity within the student body as an important aspect of the educational climate. In graduate schools of arts and sciences there is also much variation in the academic ability of students from department to department, but perhaps less concern with selecting a diverse group of students within departments than is often found in undergraduate colleges and professional schools.

The connection with the professional fields into which their students tend to move is a very significant difference between graduate and professional schools. The most prominent professions are often open only to graduates of professional schools, and exclusion from those schools constitutes exclusion from the profession. This is seldom the case in graduate programs in arts and sciences, though high achievement may prove difficult in a number of fields without the appropriate Ph.D.

These distinctions among educational levels suggest that selective admissions serve somewhat different combinations of purposes in different situations. Without arguing the merits of each, three broad purposes can be distinguished:

1. *To enroll successful students.* Where admission is selective it is most often occasioned by a surplus of applicants and experience that indicates that poorly prepared students do not ordinarily meet the scholastic demands of the program with reasonable time and effort. Thus, selective admissions most frequently has the explicit purpose of admitting those students who are most likely to do well in their studies and to obtain a degree. The objective is to improve the efficiency of the institution in producing high quality graduates.

2. *To serve other institutional purposes.* Some applicants may get preference because they are applying to programs with ample staff and facilities but too few students in a particular year. The school orchestra needs players as well as the athletic teams. Many private colleges select students partly to *maintain* a particular tradition and character; other colleges may decide to select more older students, or women, or minority students, or students with a different type of preparation in order to *change* the institutional character. In general, a college or university strives to maintain the diversity and balance in its student body that enhances the educational climate and health of the institution; that is, admissions policy is one important expression of institutional purpose.

3. *To serve other social purposes.* Institutions of higher education constitute an important public resource and also a means of accomplishing social objectives. There is considerable difference of opinion concerning the extent to which admissions policies should serve various social objectives, but institutions do select students partly to develop high level talent and research capability in particular fields, to maintain a continuous supply of graduates to the various professions, and to promote affirmative action.

It is this latter purpose that provides the rationale for special admissions programs. Faced with the need to increase enrollment of ethnic minorities and women, most selective institutions have varied or supplemented their usual admission procedures. These special admissions programs are of three general types: special recruitment of students who are underrepresented in the student body; special selection procedures, which may involve selection measures and decision processes that differ from those normally used; and special educational programs designed to help students make up any academic deficiencies.

It is the second of these with which the *Bakke* case is concerned, but the three types together indicate that selective admissions is more complicated than a simple decision about which applicants an institution is willing to enroll. Despite the importance of the admissions process, there is surprisingly sparse literature on the mechanics of admissions, especially the dynamics of actual selection procedures. There is, however, a fairly extensive literature on a variety of topics intimately related to selective admissions (Willingham, 1973a), and there are general discussions of college admissions that are well worth careful study (Carnegie Commission on Higher Education, 1973a; Dyer, 1969; College Entrance Examination Board, 1976; Thresher, 1966).

To provide some orientation for the sections that follow, it may be useful to outline the principal stages in the usual process of selective admissions:

Recruitment. Highly selective institutions often devote considerable energy to communicating a favorable image to prospective students, to searching for and encouraging applications from the most highly qualified applicants, and to providing financial assistance that will lower economic barriers. Despite these efforts, students often choose institutions on the basis of quite limited information and for superficial reasons.

Application. There are some arrangments whereby students can file a single application to a number of institutions, but in most instances individual applications must be filed with each institution. Although applications are often voluminous, students typically file several—sometimes as many as 10 to 20. These usually include transcripts, extensive personal history information, test scores, and often some form of biographical essay.

Determining admissibility. Typically, the first step in reviewing applications is to determine whether the student has satisfied all prerequisites and conditions of admission. Another important initial question is whether the student's previous record, test scores, and other information indicate reasonable likelihood of success in the institution. Such judgments may be made informally or on the basis of a statistically determined estimate of performance.

Selection. In most selective colleges, graduate departments, and professional schools, reading applications and reaching admissions decisions is an extremely time-consuming process. Judgments often involve interviews and admissions committees and are seldom made on the basis of any single piece of information.

Notification. Because of simultaneous multiple applications, the timing of admissions decisions can be very important to individiual students and is sometimes a source of confusion and controversy. Some institutions send notifications to applicants on a continuous basis ("rolling admissions"); others hold all for a single mailing—often connected with a "common reply date" upon which institutions have agreed. Some of the latter admit some students on an "early decision plan."

Enrollment. As a final step in the admissions process, students make their own decisions on the basis of offers of admissions received. Institutions typically accept some number of students in excess of available spaces in anticipation of a substantial number of "no shows" who will elect to attend elsewhere.

This process is sometimes called "the great sorting," though its chaotic nature frequently inspires more derogatory epithets. Two aspects of the process are worth noting. First, there is a great deal of self-selection on the part of the students—with respect to both where they send applications and where they finally decide to enroll. Second, multiple applications cause much uncertainty because institutions cannot tell how many and which of the students they accept will actually enroll. Both of these factors tend to limit the institution's ability to assure the particular array of enrolled students that it hopes to attract. This fact in no way relieves the institution of carrying out a defensible admissions policy; it simply makes it more difficult.

The following sections concern five major institutional settings in which selective admissions occur: selective undergraduate colleges, graduate schools of arts and sciences, law schools, medical schools, and graduate management schools. In each case, our intent is to provide some basic facts concerning application and enrollment, to describe briefly important aspects of the admissions process that especially characterize each type of institution, and to indicate the nature of special admissions programs. There follows a discussion of strengths and weaknesses of various measures used to select students, and a brief summary of some of the main points covered in this report.

2

Selective Undergraduate Admissions

Admission to undergraduate education is a concern of a large portion of the American public each year. Nearly two million young people and adults were first-time enrollees in 3,075 accredited institutions across the country in fall 1976 (Grant and Lind, 1976). These institutions serve a variety of students and educational goals through diverse programs.

Undergraduate institutions vary immensely; some practice selective admissions to a high degree, and some others not at all. But to understand current conditions in selective admissions at the undergraduate level, one must note a very important recent trend. The existence of ample (perhaps too ample) staff and physical resources, steady or declining applicant populations, and serious financial problems in many institutions has tended to create a buyer's market in undergraduate admissions.

For many colleges, admissions is not only a means of shaping the institution but, for some, a means of survival. As a result, competition among undergraduate institutions is stronger than since prior to World War II. Some institutions view admissions as a marketing and recruitment process and conduct elaborate research on student demography to determine for what students the institution has special appeal, and how it should "position" itself in the student market. Doermann (1976) has described the marketing prospects for the next 20 years, showing that the pool of students who are both academically well prepared *and* whose families have adequate resources to support them through college is very small. Simultaneously most of these institutions are making strenuous efforts to increase representation of minority students.

Although the role of financial aid programs is extremely complex (for example, Rice, 1977) and institutions have made special efforts to keep admissions decisions and financial assistance decisions separate, it is still evident that student aid policies can modify the most carefully considered admissions program. At many institutions, for example, it is common practice to spread available student assistance funds so as to attract the largest number of students or to attract especially desirable students rather than those who have greatest financial need.

Given this climate in undergraduate admissions and the prospect for even more stringent conditions over the next decade because of progressively declining cohorts of 18-year-olds, many institutions will be forced to give top priority to maintaining enrollment, and their admissions policies and practices will be designed to serve that end. These forces may have their greatest effect on the institutions viewed as moderately selective, but highly selective colleges will undoubtedly have to deal with the same programs to some degree in order to maintain their favored position.

For purposes of this report, it is at times desirable to focus attention on a fairly limited number of undergraduate institutions which, by reputation and practice, are the most prestigious and most selective. As it happens, there is a formally organized small group of institutions that provide a useful, even if not totally representative, view of the most selective colleges in the country. The Consortium on Financing Higher Education (COFHE) was formed in 1975 and currently includes 30 institutions that rank at or near the top of any of the formal yardsticks of selectivity (see Appendix A-1 for a listing). The institutions are all private and include the Ivy League colleges, the Seven Sisters, independent colleges such as Carleton, and major universities such as Duke, Northwestern, and Stanford. The COFHE institutions are a very convenient referent in this section not only because of their character as highly selective institutions, but also because COFHE has compiled considerable group data that are relevant to a description of highly selective admissions (COFHE, 1976).

Sometimes there are rumors that highly selective colleges accept only one candidate out of every eight or ten applicants. In fact, only seven COFHE institutions had an applicant/accepted ratio as high as 4:1 in 1972, or 1975, and none had a ratio higher than 5:1. The relatively high quality of applicants to these institutions, however, tends to make such ratios more competitive than they may seem. The COFHE institutions as a group accepted 40 percent of all applicants in 1972 and 1975.

To increase their chances of admission to these top institutions, many applicants file multiple applications. In 1973 and 1974, 69 percent of all COFHE applicants were accepted in at least one COFHE institution. From these data one might conclude that the majority of prospective students applying to these highly selective colleges and universities have a reasonable assessment of their own abilities and the institution's admissions expectations—another indication that self-selection plays a major role in the admissions process.

There was a time when attendance at a private secondary school was the best guarantee of admission into a highly selective college or university, but this is no longer true. According to Greene and Minton (1975), "one of the most striking changes in the admissions policies of many selective colleges (in the past 25 years) has been a 'tilt' favoring high school applicants over private school applicants" (p. 75). In 1940, 72 boys from Exeter Academy applied to Harvard and all were accepted; in 1950, 72 out of 76 Exeter applicants were accepted, but in 1960 the figure dropped to 60 of 108 and in 1970 dropped further to 38 of 95. This trend likely resulted partly from the improved quality of public high schools and partly from the conscious attempt by the selective colleges to seek a more diversified student body.

Student Population

Each spring approximately three million high school seniors

graduate from the more than 25,000 secondary schools in the United States. The National Center for Educational Statistics reports that first-time, degree-credit enrollment in U.S. colleges and universities increased from 1,740,438 in fall 1972 to 1,906,000 in fall 1976. NCES projects these enrollments to peak in 1979–1980 at 1,938,000 and drop to 1,704,000 by 1984–1985 (Simon and Frankel, 1976, p. 31). A key determinant of first-time enrollments is the number of 18-year-olds in the United States. The number is expected to peak in 1977 at 4.2 million and to return to mid-1960 level of 3.5 million by the mid-1980s. The projected decline begins to level off only after 1994.

Although the number of nonwhite 18-year-olds also is expected to decrease between 1977 and 1994, the rate of decline is much lower. In fact, in 1976 blacks constituted 13.2 percent and other nonwhites 1.7 percent of the 18-year-old population. By 1994, blacks will constitute 15.5 percent and other nonwhites 3.9 percent (see Appendix A-2 for more detail).

Each fall the Cooperative Institutional Research Program sponsored by the American Council on Education and UCLA surveys a representative group of entering college freshmen. Questions range from demographic characteristics to plans, interests, academic background, and personal preferences. According to these data, the proportion of full-time freshmen who reported that they were nonwhite or non-Caucasian increased from 10.1 percent to 13.8 percent between 1967 and 1976. During this period a significant shift occurred in enrollment by type of institution (see Appendix A-3). Two-year colleges had the highest proportion of nonwhites in 1967 (12.3 percent), but four-year colleges had the highest proportion in 1976 (15.2 percent).

Bailey and Collins (1977) analyzed their data to ascertain the effects of race and ability on college attendance patterns. They report that higher percentages of blacks than whites or Hispanics entered four-year colleges in fall 1972 immediately after high school, and that this holds for each of four ability levels (see Appendix A-4). They further analyzed distribution across institutions of high, medium, and low selectivity and concluded that, overall, "blacks tend to congregate in the lower selectivity level four-year colleges, and as compared with whites the difference is striking: nearly 71 percent of blacks who are in four-year colleges are in 'low-level' colleges, as compared to 49 percent of whites" (p. 16). At the same time high-ability blacks appeared to do considerably better than high-ability whites in gaining acceptance to the most selective schools (43 percent versus 24 percent). Nevertheless, one informal study showed that the percentage of black students applying to, and accepting offers of admission from, 13 selective New England colleges had declined over the past five years from 52 percent to 42 percent (*Brown Daily Herald,* March 30, 1977, p. 12).

In 1974, minority students constituted 11.1 percent of all COFHE applicants, 10.8 percent of all accepted applicants, and 10.8 percent of the enrolled freshmen (including nearly equal numbers of men and women). The 10.8 percent enrolled freshmen figure compares with a national average of 14.1 percent for four-year colleges, as reported in Astin's National Norms study (Astin and others, 1974, p. 41; COFHE, 1976, Appendix table I-18).

Minority students who enroll in the highly selective COFHE institutions do not typically come from impoverished backgrounds. The average gross income of the families of minority enrollees in 1974 was $17,400. But there was an $8,700 gap between minority family income and nonminority family average income ($29,100 in 1974). The annual per-student budget ranged from $6,500 to $8,000 yet only 36 percent of the fall 1974 nonminority freshmen received financial aid. Eighty-five percent of the minority students in the same entering class received aid.

The COFHE institutions admitted, on the average, 45 percent of all applicants in 1974 with virtually no difference between minority and nonminority acceptance rates. Similarly, there was virtually no difference in the percentage of accepted applicants who actually enrolled—69 percent of the nonminorities and 68 percent of the minorities.

A difference in academic achievement as determined by SAT scores was apparent between minority and nonminority groups. The mean SAT verbal score for nonminority accepted applicants was 609 and for minority applicants 534. The mean SAT math score for accepted nonminority applicants was 648 and for accepted minority applicants 570. The size of that difference can be illustrated by imagining an arbitrary cutting score. If, for example, COFHE institutions had established an SAT verbal score of 500 as an absolute minimum in 1974, 37 percent of the minority students and 9 percent of the nonminority students admitted would have been rejected. This would have reduced the percent of minority students in the entering freshman class from 10.8 to 7.8 percent, or one half of the national average.

Finally, it should be noted that national data on minority enrollments are far from satisfactory. Agencies, researchers, and the public have had great difficulty in obtaining complete and useful data (Arce, 1976). There are four major problem areas: accuracy of data, errors in usage, incompatibility of current data, and missing data (Abramowitz, 1975). These problems seriously limit sound evaluations of current circumstances in admissions.

Degrees Awarded

Data on undergraduate degrees received by minorities is also difficult to locate, but the National Board on Graduate Education (1976) reported some data for the 1973–1974 academic year. Of 989,200 baccalaureate recipients in that year, 5.3 percent were black, 1.3 percent Spanish-surnamed, 0.9 percent Asian, and 0.3 percent American Indian. The total of 7.8 percent of degrees awarded to minorities is less than the enrollment figures would lead one to expect (see Appendix A-5).

Admissions Procedures

One goal of selective undergraduate admissions programs is to create a balanced class that is academically able and sufficiently diverse to promote a stimulating environment (Kinkead, 1961; Greene and Minton, 1975). To reach such a goal admissions committees rely on both objective data and subjective considerations of a large number of personal, academic, and nonacademic characteristics and experiences.

Selective colleges use the standard recruiting strategies: high school visitations, appearance at college nights and fairs, distribution and brochures and other promotional material that highlight specific academic programs, and active recruitment by alumni. Many also make extensive use of the Student Search Service (SSS), a program of the College Entrance Examination Board that includes the names of admissions test takers who have given permission for their names to be given to inquiring institutions. In 1975–1976, twenty-six of the thirty COFHE colleges used SSS as an aid in identifying and contacting minority and other students who seemed to fit the recruiting interest of the individual colleges.

Test Scores. Each COFHE institution requires a candidate to submit scores from the Scholastic Aptitude Test (SAT). Some also accept ACT scores from the American College Testing Program. It is highly unlikely that any selective college concentrates solely on such academic performance measures as high school grades and test scores, but typically few students with below-average grades and test scores even apply.

Other Considerations. The College Entrance Examination Board asks students taking their admission tests to complete an extensive Student Descriptive Questionnaire (SDQ) concerning activities and personal characteristics relevant to admissions. This information is forwarded to colleges designated by the student along with the test scores (see Appendix F-2; the American College Testing Program has a similar feature). An additional and increasingly utilized feature of the SDQ process is the Summary Report system that provides descriptive information on students for a single institution or any group of institutions. The system has become widely used for management information and research purposes. In addition to test scores and such personal descriptive information, applicants file high school transcripts, personal references, work and activity histories, and many are urged to submit essays, portfolios, or any evidence of creative accomplishment they feel would be useful in assessing qualifications. The personal interview remains an important step in the admissions process at most selective colleges.

Use of Common Procedures. There is a little support among the COFHE colleges for any form of common application, although that procedure is used in some other consortia. Twenty-three of the 30 COFHE schools use the Early Decision Plan, whereby they grant admission to particularly promising applicants on December 15. Whether or not an institution participates in the Early Decision Plan, most selective colleges utilize the Uniform Notification Date. That is, each college holds its notifications of admission until April 15 so that applicants receive notification at the same time.

Although admissions matters are treated separately from the determination of financial need and aid awards, some admissions offices do converse with the financial aid office when it becomes apparent that aid money is running low. At that point, depending upon the philosophy of admissions at the particular institution, a qualified student with financial need is either rejected or given an "admit/deny" notification, which means that a student is admitted, but that request for aid is denied even though need has been documented.

The actual decision process differs widely among institutions, although frequently the admissions staff meets as a committee and bases decisions on guidelines established by a faculty admissions committee. Faculty are involved in the case-by-case deliberations, but frequently in a peripheral manner because of time constraints (Greene and Minton, 1975). In a smaller number of institutions— usually the most selective—faculty are centrally involved and discuss each case in detail. In still other institutions, faculty members evaluate sample cases to help set admissions policy.

In an effort to build a class with complementary strengths and talents, committees typically consider special categories of people and have done so for some years. Children of alumni, minorities, athletes, musicians, and other special cases are considered at least informally by most committees. With the expressed goal of producing a balanced class and with the realization that the actual credentials of many candidates are so similar, it is inevitable that in the final analysis the decision process is judgmental and, therefore, inherently subjective.

Special Admissions

In the 1960s many institutions, selective and nonselective, established special admissions programs. By 1970, more than 800 colleges indicated some form of special consideration for minority/poverty students (College Entrance Examination Board, 1971). Some were informal with only general goals and guidelines, whereas others were formally mandated with specific goals set.

Programs developed in the 1960s frequently included one or more of the following components: recruitment, tutoring, financial counseling and aid, academic counseling, reduction in course load, and housing aid. The U.S. Office of Education gave its support through its "trio" programs: Upward Bound, Talent Search, and Special Services for Disadvantaged Students.

A range of alternative strategies are used in admitting disadvantaged students to selective institutions. The most frequent are the use of minority recruiters, differential treatment of traditional intellective measures, heavier weight on nonintellective factors, and inclusion of minority faculty/students on the admissions committee. Nonintellective factors such as family background, income, motivation, attitude toward education, and other biographical data may prove useful for predicting college success, according to several studies (Gordon, 1970). Nevertheless, one datum that illustrates the overall high ability of selective college applicants is minority student SAT scores. Although the mean SAT total score (combining verbal and mathematical subscores) for minority applicants accepted into one or more COFHE colleges in 1973 and 1974 was approximately 150 points below the score of their nonminority counterparts (COFHE, 1976, Appendix I-21), it was still well above the average of all SAT takers.

Special Assistance

Special services and programs for disadvantaged students lost visibility in the mid 1970s, but at the federal level the financial commitment has been maintained. The budget of the Division of Student Services was increased to $70 million in 1972 and to $85

million by a supplemental appropriation in 1977. In 1976–77, 883
institutions and agencies received funds to identify, stimulate, and
support disadvantaged students. There were 120 Talent Search
agencies, 400 Upward Bound programs in colleges and universities,
350 Special Services programs, and 13 multipurpose Educational
Opportunity Centers.

Each spring four-year awards averaging approximately $5,600
are given by the National Merit Scholarship Corporation to between
550 and 600 outstanding black students for attending four-year
institutions. In 1976–1977, 1,901 such winners were enrolled in 316
colleges and universities across the nation. Forty-two percent were
attending one of the COFHE institutions. The National Scholarship
Service and Fund for Negro Students (NSSFNS) assists black high
school juniors and seniors in obtaining admission and financial aid
at postsecondary institutions. NSSFNS is a source of special guidance
rather than a primary source of funds. NSSFNS does, however,
maintain a Supplementary Scholarship Fund to help fill the gap
between students' total resources and college costs. A computerized
system is used to match students with appropriate colleges. A variety
of NSSFNS programs are provided to assist students and to improve
guidance services.

One other program worthy of mention is the Upper Division
Scholarship Program (UDSA). This program has been administered
by the College Entrance Examination Board since 1971, but will not
be continued after 1977. Funded by the Ford Foundation for six years,
UDSP has provided grants to promising two-year college graduates
for their continued studies at baccalaureate-granting institutions.
Nearly 5,000 students have been nominated by their colleges and have
received financial awards. An additional several thousand who did
not receive awards were identified as promising, and many of these
were recruited by four-year institutions. of the 5,000 students
receiving aid, 75 percent went on to public colleges and universities
and 25 percent attended private institutions. The College Board also
waives test fees, and many colleges waive application fees for
minority students.

*   *   *

This section on selective undergraduate admissions notes the declining population of 18-year-olds, the resulting buyer's market in the undergraduate setting, the competition among institutions for students, and the critical role of financial aid. Noted also is the diversity of undergraduate institutions. National data indicate that nonwhites represented a greater proportion of the entering freshman class in 1976 than in 1967. However, some data suggest that black representation in the 1976 entering classes of some selective undergraduate institutions may be less than it was in 1970.

3

Admissions to Graduate Schools of Arts and Sciences

Selective admission practices in graduate schools of arts and science contrast significantly with those in undergraduate institutions. Much decentralized, autonomous authority rests with small faculty committees in individual departments and sometimes with individual faculty members. While there are some national organizations whose primary concern is graduate education (for example, Council of Graduate Schools and the Association of Graduate Schools) these organizations do not exert as much influence over educational practices as do similar organizations in other settings (for example, Association of American Law Schools, Association of American Medical Colleges). The national organizations that influence graduate education are as numerous as the disciplines taught in graduate schools. The *Graduate Programs and Admissions Manual* of the Graduate Record Examinations Board (Graduate Record Examinations Board, 1976) lists some 82 departments and numerous interdisciplinary programs. A description of selective admissions in graduate schools is, therefore, inherently complex.

Institutions

For 1970, the Carnegie Commission on Higher Education (1973b, pp. 12, 15, 20, 22, 33, 41) counted 173 doctoral granting institutions and

453 comprehensive universities and colleges, many of which granted only master's degrees. In 1976, there were 354 members of the Council of Graduate Schools (CGS). For 243 of these CGS schools, the Ph.D. is the highest degree offered. Of these, 154 are public and 89 private (Somerville, 1976). Master's-degree-only programs, which are offered by 111 graduate schools, have assumed an increasingly important role in recent years. This change in master's programs has been coupled with increased diversity in the types of programs and in the preparation required for them.

Financial Support

In graduate admissions an acceptance without concomitant financial aid is considered by many to be equivalent to a rejection. Graduate schools have suffered sharp declines in financial support since the late 1960s. Graduate fellowship and assistantship awards decreased from 51,446 in 1968 to 18,472 in 1974 (National Board on Graduate Education, 1976, p. 107). Many special federal research programs have also been terminated and foundation grants have waned under a number of pressures. The decline in federal financial aid for graduate study relates to the decline in the job market for the products of graduate schools, since (in terms of federal incentives) there is no need to encourage Ph.D. or master's degree production when there are limited jobs available. These trends affect all graduate applicants, but especially minority students who are more likely to need financial assistance.

Student Population

Estimates of graduate school enrollment published by the National Center for Educational Statistics (NCES) show a steadily increasing enrollment during the past 10 to 15 years (Simon and Frankel, 1976). NCES estimates between 1970 and 1976 are given in Table 1 for both public and private institutions. These figures indicate a 26 percent increase in public and 16 percent increase in private graduate school enrollment between 1970 and 1976 (see Appendix B-1 for estimates from 1964–1984 for men and women and for full-time versus part-time).

Graduate enrollment in public institutions is projected by NCES to increase from 942,000 in 1977 to a peak of 1,013,000 in 1982, but a decline is anticipated in 1983 and 1984. In contrast, enrollment in private institutions is expected to increase only from 361,000 in 1977 to a peak of 369,000 in 1980, with a decline beginning in 1981 and continuing to 1984.

Table 1. Enrollments in public and private graduate
schools in the United States, 1970—1976

(in thousands)

| Year | Total | NCES estimates | |
		Public	Private
1970	1,031	724	307
1971	1,012	712	300
1972	1,066	757	308
1973	1,123	799	324
1974	1,190	852	338
1975	1,232	885	347
1976	1,268	913	355

Source: Simon & Frankel (1976).

The NCES estimates are considered optimistic by some observers (for example, National Board on Graduate Education, 1975), and some data suggest that, in fact, graduate enrollments began to level off in 1976. Somerville (1976) reports on surveys by the Council of Graduate Schools—Graduate Record Examinations Board (CGS-GREB) that show a decline in public graduate school enrollments between 1975 and 1976 and no change in private graduate school enrollments (see Appendix B-3). While the CGS-GREB surveys have limitations and the fields of study covered are probably slightly different from those in the NCES projections, they support the contention that the NCES projections may be optimistic. The 354 member institutions of the CGS grant 99 percent of the earned doctorates and 85 percent of the master's degrees awarded, and the 1975 and 1976 CGS samples are representative of the total CGS population.

The CGS-GREB surveys also show a decrease in first-time graduate enrollment of 3.5 percent between 1975 and 1976 (see Appendix B-4). However, the number of applicants to CGS institutions surveyed increased by 1.3 percent between 1975 and 1976 (see Appendix B-5). Increases and decreases in applications and enrollments by type of institution are summarized in Table 2. The CGS institutions surveyed also reported a slight decrease in the number of Ph.D. degrees awarded between 1975 and 1976 (see Appendix B-6).

Table 2. Applications and first-time enrollments in CGS surveys, 1975–1976
(in thousands)

| Institutional type | Applications (top figure) and first-time enrollments | | |
	1975	1976	Percent Change
Public Ph.D. granting	358	366	+2.1
	113	105	-6.6
Public Masters granting	62	60	-3.5
	30	29	-0.5
Private Ph.D. granting	149	151	+1.4
	39	40	+1.1
Private Masters granting	12	12	—
	5	5	—
Totals	581	589	+1.3
	187	179	-3.5

Source: Somerville (1976).

Minority Enrollments

Data on minority enrollments in graduate schools are available from five primary sources. Surveys are conducted biennially by the Office for Civil Rights (OCR) of the Department of Health, Education and Welfare, and the National Association of State Universities and Land Grant Colleges (NASULGC). The American Council on Education (ACE), and Education Testing Service (ETS) have also collected data on minority enrollments. OCR surveys were undertaken in 1968, 1970, 1972, 1974, and 1976, but the 1976 data have not yet been released. A 1971 survey by ETS was reported by Hamilton (1973), a 1972 NASULGC was reported by the National Board on Graduate Education (1976) and a 1973 ACE study of 228 doctorate-granting institutions was reported by El-Khawas and Kinzer (1974). Finally, the 1975 and 1976 CGS surveys (Somerville, 1977) collected data on minority enrollment. These surveys are not entirely comparable, and it is difficult to draw firm conclusions about trends in minority enrollment. Nevertheless, they represent the best data available. Table 3 presents percentage of full-time minority students between

1968 and 1976 for the OCR and CGS surveys only, since they cover the time span and interest. (A more detailed table summarizing the surveys will be found in Appendix B-7).

Table 3. Percent minority representation in graduate schools

Group	1968 (OCR)	1970 (OCR)	1972 (OCR)	1974 (OCR)	1975[a] (CGS)	1976[a] (CGS)
White	94.7	92.3	90.8	90.8	87.8	87.5
Black	3.4	4.2	5.3	5.5	6.7	6.4
Spanish-surnamed	0.8	1.2	1.5	1.5	1.3	1.5
American Indian	0.2	0.3	0.4	0.4	0.4	0.4
Asian or other minority	0.9	1.9	2.1	1.8	3.6	4.1

[a] Figures are based on limited response rates, which may explain the differences observed between the CGS and OCR percentages.

The OCR and CGS surveys are not appropriate for the study of total enrollment trends, since different sampling techniques were used, but they do provide percentage distributions by ethnic classification and some notion of trends in minority representation. For example, in the 1968 OCR survey (U.S. Department of Health, Education and Welfare, Office for Civil Rights, 1975), blacks represented only 3.4 percent of the full-time graduate school enrollment, in the 1974 OCR survey they represented 5.5 percent, and in the 1976 CGS survey, 6.4 percent. Spanish-surnamed students represented 0.8 percent in 1968 and 1.5 percent in 1976, and American Indians represented 0.2 percent in 1968 and 0.4 percent in 1976. By contrast, the surveys indicate that white students decreased in representation from 94.7 percent in 1968 to 87.5 percent in 1976.

There are a number of difficulties in interpreting these surveys (see Abramowitz, 1975; Arce, 1976; and López, Madrid-Barela, and Macías, 1976, for discussions of data problems). The 1968 OCR survey was limited to a relatively small number—approximately 150,000—of graduate students. The 1970 OCR survey (and presumably the 1968 OCR survey) included enrollments in professional schools and, accordingly, are not entirely comparable to the 1972 and 1974 OCR surveys. Nor can one be sure that the OCR and CGS surveys are comparable. Moreover, there is a problem with respect to inclusion or exclusion of certain groups. For example, Asian includes native-born Asians as well as Asians from other countries attending U.S. graduate schools on visas. Spanish-surnamed persons include persons from Spain as well as those from South and Central America and Cuba. Thus, the representation of Chicanos, Puerto Ricans, and other U.S. minorities is actually smaller than the surveys indicate.

CGS unpublished data show that *first-time* graduate enrollment between 1975 and 1976 decreased for all groups studied except Chicanos and Puerto Ricans. Blacks made up 7.0 percent of the first-time enrollment in the 1975 CGS survey and 6.6 percent in the 1976 CGS survey. Nonminorities made up 88.0 percent in 1975 and 88.3 percent in 1976.

Degrees Awarded

Projections of degree awards expected for men and women have been made by NCES. Doctorates awarded to men are expected to peak in 1976–1977, while doctorates awarded to women show a steady increase. By the 1984–1985 academic year NCES expects that women will earn a third of all doctorates compared with less than a fourth in 1975–76 (see Appendix B-2).

Data on doctorates awarded by ethnic classification and by citizenship status has been compiled by the National Board on Graduate Education (National Board on Graduate Education, 1976). In a sample of 29,241 doctorates awarded in 1973–74, blacks received 1,010 (3.4 percent), Orientals 2,204 (7.5 percent), and Hispanics 274 (0.9 percent). But only 846 (2.9 percent) black doctorates, 293 (1.0 percent) Oriental doctorates, and 195 (0.7 percent) Hispanic doctorates were received by U.S. citizens (see Appendix B-8).

The distribution of minorities among the graduate school disciplines is a special concern because of the low level of participation in academic disciplines such as the physcial sciences, mathematics, and engineering. Of 833 black U.S. native-born citizens who received doctorates only 62 (7.4 percent) received them in physical science, mathematics or engineering as compared with over 20 percent of white doctorates in these fields. A total of 493 (59.2 percent) of the black doctorates were received in education, but only 24.1 percent of the white doctorates were in education (see Appendices B-9 and B-10).

More recent data compiled by Altman and Holland (1977) suggest a shift away from education by blacks. Of students taking the Graduate Record Examination (GRE) during 1975-76, only 19.1 percent of blacks intended to study education as a graduate major as compared to 16.2 percent of whites. Still, only 5.4 percent of blacks responding intended to study physical science, mathematics, or engineering as compared to 9.8 percent of whites (see Appendix B-11). These distributional differences exacerbate the problem of inadequate minority representation within certain faculties (Carnegie Council on Policy Studies in Higher Education, 1975, p.23).

Admissions Procedures

Despite their heterogeneity, some common aspects of admissions policy exist in almost all graduate schools. In a survey conducted by Richard L. Burns in 1969, only 7 percent of 245 graduate schools sampled indicated that they had no overall policy. The departments reported having the major voice in admissions decisions, although the graduate dean had a veto in 52 percent of the institutions surveyed. The graduate dean's office has a primary role in approximately two-thirds of the schools in preparing announcements of admissions policy and requirements, setting deadlines, informing students of admissions decisions, informing students of fellowship decisions, and in retaining current application files. The Burns survey indicated, further, that information about admissions policies is commonly communicated through the catalog,and that specific information that is not included in the catalog is provided on request.

The majority of graduate schools reported some prerequisites that applied across all departments. Eighty-nine percent required a bachelor's degree or its equivalent and 76 percent required that it be from an accredited institution. Sixty-nine percent required a certain GPA or class rank. Less than 25 percent of the institutions replied that they required an undergraduate major in the field of graduate application or a minimum admission test score. Ninety-nine percent of the institutions required a college transcript, and 92 percent required a completed application form. Letters of recommendation were required by 52 percent, GRE Aptitude Test results by 45 percent, statements of purpose or study plans by 45 percent, and GRE

Advanced Test results by 22 percent. Personality tests, photographs, biographical sketches, and academic rating forms were rarely required and rarely used if available.

Very few departments used either the GRE Aptitude or Advanced Test results as the most important (or least important) factor in the admissions decision. In order of importance, the five most important admissions criteria reported by Burns were college transcripts, completed application forms, GRE Aptitude Test scores, letters of recommendation, and GRE Advanced Test scores. Students participated in establishing admissions policy and in selection of students for admission or fellowship awards in 25 percent of the institutions, although the student role was primarily advisory. In very few institutions did students have a vote (see Appendix B-12 for a listing of the major findings of Burns' survey).

Special Programs

The promotion of special admissions programs in graduate schools is made difficult by the decentralized nature and other traditions of those schools. As one source observed, law and medicine are "easy cases" when compared to graduate schools (National Board on Graduate Education, 1976, p. 143). A report published by the Graduate Minority Program at the University of California at Berkeley describes ways to improve admissions of minorities into graduate study and the objectives of some programs (University of California, Berkeley, 1973). One particularly effective national activity is that represented by the Graduate Record Examinations Board's Minority Graduate Student Locator Service (Educational Testing Service, 1976). This service was developed to help minority students call themselves to the attention of graduate schools and to help schools identify potential minority applicants.

The federal role in special graduate programs is somewhat different from the federal role in special undergraduate programs. The stated objective of many federal undergraduate programs is to provide every high school graduate with an opportunity to obtain postsecondary education. At the graduate level, federal policy is based more on merit and manpower needs. Special federal programs similar to those in undergraduate education are rare (National Board on Graduate Education, 1976), although some foundation support is less tied to merit and more to need (for example, the Ford Foundation minority program described below). A number of financial aid programs are described in Appendix B-13, some of which are described briefly in the following paragraphs.

The National Institutes of Health (NIH) program on Minority Biomedical Support (MBS) provides funding for research projects in institutions with a significant commitment to the education of minorities. Although the MBS program focused initially on black colleges, it was later broadened to include persons from other minority groups. In 1975, the MBS program provided support for 145 graduate students.

The National Institute of Mental Health (NIMH) sponsors several programs intended to involve minority persons in its research and training activities. One early NIMH activity consisted of a program of grants and services to universities that supported both minority students and faculty. Later NIMH programs provided student fieldwork experiences through the Institute's community mental health centers. A new fellowship program within the Alcohol, Drug Abuse, and Mental Health Administration of NIMH is administered by professional associations in sociology, social welfare, psychiatry, psychology, and nursing. The professional associations serve as a mechanism for selecting and monitoring students awarded fellowships. NIMH has also established six minority research and development centers funded at $200,000 annually. In the Social Sciences Research Training Grant program, NIMH has a stated goal of 25 percent minority enrollment.

There has also been foundation support for minority graduate education. The Ford Foundation Graduate Fellowships, designed to aid specific minority groups, is one of the more well-known programs. The program is oriented towards minority persons studying in various fields of the social sciences, natural sciences, and the humanities. These Ford fellowships currently support about 375 minority students.

*   *   *

In this section, some emphasis has been placed on the diverse and decentralized nature of education in the U.S. graduate schools.

Data presented on graduate school enrollments indicate that past projections of steadily increasing graduate enrollments until the mid-1980's may be optimistic. One study showed a decline in graduate enrollments beginning in 1976, suggesting the possibility that students may be overreacting to the recent employment picture for Ph.D.s and other graduate school products. While the data are questionable, it would appear that minorities' representation in graduate schools has increased. Blacks represented only about 3 percent of graduate enrollments in 1968 but probably more than 6 percent in 1976. A number of financial aid programs for minority students are noted, but it is clear that these have a relatively small impact on the total pool of minority graduate students.

4

Admissions to Law Schools

There are more lawyers per capita in the United States than in any other country except Israel, and the 445,000 lawyers of 1977 are expected to grow to 600,000 by 1985 (*New York Times*, May 17, 1977, p. 155). Nonetheless, there still exist unmet needs for legal services in middle class rural areas and in minority and other disadvantaged groups. These needs persist even though enrollment in law schools has almost doubled during the past 10 years. While the unmet needs vis-à-vis the increasing lawyer production seems paradoxical, it should be remembered that all law graduates do not practice law and those who do tend to gravitate toward affluent metropolitan areas.

Institutions

The total number of law schools has oscillated somewhat since about 1930, but the number of approved (accredited) schools has increased steadily. The American Bar Association (ABA) began classifying law schools as approved for the first time in the 1920s and, by 1977, there were 163 approved law schools (American Bar Association, 1976, p. 6-40). In 1930 there were a total of 180 law schools, but by 1944 this number had decreased to 159 (Hughes et al., 1973, p. 106). The table on the opposite page shows the growth in the number of accredited law schools over the past 33 years.

The most prestigious law schools have always been associated with universities. The case method forms the basic instructional procedure at most schools. The case method is significant in law schools in that it usually is accompanied by an isolation of professional training from professional practice. That is, in most law schools there is nothing analogous to clinical training in medical education. Hughes and others (1973, p. 106) describe an attempt to develop a more clinical orientation in legal education in the 1930s. but it was not successful. In recent years there has been another movement in that direction, and almost all law schools now have limited clinical training; many states have instituted laws allowing law students to practice under the supervision of an attorney. Except for a few schools, however, both the curricula and the teaching methods in law schools are primarily nonclinical.

Year	Number of ABA-accredited law schools
1944	109
1950	120
1960	132
1963	134
1975	157
1977	163

Student Population

Following World War II, enrollments in law schools boomed, and a peak 1940s figure of 57,759 occurred in 1949. Through the 1950s enrollment stabilized at around 35,000. Another increase began in about 1961, and by 1966 enrollments in ABA-approved schools had expanded to 62,556. Table 4 shows the trend in enrollments between 1966 and 1976. The increased competition for seats is demonstrated by comparing the number of persons taking the Law School Admission Test (LSAT) with the number of first-year law students (Table 5).

These figures indicate that over a 10-year period the number of persons taking the Law School Admission Test (LSAT) increased by almost 200 percent while the number of first-year places increased by only about 62 percent. While not all law school applicants take the LSAT, and many take it more than once, it serves as a rough indicator of the number of applicants. Clearly, law school admission has become much more competitive over the past 10 years. The increase in number of applications has resulted in an average increase in the quality of the academic credentials presented by applicants. Consequently, many qualified applicants must be turned away (Evans, 1977, p. 3).

Degrees Awarded

Degrees awarded and admissions to the bar have increased steadily in recent years. In 1963, there were 9,638 J.D. or LL.B. degrees awarded; by 1975, this figure had almost tripled to 29,961. And new admissions to the bar increased similarily from 10,738 in 1963 to more than 35,000 by 1975 (American Bar Association, 1976, p. 45).

Table 4. Enrollment in ABA-approved law schools

Year	Total	Women	Minorities[a]	Percent Women	Percent Minorities[a]
1966	62,556	2,678		4.3	
1967	64,406	2,906		4.5	
1968	62.779	3,704		5.9	
1969	68,386	4,715	2,933	6.9	4.3
1970[b]	82,478	7,031		8.5	
1971	94,468	8,914	5,568	9.4	5.9
1972	101,707	12,173	6,730	12.0	6.6
1973	106,102	16,760	7,601	15.8	7.2
1974	110,713	21,788	8,333	19.7	7.5
1975	116,991	26,737	8,702	22.8	7.4
1976	115,548	29,497	9,524	25.5	8.2

[a] Includes blacks, Chicanos, American Indians, Puerto Ricans, Orientals, and other unspecified minorities.

[b] Minority data not available for 1970.

Sources: ABA (1976); unpublished data for 1976 figures.

Table 5. Applicants and admissions to ABA-approved law schools

Year	No. of LSAT takers[a]	LSAT mean score	First-year law students
1966	44,905	511	24,077
1967	47,110	514	24,267
1968	49,756	516	23,652
1969	59,050	516	29,128
1970	74,092	518	34,713
1971	107,479	519	36,171
1972	119,694	521	35,131
1973	121,262	522	37,018
1974	135,397	527	38,074
1975	133,546	520	39,038
1976	133,609	525	39,218

[a] These figures include persons who repeat the LSAT, which is over 20 percent of the total in some years.

Sources: ABA (1976); unpublished data for 1976 figures.

Minority Enrollments

During this same period of increasing competition for law school seats, many law schools were making efforts to increase the enrollments of minorities. The impetus for these efforts grew out of a consideration of the numbers of minority lawyers vis-à-vis the total number of lawyers in the population. In 1970 there were only 3,845 black lawyers in the United States out of the total of 335,242 lawyers, about 1 percent (*Pre-Law Handbook,* 1972–73, p. 9). Of particular interest in Table 4 is the contrast in enrollment of women and minorities. Since 1969 women's representation in law school classes has increased almost four times to over 25 percent, while minority representation has nearly doubled. First-year law school enrollments in ABA-approved schools, by minority group, are given in Table 6. These first-year enrollment figures show increases in total enrollments for blacks, Chicanos, and other minority groups. When considered in terms of percent representation, however, the increases occur only until about 1972 for blacks and Chicanos. Other minorities show steady increases in representation between 1971 and 1976. The representation of women in first-year law classes increased from 11.8 percent in 1971 to 28.1 percent in 1976. Further details are given in Appendices C-1 and C-2.

Attrition of minority versus nonminority students from law schools can be estimated from enrollment data given in each annual ABA report of law school statistics. That is, the difference between second-year enrollments and first-year enrollments for given law school classes in the same law schools provides an estimate of attrition. Table 7 shows that the attrition rate for minorities, while almost twice that of all students for the law classes entering in 1971 (23 percent versus 13 percent), was down to 17 percent for classes entering in 1975.

Admissions Procedures

Until the post–World War II period, records of undergraduate performance and letters of recommendation were the primary information used in law school admissions. As the number and diversity of applicants began to increase rapidly, however, schools found it more difficult to compare credentials, and there were too many applications to process in the customary way. In recognition of

LEWIS AND CLARK COLLEGE LIBRARY
PORTLAND, OREGON 97219

Table 6. First-year enrollments in ABA-approved law schools by minority group

Year	Total	Black	Chicano	Other minorities[a]
1969	29,128	1,115 (3.8%)	245 (0.8%)	
1970[b]	34,713			
1971	36,171	1,716 (4.7%)	403 (1.1%)	443 (1.2%)
1972	35,131	1,907 (5.4%)	480 (1.4%)	546 (1.6%)
1973	37,018	1,943 (5.2%)	539 (1.4%)	626 (1.7%)
1974	38,074	1,898 (5.0%)	560 (1.5%)	838 (2.2%)
1975	39,038	2,045 (5.2%)	484 (1.2%)	884 (2.3%)
1976	39,218	2,128 (5.4%)	542 (1.4%)	991 (2.5%)

[a] Includes Puerto Ricans, American Indians, Asian Americans, other Hispanic groups, and other unspecified minorities.

[b] Minority data not available for 1970.

Sources: ABA (1976); unpublished data for 1976 figures.

Table 7. Attrition rates for minority students in law school

Year Entered	First-year enrollment		Second-year enrollment		Attrition rate (in percent)	
	All students	Minority	All students	Minority	All students	Minority
1971	36,171	2,567	31,077	1,988	13	23
1972	35,131	2,934	30,980	2,287	12	22
1973	37,018	3,114	33,489	2,602	10	16
1974	38,074	3,308	34,227	2,639	10	20
1975	39,083	3,413	35,189	2,846	10	17

Source: Adapted from: Brief Amicus Curiae for the Association of American Law Schools in Regents of the University of California v. Bakke (Supreme Court of the U.S., 1977.

these problems, a small number of law schools affiliated in 1947 to develop a common measure to facilitate comparisons among students. The measure developed was the Law School Admission Test (LSAT).

Only 18 law schools required the LSAT in 1948, but by 1968, 90 percent of law students were enrolled in law schools requiring the LSAT (Schrader, 1968, p. 25). In 1977, all schools accredited by the ABA required the LSAT. The increased use of the LSAT was related both to its demonstrated predictive capabilities and to the increased number of applications to law schools. To handle large numbers of applications in an economical, efficient and equitable manner, the Law School Admission Council (LSAC) established a Law School Data Assembly Service (LSDAS) which provides member law schools with LSAT scores, biographical data, copies of official transcripts, and a transcript analysis.

Some law schools, for example, use the LSDAS or similarly organized information to place all applicants into one of three groups based on a numerical index developed from the LSAT score and undergraduate grades. These groups are sometimes labeled as: (1) Presumptive Admit, (2) Presumptive Deny, and (3) Hold (Evans, 1977, p. 47). Applicants are moved into or out of these three groups after study of other information in their application folders. The Presumptive Admit category indicates that there exists a strong presumption to admit applicants initially placed in it on the basis of the numerical index. Similarly, the Presumptive Deny category implies a proclivity to deny admission. Applicants in the Hold category, however, receive an extensive review and many factors other than academic credentials are considered. Schools that follow this procedure vary with respect to the proportions of applicants placed in the three categories and with respect to the factors that are considered. Many law schools shy away from mechanical procedures, preferring to avoid sorting based on numerical indices.

Turnbull and others (1976) described and analyzed the procedures used at five anonymous law schools in detail and compared these five schools with a large national sample. These schools included public and private schools as well as large and small schools, and they were chosen to represent a variety of admission techniques. Admissions officials at the five schools were interviewed and a random sample of 250 individual files were selected from the 1971 applicant pool at each school. Questionaires were sent to most other law schools in the United States so as to compare the five law schools in the study with law schools in general. The majority of the law schools studied used some form of admissions index based upon a combination of undergraduate grades and LSAT scores, but rigid use of numerical indices was rare.

The following quotation, from Gellhorn and Hornby (1974), further illustrates law school admissions procedures:

The process of actual decision-making cannot be ... easily catalogued. The practice among schools is ... varied and frequently varies from year to year within a school as membership on admissions committees rotates. Seldom does a school's catalogue reveal its selection method. Our experience suggests, however, that several practices are common. ...

Typically, a law school's admissions committee relies heavily (but not mechanically) on an admissions index based on the applicant's undergraduate grade average and LSAT score. Some schools weigh each factor equally, while others give predominance to one or the other. Moreover, the committee members and director may themselves assign different weights to grades and test scores, so that such assessments may differ markedly even within an institution. If the applicant's undergraduate school or course load is considered particularly rigorous or lax, the significance of the grades may be adjusted.

Most state-supported schools give considerable preference to in-state residents. Preference may also be given to those with additional experience after law school, a strong record of extracurricular activities, or success in the face of adversity such as a physical handicap. Letters of recommendation are generally required but are seldom given substantial weight. They are usually viewed as self-serving documents since the applicant selects his sponsors. Few schools rely on personal interviews for evaluating applicants.

Financial aid requests generally are not considered with the application and a student's economic situation plays a role only where the student's success would seem to indicate strong motivation. Occasionally a school will seek to summarize these subjective criteria in a "personal index" using a point scale. This point assignment is added to the objective admissions index (of grades and LSAT score) to reach a composite total for comparative evaluations in deciding close cases [pp. 977-978].

Appendix C-11 contains a brief description of procedures used at the University of Virginia law school, and Appendix C-12 presents admissions information given in the *Pre-Law Handbook* (Association of American Law Schools, 1976) for the Harvard Law School. Even with details usually unavailable, such as those for the University of Virginia, one find that a complete understanding of law school admissions procedures is somewhat elusive. It is perhaps more useful to turn to data on the actual outcomes of procedures nationally.

Minority Admissions

Evans (1977; see Appendices C-3 through C-10) presents some detailed data on 1976 applicants to law schools categorized by undergraduate GPA strata as well as LSAT score ranges. The total number of applicants for whom LDAS reports were sent in 1976 was 76,061, and it was possible to relate this total to the number of applicants who received offers *from at least one ABA approved law school*. Acceptance rates, by group, in 1976 based on Evans' data were:

Group	Applicants	Offers	Acceptance rate
Total	76,061	43,513	57%
Men	54,473	30,531	56%
Women	21,588	12,953	60%
Blacks	4,299	1,697	39%
Chicanos	1,085	510	47%
Unspecified minorities	3,683	1,892	51%
Whites	66,994	39,284	59%

For further details, see Appendices C-3 through C-9. One may also compare acceptance rates within undergraduate GPA ranges as in Table 8. In some of the GPA ranges (for example, 3.00–3.24) acceptance rates were quite uniform in 1976, but in other GPA ranges (for example, 2.00–2.24) there was considerable disparity. Acceptance rates within LSAT score ranges are given in Table 9, where the greatest disparity in acceptance rates also occurs in the lower-ability ranges. But whereas whites with low GPAs were preferred over minorities with low GPAs, minorities with low LSAT scores were preferred over whites with low LSAT scores. Probaly most meaningful for comparison are acceptance rates for categories of applicants based upon *both* undergraduate grade averages *and* LSAT scores, as shown in Table 10. Blacks and Chicanos had higher acceptance rates in 1976 than either whites or other minorities for all the categories shown. Blacks and Chicanos with very high GPAs and reasonably good LSAT scores (500-600) had a 100 percent rate of acceptance. See Appendix C-10 for further comparisons of this type.

Table 8. Acceptance rates within undergraduate GPA ranges (in percent)

GPA range	Black	Chicano	Unspecified minority	White
3.74+	86	90	83	91
3.50−3.74	77	85	75	83
3.25−3.49	69	69	67	72
3.00−3.24	61	61	59	60
2.75−2.99	45	50	46	48
2.50−2.74	34	33	35	37
2.25−2.49	25	26	30	28
2.00−2.24	14	12	12	21

Table 9. Acceptance rates within LSAT score ranges (in percent)

LSAT score range	Black	Chicano	Other minority	White
650−699	89	100	89	88
600−649	85	85	82	81
550−599	87	86	72	67
500−549	77	69	56	47
450−499	63	59	43	27
400−449	43	35	25	14
350−399	25	19	12	6

Table 10. Acceptance rates within GPA and LSAT ranges (in percent)

	LSAT score range							
	500−549				550−599			
Undergraduate GPA	Black	Chicano	Other Minority	White	Black	Chicano	Other Minority	Whit
3.74+	100	100	90	83	100	100	88	91
3.50−3.74	94	94	69	72	100	100	84	87
3.25−3.49	90	77	65	60	96	90	87	80
3.00−3.24	90	84	60	50	96	95	77	69
2.75−2.99	84	77	56	40	97	100	67	58
2.50−2.74	82	54	42	31	80	54	49	48

Source: Evans (1977).— See Appendices C-6 through C-10 for further details.

Special Admissions

The greater acceptance rates for minority applicants with lower numerical indices reflect the trend toward admissions programs in which numerical indicators are given less emphasis than other factors in the folders of applicants who have identified themselves as minorities. Some indication of the way these programs work can be obtained from records made public by litigation. In *DeFunis v. Odegaard*, for example, minority applicants who would normally have been included in the Presumptive Deny group, based on numerical studies, were considered by a special minority admissions committee which included minority students. Therefore, in effect, there existed no Presumptive Deny group for minorities.

Special Programs

Another approach that has been used to increase enrollments of minorities in law schools is that of special recruitment and training programs. The Law School Admission Council sponsors a Candidate Referral Service that is similar to the Graduate Record Examinations Board's Locator Service and the AAMs Minority Student Registry. The Council on Legal Educational Opportunity (CLEO) is a federally funded program sponsored jointly by the American Association of Law Schools, the National Bar Association, the Law School Admissions Council, and La Raza National Lawyers Association (*Pre-Law Handbook*, 1976–77). CLEO sponsors summer study programs for minority students interested in entering law school. These summer courses at law schools throughout the country consist of six weeks of study in writing and legal reasoning. In addition to CLEO programs, a number of individual law schools offer preparatory programs for minority applicants. Other support activities, such as tutorial programs, part-time work in law firms, and financial aid have been described by the Association of American Law Schools (1970.)

*   *   *

The data on law schools show a rapidly increasing enrollment over the past 10 years accompanied by increasing competition for admission. The increased competition means that many applicants who would have been admitted in previous years are not admitted now. The impact of several national law organizations on the process of selection for law school admission and minority recruitment is of selection for law school admission and minority recruitment is evident. Cooperative efforts by these national organizations have yielded some unique activities, such as that exemplified by CLEO. Another highlight of this section is the availability of complete data on law school applicants for one recent year. These data are instructive of the nature of student selection in these schools. Since 1969, minority representation in U.S. schools has almost doubled. More dramatic increases in enrollment representation have occurred for women, however. In 1966, women represented only about 4 percent of total law school enrollments, but in 1976 they represented more than 22 percent. For the first-year class entering in the fall of 1976, women made up 28 percent of the total.

5

Admissions to
Medical Schools

Medical school admissions committees attempt not only to select those individuals most likely to become good physicians but also those most likely to serve societal needs for health care delivery. Since there is an excess of academically qualified applicants, increasing attention in selection is paid to personal qualities of applicants. One such shift has been the selection of an increased proportion of underrepresented minorities entering medical school classes.

The medical school curriculum leading to the M.D. degree generally requires four years. The purpose of undergraduate medical education is to provide preparation for further medical training. Thus the broad curriculum includes both basic medical sciences and extensive clinical training. Virtually all medical school graduates enter graduate medical educational programs for further training of one to seven years in a particular medical speciality.

Although admissions to medical school have almost doubled in the last decade there exists a demand for physicians that has not been satisfied. The ratio of white physicians to the white population is 1 to 538; however, the ratio of black physicians to the black population is 1 to 4,100. These differences are further exaggerated in certain regions of the country. For example, the ratio for blacks in Georgia is 1 to 8,903 (*New York Times*, May 10, 1977, p. 12). Similar situations exist for other minority groups and in diverse settings (for example, inner city and rural areas), and there has been a concerted effort by individual medical schools (Johnson, Smith, Tarnoff, 1975; Ode-

gaard, 1977) and by the Association of American Medical Colleges
(1975) to increase the number of qualified applicants from groups
currently underrepresented in medical education. A further aim is to
select individuals likely to practice in poorly served areas and in
primary care specialties.

Student Population

Table 11 summarizes medical school enrollment between 1966 and
1976. The number of applicants to American medical schools has
increased dramatically from 18,250 for the class of 1966-67 to 42,155
for 1976-77. Although the number of places in medical schools has
increased from 8,991 to almost 16,000, only 37.4 percent of applicants
were accepted in 1976. Half of the applicant pool had been accepted
10 years earlier. It is interesting that the number of applicants
decreased slightly for the first time in a decade in 1975-76 and
another decrease occurred in 1976-77. The average number of
applications per individual increased from 4.8 in 1966 to 8.5 and 8.6 in
1974 and 1975, respectively (see Appendix D-1). The increasing
disparity between the number of applicants and the number of
entering places in medical school has resulted in increased competition among premedical students and major problems for the rejected
applicants, many of whom have not seriously considered alternative
careers (Levine, Weisman, and Seidel, 1974).

Minority Enrollment

The proportion of underrepresented minorities in entering medical
classes increased from 3.0 percent in 1968 to a high of 10.0 percent in
1974 (see Table 12 and Appendix D-2) but dropped to 9.0 percent in
1976. The proportion of women entering medical schools during the
same period rose from 9.0 percent to 24.7 percent (somewhat similar
to the figures for law schools—5.9 percent women students in 1968
and 25.5 percent in 1976). Of 2,288 blacks who applied for admission
to medical school for the 1975-76 first-year class, 945 (41 percent)
were accepted; of 427 Chicano applicants, 220 (52 percent) were
accepted; and of 34,868 white applicants, 12,985 (37 percent) were
accepted. For other groups, 32 percent of Orientals were accepted, 42
percent of mainland Puerto Ricans, 36 percent of Commonwealth

Table 11. Medical school applicant data, 1966—1975

First-year class	Number of applicants	Accepted applicants	Percentage of total applicants accepted
1966—67	18,250	9,123	50.0
1967—68	18,724	9,702	51.8
1968—69	21,118	10,092	47.9
1969—70	24,465	10,547	43.1
1970—71	24,987	11,500	46.0
1971—72	29,172	12,335	42.3
1972—73	36,135	13,757	38.1
1973—74	40,506	14,335	35.4
1974—75	42,624	15,066	35.3
1975—76	42,303	15,365	36.3
1976—77	42,155	15,774	37.4

Table 12. Medical school first-year enrollment data, 1966—1977

First-year class	First-year enrollment	First-year underrepresented minority enrollment[a] cohort groups		Women	
1966—67	8,991				
1967—68	9,473				
1968—69	9,863	292	(3.0%)	887	(9.0%)
1969—70	10,422	501	(4.8%)	948	(9.1%)
1970—71	11,348	808	(7.1%)	1,256	(11.1%)
1971—72	12,361	1,063	(8.6%)	1,693	(13.7%)
1972—73	13,677	1,172	(8.6%)	2,284	(16.7%)
1973—74	14,159	1,301	(9.2%)	2,790	(19.7%)
1974—75	14,763	1,473	(10.0%)	3,275	(22.2%)
1975—76	15,295	1,391[b]	(9.1%)	3,647	(23.8%)
1976—77	15,616[c]	1,400	(9.0%)	3,858	(24.7%)

[a] Includes blacks, American Indians, Mexican-Americans, and mainland Puerto Ricans.

[b] Approximately 200 of these students were enrolled at the two traditionally black medical schools.

[c] Estimated at 99 percent of the accepted applicants for 1976-77.

Sources: See Appendices D-1 and D-2 for data up to 1975-76, and Waldman (1977) for 1976-77 data.

Puerto Ricans, and 32 percent of Cubans (see Appendix D-3 for more details). In 1976-77, 39.1 percent of black applicants and 38.9 percent of white applicants were accepted (Waldman, 1977, pp. 15,16).[1]

Historically, attrition from medical schools has been low. More than 95 percent of entering medical students eventually receive the M.D. degree (*American Medical Association*, 1976, p. 2964). Johnson, Smith, and Tarnoff (1975) studied retention rates for various racial and ethnic groups in the 1970 and 1971 entering classes (see Appendix D-4). A general conclusion of this survey is:

> Although differences in total attrition by race are not very sizable, greater disparities exist regarding immediate promotion from the first to the second year class. Black medical students had a lower than average immediate promotion rate, which means that more blacks will take an extra year to graduate than will students from other groups. The immediate promotion rate for blacks was approximately 80 percent for the classes in this study. This compares with about 96 percent for white students [p. 738].

Admissions Procedures

Admissions policy is locally determined by each medical school. During much of the 1960s the emphasis in selection was on academic achievement and aptitude. The aim had been to select applicants most likely to complete medical school successfully (Erdmann, 1971). Now, with an excess of academically qualified applicants and increasing concern for social needs, admissions committees place more emphasis in selection on personal qualities of applicants. They have increased interest in selecting applicants most likely to enter primary care specialties and/or to practice in geographic areas which are underserved. Attempts are made to broaden the socioeconomic diversity of entering medical classes and to expand educational opportunities for racial/ethnic groups underrepresented in medicine

[1] This report, recently released by the Association of American Medical Colleges, shows also acceptance rates within specific college GPA ranges and MCAT scores for different ethnic groups. These data illustrate affirmative action policies in medical school admissions and are in many ways similar to those compiled by Evans (1977) for law school applicants.

continue (Cuca, 1976; Association of American Medical Colleges, 1977). Interviews are widely used as a means of collecting personal information. Admissions committees generally agree that such attributes as stamina and the ability to relate to people are important for medical education and practice. Public medical schools give strong preference to applicants from particular state(s) of residence. See Appendices D-5 and D-6 for statements on admissions procedures for two medical schools.

Preliminary Screening. Generally, applicants are given preliminary screening on the basis of some or all of the following: biographic and demographic data and a personal statement included in the application, previous academic record, and Medical College Admission Test scores. If an applicant is judged to be a good prospect for admission, an interview typically is arranged with medical college faculty, students, alumni, or others. Letters of evaluation by the preprofessional advisor or a college faculty member are also considered at this time. Particularly important in some schools are recommendations from premedical college committees, who represent a formal part of the admissions structure. Evidence of having sought and obtained relevant work experience is considered favorably.

Admissions Committee. Final decision on the selection of a particular applicant is usually made by the admissions committee, which meets to consider all available information about the individual. Unfortunately little has been published recently on committee structure and function (Cuca, 1976). However, admissions committees generally include both basic science and clinical faculty. In addition, most committees also have one or more medical students, residents, and practicing physicians. In recent years admissions committees have included increased representation of minorities and women.

Prerequisites. English, biology, inorganic and organic chemistry, and physics are the college courses required by most medical schools. Specific prerequisites for individual medical schools are listed in *Medical School Admission Requirements* (Association of American Medical Colleges, 1977). Though no particular undergraduate major is required, about 71 percent of applicants accepted in 1975 majored in biology, chemistry, physics, or a related science field. Appendix D-7 lists the numbers of accepted applicants by major. As in other selective admissions settings, the previous academic record is an important factor in selection. In reviewing the academic record admissions committees consider such factors as course load, difficulty of program, sending college, and extent of work and extracurricular activities.

Admissions Tests. The Medical College Admission Test (MCAT) used from 1946 through 1976 contained four sections: Verbal Aptitude, Quantitative Aptitude, Science Achievement, and General Information. Scores ranged from 200 to 800, with a mean of 500 and standard deviation of 100 (Erdmann, 1971). The "New MCAT," administered for the first time in 1977, reports six scores: Biology, Chemistry, Physics, Science Problems, Skills Analysis—Reading, and Skills Analysis—Quantitative. The science tests assess the understanding of concepts and principles from the four prerequisite courses in science which had been judged as important for entering medical students. While the biology, chemistry, and physics tests contain relatively short multiple-choice questions, the science problems tests involve longer problems in a medically relevant context. (See Appendix F-1 for a sample set of items from the new MCAT.) The skills analysis tests assess skills in the comprehension and use of written and quantitative materials. The score scale used is a 15-point scale (Littlemeyer, 1976).

As the acceptance ratio has declined, both MCAT scores and undergraduate grades of entering students have shown an upward trend over ten years. Mean scores on MCAT subtests and GPAs by self-described racial/national background for accepted applicants of 1975–76 are highest for those individuals describing themselves as Caucasians or Oriental Americans. Average test scores recorded were somewhat lower for those identifying themselves as blacks, Puerto Ricans, American Indians, and Mexican Americans. A similar pattern is evident in average GPAs (Appendix D-8).

Grades. Appendix D-9 indicates the proportion of entering medical students with grade point averages (GPAs) in each of three categories —A (3.6–4.0 on a four-point scale), B (2.5–3.5), and C (less than 2.6).

Interviews. At 113 of 116 medical schools, more than 90 percent of the students entering in 1976 were interviewed (Association of American Medical Colleges, 1977). The format and content of the interview and the report and its role in admissions decisions vary among medical schools. The use of other measures such as letters of evaluation and application information also varies.

Application Service. The American Medical College Application Service (AMCAS), operated by the Association of American Medical Colleges, provides a centralized service that facilitates application to 89 participating medical schools. AMCAS collects and processes application materials and distributes them to medical schools designated by the applicant. In addition, AMCAS provides summary reports of various types to medical schools (American Medical College Application Service, 1977).

Special Programs

In 1968, the Assembly of the Association of American Medical colleges recommended that medical schools admit increased numbers of students from geographic areas, economic backgrounds, and ethnic groups that were then inadequately represented (Association of American Medical Colleges, 1970). The Comprehensive Health Manpower Training Act (Public Law 92-157) further encouraged the enrollment of individuals expected to help overcome problems of geographical and specialty maldistribution. The Health Professions Educational Assistance Act of 1976 (Public Law 94-484) provides funding to health profession schools for the recruitment and retention of individuals from disadvantaged backgrounds. Public Law 94-484 also has some controversial aspects; one of these is that it also requires acceptance into U.S. medical schools of some students who have studied in foreign medical schools to qualify for federal funding.

AAMC has received substantial funding from the Office of Economic Opportunity for the recruitment and training of under-represented minority students (Johnson et al., 1975). A Robert Wood Johnson Foundation grant of ten million dollars for similar purposes also specified females and those from rural areas (Association of American Medical Colleges, 1973).

Information Aids. Minority Student Opportunities in United States Medical Schools, 1975–76 (Association of American Medical Colleges, 1975) was written for minority students contemplating a medical career. This book describes each medical school in terms of (1) recruitment programs, (2) admissions policy and procedure for minority applicants, (3) special academic assistance programs, and (4) financial aid. *The Simulated Minority Admissions Exercise,* developed by AAMC, is a workbook designed to aid admissions committee members in the selection of nontraditional applicants on the basis of application information and interview reports. The workbook provides experience and training in judging those noncognitive characteristics which predict medical school success for disadvantaged students (D'Costa and others, 1974).

Through the Medical Minority Applicant Registry, established by AAMC, basic biographical information about MCAT examinees who have identified themselves as belonging to a minority group or low income family is circulated to all medical schools. Medical schools can then correspond directly with particular students.

Special Admissions. While some schools have no special recruitment programs for minority applicants, many have extensive recruitment programs. A few admissions committees have a subcommittee which considers minority students and in some cases nonminority applicants who are economically or educationally disadvantaged. Such a subcommittee may be empowered to make the final selection or may only make recommendations to the full admissions committee on the selection of minority applicants.

Student Assistance. Academic assistance is generally based upon need and more than half of American medical colleges report offering special summer programs for students in need of remedial help prior to matriculation. Tutorial help is generally available. Odegaard (1977), in reviewing the experiences of a decade of minority admissions to medical school, pointed out the value of carefully designed programs to remedy the deficiencies in preparation among many entering minority students. Financial assistance is also awarded on the basis of need. However, need for financial aid is not generally considered in making selection decisions.

*   *   *

The enrollment picture for the past decade in medical schools is quite similar to that of law: Although the number of places has increased dramatically, the competition for those places has also increased. Enrollment of underrepresented minorities increased from 3 percent in 1968 to 9 percent in 1976, but enrollment of women increased much more proportionally—from 9 percent to almost 25 percent. One difference between medical and law schools is to be found in current acceptance rates. Medical school acceptance rates for 1976 were approximately equal for both blacks and whites (about 39 percent of each group were selected). In the previous section we saw that law school acceptance rates were 59 percent for whites but only 39 percent for blacks. It is not clear whether this difference reflects a difference in minority student qualifications across fields or a difference in selection policies. It is also possible that minority medical school applicants are more self-selective than are minority law school applicants. But it would also appear that medical schools are making much more use of a broad set of qualities and objectives in choosing students. More use is made of interviews, for example, and other subjective judgments.

6

Admissions to Management Schools

Although they are usually associated with business, management schools provide training for administrative work in many settings including, for example, business, government, education, and health care. In recent years the trend has been toward consolidating management training as a general discipline that transcends institutional interests. Accordingly, many former graduate schools of business administration are now schools of management. As a profession, management contrasts significantly with law and medicine, the traditional professions. Schein (1972, pp.10,11) observed that management does not necessarily conform to the usually cited prerequisites of professionalism. It is not entered with a strong sense of calling, managers do not have the traditional client relationship of law and medicine, managers are not autonomous, and managers do not eschew self-advertisement. Nevertheless, management is recognized as one of the fastest-growing professions.

Institutions

A large variety of institutions teach management of one kind or another. These include undergraduate as well as graduate schools and a variety of special types of management. Only *graduate* schools of management are considered here. The principal guide for prospective graduate management students, *Graduate Study in Management,* published by the Graduate Management Admission Council (GMAC, 1976), lists 359 schools that offered graduate management training.

Despite considerable diversity, graduate schools of management have some common features. Most offer a professional approach to education at the master's degree level (primarily, the MBA). Different instructional methods are used, such as the case method of law and the management science approach. Most MBA degree programs require two full-time academic years, and many have part-time programs that take longer to complete. Candidates for the MBA may enter with many different undergraduate backgrounds, and many, if not most, enter without having had previous management courses. Although much of the training is oriented toward an executive role for graduates, most do not end up in positions of line responsibility. One survey showed that only 20 percent of MBA graduates characterized their positions as line positions, while 40 percent described their roles as staff, 11 percent as specialists, and 29 percent as some combination of line, staff, and specialist.

Student Population

Enrollment for master's and doctor's degrees in business and management, based on NCES data as reported by Grant and Lind (1976, p.86), increased fourfold between 1960 and 1973:

Year	Number of students
1960	25,342
1965	50,920
1970	87,487
1971	97,359
1972	98,762
1973	107,874

The 1973 enrollment consisted of 69,638 first-year students of which 22,938 (33 percent) were full-time men, 2,748 (12 percent) were full-time women, and 43,952 (63 percent) were part-time students (see Appendix E-1 for more details). In 1971-72, 30,433 master's degrees and 902 doctor's degrees were awarded (see Appendix E-2), and in 1972-73, 31,166 master's degrees and 932 doctor's degrees were awarded (see Appendix E-3), according to the data given by Grant and Lind. Data from the GMAC group of schools provide a similar picture. Table 13 shows candidate volumes from GMAT administrations for the past nine years and percentage of women for the past five years. Turner (1977) projected a moderate increase in graduate management school enrollment through about 1981, a steady-state period for five or six years, and then the beginning of a decline. Since some candidates take the GMAT more than once and since some GMAT takers may also apply to other kinds of schools (for example, law), the figures in Table 13 cannot be interpreted precisely. But they do serve to indicate increasing interest in management.

Table 13. GMAT candidate volume, 1967—1975

Year	GMAT tests	Percentage of Women
1967—68	58,573	
1968—69	69,296	
1969—70	86,172	
1970—71	87,516	
1971—72	83,915	8
1972—73	91,851	12
1973—74	104,742	16
1974—75	128,538	19
1975—76	137,717	22

Source: GMAC (1977, p.2).

Minority Enrollment

One of the earliest surveys of minority enrollment in graduate management study was by Hamilton (1973) at ETS in 1971-72 of 37 graduate business schools and 10,833 students. This survey showed these percentages: 2.2 percent black, 0.3 percent American Indian, 0.8 percent Chicano, and 0.9 percent Oriental for a total minority enrollment of 4.2 percent in 1971–72 (see Appendix E-4).

Larger samplings of schools and students have been made by the American Assembly of Collegiate Schools of Business, AACSB (1975), and AACSB (1977). The first AACSB survey included master's and doctoral level students in 206 AACSB member schools in 1973-74. Of 31,290 master's level students surveyed, 3.4 percent were blacks, 1.1 percent American Orientals, 1.1 percent Spanish Americans, and 0.3 percent American Indians. Foreign students made up 7 percent of the enrollment and were not included in American minority counts (see Appendices E-5 and E-6).

The second AACSB study surveyed a somewhat larger number of schools (300) and students. This survey included 76,123 master's and 1,177 doctoral level students enrolled during the 1975-76 academic year. A slight increase in blacks (3.7 percent) and a slight increase in Orientals (1.7 percent) was indicated, but observed percentages of Spanish Americans remained the same (1.1 percent) and American Indians decreased to slightly less than 0.2 percent (see Appendix E-7). The 1974 survey by the Office of Civil Rights (DHEW, 1976) is also useful for comparison. The OCR reported a total of 112,317 students in graduate business and management schools, 40,000 of whom were full-time and 72,317 of whom were part-time. Of full-time graduate students in business and management, 4.4 percent were blacks, 2.3 percent Asian American, 1.0 percent Spanish-surnamed Americans, and 0.2 percent American Indians. Of all students, 4.0 percent were blacks, 1.8 percent Asian American, 1.1 percent Spanish-surnamed Americans, and 0.2 percent were American Indians (see Appendix E-8).

Despite some differences in semantics and classification of students, these four surveys are summarized in Table 14. The consistency in the percentage figures is remarkable considering the differences in the quality of the samples, the way questionnaires were worded, and classification problems. It suggests an increase in minority enrollment in the early 1970s but a leveling off in 1974 and 1976. The Hispanic representation is constant at 1.1 percent for the last three surveys even though a variety of terms was used in the

Table 14. Comparison of minority representation in graduate
business school enrollments

Survey	Academic year	Blacks	Hispanic	American Indian	Asian American	Other	Total
ETS	1971–72	236 (2.2%)	84 (0.8%)	30 (0.3%)	99 (0.9%)	10,300 (95.1%)	10,833 (100%)
AACSB	1973–74	1,077 (3.4%)	340 (1.1%)	82 (0.3%)	345 (1.1%)	29,446 (94.1%)	31,290 (100%)
OCR	1974–75	4,445 (4.0%)	1,203 (1.1%)	259 (0.2%)	2,077 (1.8%)	104,333 (92.9%)	112,317 (100%)
AACSB	1975–76	2,832 (3.7%)	828 (1.1%)	112 (0.2%)	1,273 (1.7%)	71,078 (93.4%)	76,123 (100%)

surveys for this category (for example, Spanish-surnamed Americans; Chicano, Puerto Rican, and Spanish; Spanish origin; Spanish Americans).

Degrees Awarded

The AACSB surveys also included data on degrees awarded in member schools responding. Of the 14,155 master's degrees awarded in 1973-74, 3.8 percent were awarded to blacks, 1.5 percent to Spanish Americans, 0.4 percent to American Indians, and 0.7 percent to Oriental Americans (see Appendix E-9). Of 22,790 master's degrees awarded in 1975-76, 3.2 percent were awarded to blacks, 1.1 percent to Spanish Americans, 0.1 percent to American Indians, and 1.9 percent to Oriental Americans (see Appendix E-7). The AACSB percentages would indicate that, between 1973 and 1976, American Indians decreased in their representation of master's degrees in business and management, blacks and Asian Americans increased their representation and Hispanic representation remained the same.

Admissions Procedures

The Admission Council for Graduate Study in Management publishes an annual *Guide for Prospective Students* (GMAC, 1976). The procedures described do not appear to substantially differ from those used for law school admission, even though different student qualities are emphasized. The usual transcripts from college are required, an admission test score (the GMAT), and letters of recommendation are required. Interviews are desirable but not required. Some emphasis is given to the flexibility with which applications are reviewed. The qualities of students desired for graduate management schools are probably slightly different from those desired for law schools and somewhat different from those desired for other fields. As in law, a premium is placed upon communication skills, both written and oral. Most graduate schools of business expect a certain degree of analytic proficiency, especially quantitative abilities. And most view social and interpersonal skills as especially important. Management schools also value, particularly, such qualities as initiative, persistence, and planning ability. Probably more than in any other discipline, actual work experience is highly valued, but this is not true for all schools.

A 1971 survey by the Graduate Business Admission Council (GBAC, 1972) indicated that the most important consideration in admission for a majority of the GBAC schools was the GMAT score and the undergraduate grade-point average. Sixty-two percent of the schools required a minimum undergraduate score on the GMAT and 69 percent required a minimum grade-point average. Work and military experience were moderately important considerations, but neither geographic balance nor in-state versus out-of-state representation was considered important in selecting entering classes. Approximately 75 percent of the schools in the GBAC survey used letters of recommendation, but only a few used a rating scale to evaluate the letters. Various personal factors were also evaluated: interpersonal capabilities, maturity, leadership, motivation, determination, and work/military experience. About one-fourth of the schools interviewed over 50 percent of applicants.

Special Admissions and Programs

Although perhaps not to the degree that medical and law schools have, graduate management schools have been expending considerable effort to increase representation of blacks, American Indians, Spanish Americans, Asian Americans, and other minority groups. These efforts include special recruitment programs to attract students, special financial aid programs, special support services to aid minority students while in school, and special job placement programs. Beyond the efforts being made by individual schools, organizations have been set up specifically to aid minority students. These organizations include Program ABLE, ASPIRA of America, the Consortium for Graduate Study in Management (CGME) (which uses financial contributions from business firms), and the Council for Opportunity in Graduate Management (COGME).

In the GBAC (1972) survey, well over half of the schools responded that they actively recruited minority students. Recruiting was conducted through visits to undergraduate colleges by students, faculty, and admissions officers, and through newspaper advertising. But only 31 percent of the schools thought that their recruiting efforts were effective. Several schools reported that they waive the GMAT for minority and foreign students if a student is applying for financial aid or if the undergraduate grade-point average is high enough. Forty percent of the responding schools reported that they gave exemptions from application fees or tuition deposits, and half of these did so for minority or low-SES applicants.

*   *   *

Enrollment in graduate management schools increased rapidly during the past several years, women increased substantially in their representation, and minority representation increased some. Although the survey data for minority enrollments in graduate management schools are less extensive than those available for other settings, the indication is that minority increases are less demonstrable in management than in law and medicine. But unlike law and medicine there are many routes to management careers other than graduate management schools. The lower minority increases in graduate management schools, therefore, may be the result of a tendency for minorities to opt for direct entry into management careers rather than to defer entry until completion of a graduate management degree.

7

Use and Limitations of Selection Measures

The preceding sections have presented a brief overview of selective admissions in five institutional settings. In each of these, critical issues related to the *Bakke* case concern the measures actually used to select students and determine to what extent those measures are useful and defensible. Four classes of measures come into play.

First, there are administrative and educational prerequisites. Educational prerequisites include diplomas, course requirements, credit hours, and so on. Such prerequisites may be important to the institution and they may inconvenience some students, but as selection measures they do not typically have a heavy bearing on which applicants are or are not selected. Also, prerequisites are more concerned with educational philosophy than with selective admissions and are therefore not especially germane to the present discussion.

Second, a critical class of selection measures includes the traditional indicators of academic competence, particularly previous grades and standardized examinations. This discussion focuses especially upon this second class of selection measures, since these variables are used most explicitly to compare students in a competitive admissions situation and there is considerable empirical evidence that bears upon their evaluation.

A *third* class of selection measures includes personal qualities that may be critical in completing a very demanding program and successfully pursuing a responsible career: integrity, diligence, special accomplishments, interpersonal skill, a highly developed talent, and so forth. These personal qualities are often very important in admissions though they tend to be judged subjectively and there is little evidence concerning their character and use.

A *fourth* class of potential selection measures includes background characteristics such as age, sex, place of residence, race, school previously attended, father's occupation, religion, or virtually any such information that is available and is for some reason useful for categorizing applicants in a given institutional setting. This fourth class of selection measures is important because of its relationship to the second and third and because of the immensely important social and legal issues raised by the use of background characteristics in selective admissions. Thus, this discussion takes the fourth class into account to some extent though the larger social and legal issues generally lie beyond the intended scope of this report.

Measures used in selective admissions need to be evaluated on several bases. *Validity* is often considered the most important basis for evaluators. It refers to the reasonableness of the measure as well as its effectiveness in differentiating among students who are and are not likely to succeed. *Fairness* refers especially to whether students have a reasonable opportunity to meet a particular admission standard and whether imposition of the standard has an adverse impact on some students that is unrelated to the demands of the educational program. *Feasibility* refers to whether reliable measurement is a practical possibility, whether the cost of such assessment is within reason, and so on. *Secondary effects* refers to the positive or negative effect the use of an admission standard has upon the health of the educational institution, upon its feeder schools, or upon professions for which it serves as the principal or only mode of entry.

It is important to bear each of these considerations in mind in the following discussion of strengths and weaknesses of different selection measures. Special attention is given to the validity and fairness of traditional academic measures because of their importance in the selection process and the fact that large amounts of data are available that bear on those issues.

Traditional Academic Measures

Strengths and Weaknesses of Grades. In selective admissions the first question is frequently whether the applicant shows sufficient academic promise to handle the scholastic demands of the program. Faculties, measurement specialists, and selection committees usually agree that the previous academic record of the student is the most relevant source of information for judging academic competence. Furthermore, grade-point average (GPA) or rank in class tends to be a more accurate predictor than test scores at the undergraduate level. (The reverse tends to be true in graduate and professional schools.) Some illustrative data concerning validity are discussed in the following section.

Aside from considerable evidence of predictive validity, there is strong logic supporting the use of GPA as a principal means of selecting students. Once admited, ability to earn good grades is, after all, what will keep the student in school. A very large amount of research in the military, in business and industry, and in education bears out the dictum that past behavior is usually the best predictor of future behavior.

The intrinsic appropriateness of using GPA or academic rank as a selection measure is further argued by considering the role of grades in the educational system. To some degree they reflect student motivation. The motivational element in grades is probably enhanced when excellence in school work is publicly rewarded by assigning heavy weight to outstanding grades in admitting students to prestigious institutions. Put another way, *not* giving special attention to previous grades in selecting students would doubtlessly result in significant changes in education generally and adversely affect many students' interest in academic achievement.

Despite these obvious strengths, GPA has significant weaknesses as a basis for evaluating candidates for admission. By far the most important is the lack of comparability of grades among instructors, departments, and institutions. Experienced faculty and college administrators are very much aware that one B is not necessarily equal in value to another B. This problem is manifested in various ways.

One is the systematic but arbitrary changes that can be observed in grading patterns. In recent years the tendency toward grade inflation has been widely observed throughout higher education (Suslow, 1977). There was a very similar trend some 10 to 15 years earlier, though it worked in the opposite direction and was less apparent. In that period many institutions became increasingly selective and admitted students who were more and more able, but their average freshman grade tended to remain at the same level (for example, see Aiken, 1963). This tendency for grades to slide up and down and the fact that grading patterns are often observed to vary widely from department to department are likely to have a common explanation; that is, that faculty tend to award a standard distribution of grades to the students they see in their classes rather than to maintain some absolute sense of what constitutes good performance.

A dramatic example of the noncomparability of grades lies in the substantial differences among the grade scales of different institutions. It is not difficult to find instances in which the average freshman grade in two institutions is the same though their respective classes vary in mean performance on a scholastic ability test by as much as three standard deviations (see Appendix G). Such institutional grading variations have been thoroughly documented in both secondary schools and higher education. As Linn (1966) and others have shown, grading variations significantly reduce the validity of GPA as a predictor though the effect is largely corrected through use of an admissions test in combination with GPA. That lowered validity reflects a serious problem—namely, the inequity that grading variations build into the use of GPA as a predictor. Thus, applicants coming from schools or institutions with able students and tough grading standards are clearly at a disadvantage if GPA or class rank is the only measure of academic competence to which the admissions officer can refer.

Another weakness in the use of grades as a predictor concerns the limited discrimination offered by grades. In very selective programs most serious applicants have very high grade averages. This circumstance clearly limits the usefulness of fine distinctions among GPAs and lowers the validity coefficient for GPA, but it would be quite incorrect to infer from this that the GPA is not serving a useful purpose in helping to identify a pool of able applicants.

A more subtle weakness in GPA as a predictor is the fact that there tends to be little discrimination among different types of grades; that is, to a surprising degree individual students tend to make generally similar grades in different types of courses. This may be because faculty are influenced by an academic "halo" when assigning grades

(French, 1951), or possibly because students tend to compensate by working hard in (or avoiding) courses in areas that are difficult for them. In any event the practical effect of this homogeneity has been to make it difficult to produce any additional types of information from grade transcripts (for example, special types of averages such as one based upon courses in the major) that consistently add anything to the predictive usefulness of the overall grade record (Willingham, 1963; Reilly and Powers, 1976).

Strengths and Weaknesses of Tests. The second broad category of traditional measures of academic competence is the objective examination. Virtually all selective institutions of the types considered in this report (including the selective undergraduate) require their applicants to take one or more examinations.

One strength of objective examinations is the importance of the types of competence represented. Almost all tests place heavy emphasis upon verbal comprehension and quantitative ability (at their simplest levels, reading and skill with numbers). These represent cognitive abilities developed over a long period of time that have consistently proven to be generally useful predictors of scholastic performance in a wide range of situations. Institutions (of arts and sciences in particular) often require additional achievement tests covering knowledge of subject matter and methods in fields pertinent to the student's preparation and educational plans.

Broad applicability represents a second important strength of standardized examinations. The United States takes pride in its highly decentralized and pluralistic system of education. Unlike most developed countries where the schools tend to work from a common syllabus, diversity is here the rule with objectives, curriculum, and standards varying according to community or institutional need and design. Thus, the United States has a special need for standardized measures of academic achievement that other nations do not share. In fact, the selective universities instituted the first common admissions examination near the turn of the century precisely because diversity among schools and colleges had created an impossible task in evaluating credentials and admitting students to college (Fuess, 1950). Eventually, common admissions examinations became the common currency that encouraged many first-rank universities and professional schools to accept applicants from "unknown" schools and to thus diversify their student bodies. Not too many years ago admissions tests were widely credited as a primary means of identifying talent and promoting fair access in a heterogeneous educational system.

This suggests a third strength of standardized tests—their tendency to free students from what David Riesman has called the "personalism" of school authorities, college personnel, and even parents. The existence of objective tests makes it more difficult for a teacher to grade down a good student for personal reasons, or a counselor to blackball a student, or a parent to rationalize that a bright child should not go to a good school. And tests likely save many from the fickle prejudice of the interviewer who is envious of beauty or sets aside those lacking in charm.

So much for strengths; there are also weaknesses to consider. Many criticisms are leveled periodically at objective tests. Some are important and some are trivial; some are legitimate and some are spurious. The purpose here is not to sort out all of that commentary, but to consider briefly information relevant to a few major concerns about the use of standardized tests in selective admissions. In some minds, tests have two major weaknesses: They are invalid for predicting success and they are unfair to some minority groups. There is a large amount of available data pertinent to these two points, and in both cases the data support the contrary view. Since validity and fairness are closely related and the data concern both tests and grades, these issues will be discussed in a following section.

Perhaps the most persistent criticism of standardized tests is that they measure unimportant knowledge and rote recall, and that they penalize the deep-thinking, very able student. True, many tests contain trivial items, and some widely used tests are not nearly as good as they ought to be, but for the most part, standardized tests used nationally for selection purposes are carefully constructed. Furthermore, present-day tests of this sort measure cognitive processes that are considerably more complex than simple recall of facts (see Appendix F-1 for examples). Moreover, available evidence indicates that the very able students typically make the very highest scores (Chauncey and Hilton, 1965).

The fact that admissions tests used nationally need to reflect fairly the various curricula across the country does suggest a weakness. That is their limited connection with short-range instructional objectives and the limited relevance students often perceive between the tests and the particular material they have personally been exposed to in school. This is unfortunately true because students study different subjects. Even in the case of an achievement examination covering only one subject, if it contains a fair sampling of topics for all students taking the examination, it may not match very closely what any one student has studied. So in order to be fair, admissions tests such as the SAT and LSAT emphasize broad scholastic abilities developed over a long period of time, and they are not intended to represent the instructional outcomes of particular courses or curricula. This approach has the advantage of providing a standard scholastic yardstick, but it does carry with it the weakness of the test appearing somewhat abstract to students used to classroom tests on specific topics.

There is another related weakness of standardized admissions tests. Despite the diversity of human talent, tests focus upon somewhat limited types of competence. There are good reasons for that focus. Scholastic competence is itself somewhat narrow and these admissions tests concentrate on the abilities that have been demonstrated to do the best job of predicting scholastic success. Furthermore, time and again research has shown that other abilities that might reasonably be measured do not add significantly to the accuracy of estimating future academic performance. Nonetheless, it has rightly been argued that the measurement of talent can and should be broadened. That argument is taken up in a subsequent section.

Validity. Two aspects of validity deserve particular attention. Construct validity is concerned with whether the actual content and character of the examination are appropriate for its intended purpose. Predictive validity is concerned with the accuracy with which subsequent performance is forecasted, that is, a demonstrated statistical relationship between the predictor and a suitable criterion.

Predictive validity has always had the greater emphasis in evaluating admissions tests, both for educational programs and employment. The 1970 Equal Employment Opportunity Commission (EEOC) guidelines for employee selection strongly advanced the view

that prediction studies were much the preferred form of test validation. The guidelines had a strong effect on the use and interpretation
of employment tests, and due to the similarities between employee
selection and college admissions, it was assumed for a time that predictive validity would overshadow other forms of validation in
education as well. Recent court decisions have, however, altered
this emphasis in fundamental respects.

Particularly in the case of *Washington v. Davis* in 1976 the
Supreme Court wrote a decision with far-reaching implications for
the use and interpretation of standardized tests. The court ruled that
it was permissible to use a verbal ability test in the selection of candidates for police training in Washington, D.C. The decision included
these important points: (a) tests should be evaluated on the basis of a
rational analysis of all the evidence, and such analyses may or may
not include a prediction study; (b) performance in training is quite
appropriate as a criterion (as opposed to longer-range job performance); (c) it is appropriate to test for key abilities rather than all
skills that a job may involve; and (d) it is appropriate to use a general
aptitude test if justified on rational grounds, and not necessary to
measure specific aspects of job performance. (See Manning, 1977, for
a detailed discussion of this and related legal decisions bearing upon
test use.)

The clear implication is that it is quite appropriate for college
admissions tests to focus upon general abilities required for success
in educational programs and that the reasonableness of test content
may be as appropriate a method of validation as a prediction study.
Thus, if there is good evidence that a test measures mathematical
reasoning and a graduate faculty has good reason to believe that this
particular competence is important to success in its departments,
that rational analysis may be adequate justification for using the test
in selection.

This view of test validation is sound from a measurement standpoint; it is also realistic. In many situations test data are available for
so few individuals that a formal prediction study is out of the question. Furthermore, the poor criteria that are sometimes available for
a prediction study may well cast doubt on whether the particular
study is a sound basis for evaluating the usefulness of the test. Despite
these limitations, prediction studies represent the most direct way

to insure that use of the test results in the selection of those students who are more likely to succeed. For that reason thousands of prediction studies have been carried out and many more will doubtless follow.

Table 15 shows characteristic validity coefficients for four widely used admissions tests and GPA (see note 2, Appendix G, for detailed data). These data indicate that the previous GPA is typically the best single predictor at the undergraduate level, and admissions tests tend to be the more valid selection measure in graduate and professional schools. The data also show that the test plus GPA give better prediction than either one taken alone, that estimation of success in undergraduate school is more accurate than at the graduate and professional level, and that even the best predictors available are far from perfect.

Effectiveness of Prediction. How effective is this level of prediction? The following hypothetical figures represent one meaning of a validity coefficient of 03.40:

Percentage of students at different performance levels after admission

Standing on predictor:	*Bottom fifth*	*Middle three-fifths*	*Top fifth*
Top fifth	7	55	38
Middle three-fifths	18	64	18
Bottom fifth	38	55	7

These numbers indicate, for example, that for students standing in the top one-fifth on the predictor, many would rank in the top one-fifth of their class after admission (38 percent) and few would rank in the bottom fifth (7 percent)—considerably better than chance but certainly not nearly one-to-one correspondence. Figure 1 provides an alternate view of correlations of approximately the same magnitude. This figure, based upon actual data from the National Research Council, shows that high scores on the GRE Advanced (subject field)

Table 15. Characteristic validity coefficients for admission test scores and
previous grade record (GPA) for predicting subsequent grades in four institutional settings

			Median Validity Coefficients		
Admission test	*Type of School*	*No. of Schools*	*Total test score*[a]	*Previous GPA*	*Both predictors combined*
SAT	Undergraduate	51	.40	.55	.62
GRE	Graduate arts and sciences	24-30	.33	.31	.45
LSAC	Law	116	.36	.25	.45
GMAT	Graduate management	67	.29	.21	.38

[a] Where applicable, total test score represents a composite of verbal and quantitative scores; see note 2, Appendix G, for further information concerning the studies.

Test are no guarantee of obtaining the Ph.D., but applicants with high scores are much more likely to do so than are those with low scores. While the accuracy of predicting success in Ph.D. attainment on the basis of the Advanced Test score is obviously not perfect, available evidence suggests that the predictions based upon other selection measures such as undergraduate GPA and recommendations are considerably less accurate (see Appendix F-5).

It is also important to note that the effectiveness of a predictor depends not only upon the magnitude of the validity coefficient but also upon the proportion of applicants selected. When, for example, half of unselected applicants can be expected to be successful, then the following would obtain: If only 20 percent of the applicants could be accommodated, a predictor with a validity of .45 would increase the overall success rate from .50 to .75; if 50 percent of the applicants could be accepted, the predictor would have to have a validity of .70 to attain a success rate as high as 75 percent (Tiffin and McCormick, 1974, p. 598). Thus, highly selective schools stand to profit from the use of even moderately valid predictors.

At the graduate and professional level, in particular, validities are often no better than moderate. Why is this so? First, there is some *inherent unpredictability* of success in any educational program. This is necessarily true because the measures used to select students cannot possibly include more than a part of the abilities and perfor-

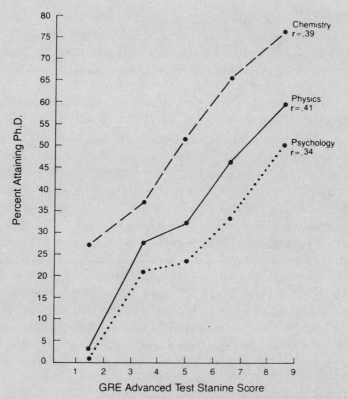

Figure 1. Proportion of students at various levels of GRE Advanced Test scores in chemistry, physics, and psychology who attained the Ph.D. within 10 years (adapted from Creager, 1965).

mance demands represented in the criteria of success. Furthermore, there are fortuitous events and changing motivation that are impossible to foresee but may markedly affect the performance of individual students.

A second reason for only moderate validity in some situations is the ever-present *criterion problem.* The usual criteria are grades and degree attainment. All the problems of grades as a predictor that were previously cited tend to apply doubly to grades as a criterion because at higher educational levels grades tend to be taken less seriously by faculty, or they are concentrated in the A and B category, or they vary more haphazardly from instructor to instructor. In a recent analysis Goldman and Slaughter (1976) presented data suggesting that the validity of undergraduate admissions tests would be substantially higher were it not for such criterion problems. In most programs degree attainment is a very important measure for administrative purposes, but is often a somewhat ambiguous criterion because some students drop out for sundry reasons not necessarily related to competence.

A third reason for moderate validities is *restriction of range*. In a highly selective program there is typically a fairly narrow range of ability among those students selected, particularly on those measures that were used in selecting the students. This narrow range can substantially lower the apparent validity of a selection measure, though the accuracy of estimating the students likely criterion performance is not thereby affected. Such restriction of range is assumed to account in large part for the generally lower validity coefficients previously noted at the graduate and professional level as compared to the undergraduate level. The effect is easily seen in Figure 1. If most admitted students cluster at the higher score levels, there will clearly be little difference among those students in probability of degree attainment that is associated with test score level. The figure makes clear, however, that such a limited relationship between the two measures in the restricted group admitted does not mean that students with much lower test scores would be just as likely to succeed. (See note 3, Appendix G for a hypothetical example and some illustrative validity coefficients in variously restricted groups.)

Finally, an uninteresting but very real reason for some low validity coefficients is simply *statistical fluctuation* due to small samples. As statistics go, the correlation coefficient is relatively unstable, especially in small samples. Since samples are often small in graduate and professional schools, a considerable number of individual validities can be expected to be out of line (too high or too low) purely on a chance basis.

Tests, Grades, and Life Success. There is one other important issue concerning the validity of traditional academic measures. Several writers (Hoyt, 1965, in particular) have cited evidence suggesting that college grades and standardized test scores are related to one another but bear little relationship to "life success" or performance in the real world. Many such studies show weak relationships, but much of this work is methodologically flawed or complicated by serious criterion problems. Nonetheless, much has been made of this presumed lack of relationship between academic performance and real life performance, and the question deserves attention.

First, it should be said that admissions tests are designed explicitly to predict success in school, not success in later life, and the *Washington* v. *Davis* (1976) decision confirms the appropriateness of validating such tests against school performance. Second, it is certainly true that no one expects schooling to be the same as working and that success in life depends heavily upon character, drive, good fortune, and many other factors in addition to the intellectual competence that is heavily represented in grades and ability tests. But finally, it is certainly reasonable to assume that such intellectual competence is *one* of the important determiners of life success and that one should be able to find confirming evidence in a positive, though undoubtedly limited, association between aptitude tests and significant markers of life success.

Research on this question is complicated by many factors and it is much beyond the scope of this report to speculate as to why tests may show a stronger association with some measures of life success than others. It is possible, however, to cite a few instances in which such a relationship is clearly demonstrated. It has been shown, for example, that obtaining the Ph.D. is very strongly related to general intellectual ability. In an analysis of most of the Ph.D. recipients in the United States in a particular year it was found that for every Ph.D. in the normal intellectual range of intelligence there were 189 at the highest level of standard aptitude tests (Harmon, 1961, p.1297). Focusing upon a less academic criterion of success, Kallop (1951, p.1299) reported data indicating that the likelihood of being listed in *Who's Who* was more than 10 times as great for individuals scoring above 696 on the SAT as for those scoring below 450. (See note 4, Appendix G, for both sets of data.)

From a broad social perspective one of the most significant questions concerning the relationship between intellectual ability and performance in later life is whether the most academically able tend to achieve the highest levels of occupational status. Substantial relationships between ability and occupational status have been well documented (Duncan, Featherman, and Duncan, 1972). The classical Terman study provides an interesting illustration.

Fifty years ago, Lewis Terman (1925) initiated a longitudinal study of especially gifted individuals. He identified some 1,500 California school children, all of whom scored in the top one percent on a general test of intellectual ability. With admirable persistence he followed practically all of that sample through adulthood. Their broad-ranging interests and outstanding achievements belied the common assumption some years ago that very intelligent children seldom lived up to their test scores. These high scorers exhibited a remarkably high incidence of scientific, literary, and civic accomplishment. Table 16 illustrates the marked difference in occupational attainment of this group as compared to the general population.

Table 16. Occupational status in 1960 of Terman gifted males at age 50
as compared with males in the general population

Occupational status	Percentage of Males in general population[a]	Percentage of Terman gifted males[b]
Professional	11	47
Official, managerial, semiprofessional	13	40
Retail business, clerical, skilled trades	32	11
Agricultural	10	2
Semiskilled, unskilled	34	1
Total	100	100

[a] From *Statistical Abstracts*, 1968.

[b] From Oden, 1968, p. 16; this group was identified 40 years earlier as ranking in the top 1 percent in general intellectual ability.

Fairness. As the *Bakke* case well illustrates, the question of what is fair in admitting students to highly selective educational programs is extremely complex. For the purposes of this report we are concerned with only a narrow aspect of fairness—whether the assessment process is fair. Even this restricted topic involves numerous technical complications and value conflicts and has inspired a substantial literature. It is only possible to provide a brief overview of major lines of work.

Fairness in the measurement process can be viewed as a question of whether selection measures are free from bias with respect to their content, the accuracy of the predictions they yield, and/or the way they are used in selecting students. All three questions apply to any type of selection measure but they have been examined primarily with respect to tests and grades.

Since blacks and some other minorities tend often to have scores below the average of other groups on admissions tests, the question of whether the content of such tests is biased against minorities naturally arises. In the sense that the test may reflect a biased social order the answer is clearly yes. The content of the tests is intended to represent important outcomes of the mainstream educational system and the abilities necessary to do well in that system. To the extent that some members of a minority group have suffered social and educational disadvantage, they would be expected to find the test difficult, and a well-developed test should reflect the educational disadvantage a person has experienced.

A pertinent measurement question is whether a test contains *some* items that are unusually difficult for a particular minority group. If so, the test might prove to be biased because it contained items that the minority group did not have an opportunity to learn or would be expected to miss because of cultural differences. There have been a number of studies that have examined the difficulty of test items for different groups of examinees (Cleary and Hilton, 1968; Angoff and Ford, 1973; Breland and others, 1974), but this research has had very limited success in identifying biased items. A typical result is to find, for example, that all items of an admissions test are consistently somewhat more difficult for a group of black students (see note 5, Appendix G for an illustration).

A second form of possible bias concerns the accuracy with which scholastic performance is predicted. Do test scores and previous GPA give a realistic picture of how minority students are likely to perform, or is the actual performance of the students underpredicted, perhaps because test scores are spuriously low? Table 17 shows results that are common to almost all studies of predictive bias. Linn (1974 pp.27,29) comments on these data as follows: "Although the common expectation (assuming a biased test) is that a single predictive system, based on all students or only on majority students, would *underpredict* the actual grades of black or Mexican-American students the result is uniformly in the opposite direction. That is, on the average, law school grades of black students or of Mexican-American students are overpredicted by the equation for the white students, or by a common equation based on both groups of students (pp. 27 and 29). (See note 5, Appendix G for additional data.)

Table 17. Predicted and actual first-year law school grades for black and Mexican American students (from Schrader and Pitcher, 1973 and 1974)

Study and school	Predicted average grade[a]	Actual average grade	Amount of overprediction
Blacks			
1973 A	39	36	3
1973 B	42	37	5
1973 C	40	38	2
1973 D	40	36	4
1973 E	40	38	2
1974 D	36	33	3
1974 E	39	36	3
1974 F	39	37	2
1974 G	44	42	2
1974 H	40	36	4
1974 I	38	33	5
1974 J1	40	35	5
1974 J2	40	36	4
Mexican Americans			
1974 A	40	36	4
1974 B	49	44	5
1974 C	41	38	3

[a] Predictions were based on undergraduate GPA and LSAT scores, using combined groups composed of whites and minority groups. Grades were scaled to a mean of 50 and a standard deviation of 10 for the combined group within each school.

A third form of possible bias concerns not the selection measures themselves but how they are used in admitting students. The classical and accepted model of fairness in selection has been to select those students with the highest predicted performance (using separate prediction equations for any subgroups that are shown to have significantly different equations). Thorndike (1971) demonstrated, however, that while that accepted procedure was fair to individuals it was not necessarily fair to groups. He showed that under assumptions not out of line with known conditions, the usual selection procedure can result in selecting a smaller proportion of the minority group who could succeed as compared to the proportion of potentially successful majority students that is selected. Having shown the usual selection model to be unfair in that sense, Thorndike offered a selection model that would offer group equity in the way he defined it.

Subsequently, it has become apparent that group equity can be defined in various defensible ways, and several writers have suggested alternate selection models based upon different definitions of fairness. These are described in detail by Linn (1973) and by Novick and Ellis (1977). The latter authors argue that all of these models pose serious technical difficulties and incorporate internal contradictions (for example, one minority group achieves equity at the expense of another minority group). Another problem is that all such models assume that admissions can and should operate as a highly mechanistic process with little judgment applied to individual cases.

Although the group equity models may offer only limited progress toward practical solutions, they have proven valuable in demonstrating serious inconsistencies between individual and group equity, and in clarifying that the fairness problem has no strictly technical solution since the technical alternatives are invariably embedded in value issues. (For example, with candidates from various racial groups, relatively speaking, how important is it to avoid selecting students who would fail or to avoid rejecting students who would succeed?)

Other Important Measures and Methods

The traditional academic selection measures receive considerable attention because they have a clearly accepted rationale and function in the admissions process, they are quantified variables that can be objectively evaluated, and there is a correspondingly large body of research information about them. But as emphasized earlier, there are a variety of other measures, particularly those concerning personal characteristics of students. These play an important role in selection, partly because predicting success is more complicated than it first seems, and partly because there are institutional and social objectives in addition to the primary objective of selecting the best students.

Often these other measures enter into the selection process in a subjective manner. Assessment of some student qualities is inherently subjective; some other characteristics may be stated quite objectively but require subjective judgment to decide how importantly they bear on the selection decision. Depending upon the measure and the institution, a particular measure may be routinely considered for every student or applied more selectively. It is fairly common, for example, to use traditional academic measures to identify a group of applicants who are clearly admissible, and another group who are clearly not qualified (counterindications being considered in both cases). A variety of other criteria are then used to select students within the remaining gray area.

There is a great variety of information and measures that can and often do bear on admissions decisions. It is useful to consider a few broad classes of measures and also several assessment methods that differ from the familiar objectively scored tests and GPA. Despite the format of this discussion it is important to recognize that the traditional academic measures and the more subjectively applied measures are by no means mutually exclusive and that institutions consider all information about each student. Furthermore, the national testing programs have made various efforts in recent years to broaden the information they provide to institutions concerning the student's qualifications and characteristics. It is sometimes assumed that the use of alternate selection measures or methods can affect markedly the proportion of minority group students selected. It is not at all clear that disadvantaged groups would do relatively better on other educationally relevant criteria, but due to the fact that different criteria are not perfectly correlated, the use of alternate criteria can, to some extent, broaden the diversity of students selected.

It is also important to note that selecting a freshman class on one measure has rippling effects on other characteristics of the class. Webb (1966) demonstrated in one institution, for example, that increasing selectivity on GPA and test scores systematically altered the measured personality of entering freshmen toward increased independence, enthusiasm, open-mindedness, and broader intellectual interests.

Other Selection Measures. In addition to traditional measures three types of information about applicants are usually considered important. These include information about personal qualities, accomplishments, and background characteristics. Some of this information comes from national testing programs, some from personal contact between student and institution, and some from the formal application plus its attachments and endorsements. These sources are complementary, each serving functions the others cannot perform well.

It is in the highly selective colleges, universities, and professional schools in particular that personal qualities are considered especially important. Many institutions require autobiographical essays or personal interviews in search of the student with maturity and integrity as well as verve and personableness. Such aspects of character are often considered critical in admitting applicants to the service professions.

Also many institutions have long sought in such personal traits the key to the motivation that carries some students to achieve highly and persistently while others of seemingly equal ability languish and fail. Off and on personality tests are seen as a possible solution, though they harbor serious technical problems and ethical dilemmas that Messick (1964) has described well. The College Board even had to warn its member colleges about the use of such tests (College Entrance Examination Board, 1963), and in recent years assessment of personal qualities has been recognized to be quite inexact and best left to carefully considered subjective judgment.

Personal characteristics of students bear upon admissions in other important ways. A student's special educational interests and plans may argue for or against admission. A small graduate department, for example, may have much to offer one advanced student and little to another. Also a student's life history may reveal extenuating circumstances that argue for admission; for example, having overcome unusual hardship or having had unusual experiences of value to the future education of the student and his or her classmates.

Accomplishments and developed competences of students represent another broad category of qualifications that are important in admissions. Various writers have argued that typical tests used for graduate and undergraduate admissions place undue emphasis upon a strictly scholastic view of education, do not recognize a diversity of purpose among disciplines and institutions, and do not recognize the clear fact that the educational objectives of most faculty and most institutions are broader than pure academic competence (Wing and Wallach, 1971; Richards, Holland, and Lutz, 1967; Baird, 1976a; Wallach, 1976; Willingham, 1974).

Through the application process the student does present a good deal of information concerning personal accomplishments and educational development. These include the nature of academic preparation, honors achieved, extracurricular activities, work history, and so on. Valuable as such information is, it seldom has the salience of traditional quantified measures, and few institutions have worked through a rationale and procedure for insuring that evidence of student accomplishment is employed in selection decisions in ways that are effectively related to educational objectives of the institution.

There has been a variety of efforts to develop more systematic procedures for recognizing the unusual achievement, developed skills, and independent learning that often occurs out of the classroom (Baird, 1976b; Knapp, 1977; American College Testing Program, 1973; Wallach and Wing, 1969). Much of this work has dealt with such questions as how to make clear the character of such learning, how it relates to personal and educational goals, and how to give it greater weight in the educational process. Such emphasis has important strengths: a useful broadening of the definition of talent in American society, more assurance of equity to students through greater opportunity to use their competences, and greater likelihood of selecting more successful students. This work will doubtless continue on individual campuses and in national agencies, but there are various weaknesses to overcome: how to develop assessment methods that are flexible but also objective, how to verify authenticity of learning, how to measure fairly the quality and depth of learning.

Biographical data is a third general category of important information about candidates for admission. Such data always include demographic information but may also include a wide variety of personal characteristics, interests, and experiences of the sort requested on most admissions applications and questionnaires that accompany admissions testing programs (see Appendix F-2, for example). Biographical data are used for various administrative purposes having little to do with actual selection among applicants, but such information can affect selection in several important respects.

Some demographic or categorical information, for example, place of residence, academic status, age, and so forth may have a direct bearing upon admissibility in particular institutions or programs. Other variables such as sex and religion are acceptable bases for selection in some special purpose institutions and quite unacceptable in others. Finally, other constitutionally suspect variables such as race and ethnic background lie at the heart of the *Bakke* case.

A number of investigators have demonstrated that, properly weighted, information concerning interests, plans, and experiences can improve prediction of academic success by an amount that is often statistically significant but limited in practical value (see Freeberg, 1967; and Baird, 1976a for example, for reviews of research). Some studies of biographical questionnaires (for example, Anatasi, Meade, and Schneiders, 1960) have included items referred to above as accomplishments, and have demonstrated that they could be used to predict educational outcomes other than grades that are valued by the institution.

A strength of biographical questionnaires is their flexibility and economy, but they are subject to faking, and use of some demographic information raises ethical as well as legal questions. As a result, biographical information has tended not to be used mechanically to predict success or exclude students, but rather as a subjective aid in forming overall judgments in selection. This is an illustration of the often important relationship between the content of selection information and the method by which it is assessed.

Other Methods of Assessment. The traditional selection measures, tests and GPA, involve assessment techniques that are relatively objective and standardized compared to other selection measures just described. The latter involve less formal modes of assessment that might be characterized as three types: personal appraisal, free response methods, and self-reports.

Personal appraisal refers to one person's evaluation of another on the basis of direct personal acquaintance. The most common examples are interviews and personal recommendations. The interview has always been a source of great controversy. Some institutions feel that interviews are critical for appraising personal qualities but research has cast a good deal of doubt on the validity of interviews intended to predict future behavior; that is, for selection purposes (Ward, 1955; Wright, 1969). Recommendations have enjoyed great favor though confidence in their usefulness has tended to erode in recent years, partly because of legislation requiring disclosure and partly due to questionable validity (see Appendix F-5, for example). Important weaknesses in personal appraisal are the fact that it is difficult to achieve consistency, judges are sometimes biased, and appraisal is often not focused effectively upon the specific type of evaluation that the judge is capable of making.

While personal appraisal is based upon the judgment of a third party, the free-response and the self-report methods both refer to information supplied by the student. In both cases, however, the student's information typically requires some evaluative judgment in interpretation. Free-response methods include any form of assessment in which there is no single answer, and the student has wide latitude in framing the nature of her or his response. This mode of assessment includes some formal tests (for example, so-called divergent tests of scientific thinking), but the obvious example in admissions is the frequently required essay. Evaluation of any type of free-response material is difficult, time-consuming, and expensive, but the important special strength of this type of material is the fact that, unlike most measures of academic competence, it requires the student to create a solution rather than recall a correct answer. The relevance to demanding real-life situations is apparent.

The self-report is a third form of assessment that is widely used. Much of the material in college application blanks falls into this general category, and there is a variety of special-purpose questionnaires and inventories that can be useful in collecting pertinent information quite efficiently. Efficiency and flexibility are special strengths of this method of assessment; accuracy can be a weakness (see Baird, 1976a for an extensive review of self-report measures).

These various modes of assessment tend to have one important quality in common—the need to apply subjective judgment, either in evaluating information or in deciding what implications it may have regarding the admission of a student. It is clear that much of the decision process in admissions is necessarily subjective, and it is therefore important to appreciate the strengths and weaknesses of such judgment.

The special strengths of subjectivity have to do with the value of human judgment generally and the importance of giving attention to the unique qualities and concerns of people as individuals. Thus, a great strength of subjective judgment lies in its flexibility regarding the content of assessment and the capacity to select information that appears most relevant to the decision at hand. Appropriate subjective judgment regarding a candidate's credentials provides some balance to potentially mechanistic objectivity. In the process of applying good judgment judiciously, an institution also sends a message to future candidates concerning its interest in all aspects of character and competence and its unwillingness to decide a candidate's status on the basis of any single piece of information.

There are major weaknesses in subjective judgment, and these are especially connected with the problems of equity and fairness. When important decisions about people are left to personal judgment, the door is open to all forms of social bias. Use of subjective assessment tends to encourage faking by the applicant or other forms of beating the system. Those who do beat the system create inequities for those who do not. Also the relative unreliability of many forms of subjective judgment can easily impair the fairness of decisions reached. The expense and time required to guard against these weaknesses may be considerable from a practical standpoint.

This array of strengths and weaknesses in some of the most critical aspects of assessment in selective admissions underscores the complexity of the process and the issues. A main implication is the need to develop an improved understanding of the role of subjective assessment in selective admissions. Undue concern with the defensibility of procedures might lead some to urge using only GPA and test scores with an unequivocal cut-off, or possibly those measures plus others that obviously fit that mold. Such a limited view of permissible selection procedures would undoubtedly undermine the strengths and compound the weaknesses of the present admissions process.

It would seem that a wiser approach would be to work toward ways of insuring that the use of subjective judgment in selective admissions is sound in principle and application. There is no inherent reason why subjective judgment need be capricious or unaccountable to the rules of reason, equity, and public scrutiny. More is possible and should be done to incorporate a desirable degree of objectivity in selecting students so as to represent the diverse personal qualities important to institutions and also to protect individual rights. What seems needed is a more formal and systematic process for bringing considered judgment to bear on selection decisions in a manner that is open and fair and also educationally valid.

8

Summary

Admission to highly selective educational institutions is an important social issue and also a matter of much personal interest to many people. There are a host of familiar problems in the admissions process: inadequacies in the information and guidance students receive, cumbersome application procedures, serious finanical barriers for many students, and so on. Important as such problems may be, it has not been the intention to deal here with all aspects of admissions. The purpose of this report has been rather to provide an overview of selective admissions in several institutional settings, to describe briefly the general nature of special admission programs for underrepresented groups of students, to report available statistics on admission of minority and majority students, and to describe briefly information concerning strengths and weaknesses of measures used in selecting students. This summary draws attention to a few highlights and implications from the foregoing pages.

One conclusion we draw from the experience of preparing this report is a renewed realization of the paucity of information concerning several of the questions addressed here. In particular, there exists very little published information concerning the details of the selection process as it occurs each year in numerous institutions. Detailed information on the practices of institutions has come more out of litigation than out of any other source. The litigation usually involves isolated institutional cases and, as such, is not altogether useful in describing admissions generally. The typical lack of clear published standards for selective admissions is no great surprise. Many institutions have preferred not to disclose precise selection methods used for fear this would inhibit their flexibility to make sound decisions. There is no reason, however, to assume that an open process cannot include appropriate human judgmental factors.

It is evident, however, that the process by which institutions select students is complex and varies from situation to situation. To a considerable degree the process is complex and variable because selective admissions serves several purposes, and these purposes vary somewhat from institution to institution. In selecting students the interest is not only to enroll the most competent but to serve other institutional responsibilities as well (for example, to supply graduates in different fields).

As a result, academic ability as measured by grades and test scores is a major basis for selecting students but by no means the only consideration. Many other aspects of the student's experience and personal qualities come into play, including race and other background variables. Use of the latter variables as a basis for admissions gives rise to the controversial social issues represented in the *Bakke* case. As is true with college admissions generally, there is very little published information that provides an overview of institutional practices with regard to preferential admission or special efforts to enroll women and minority students. There is, however, a good deal of statistical information concerning enrollment trends and other outcomes of the admission process, though these data are not entirely adequate.

There are two basic types of data that are of interest. The first and most popular consists of the proportions of persons from different groups that are represented in the enrollments and degree awards of institutions in different categories. A second is that showing the rates of acceptance of individuals classified by ethnic groups and by evidence of academic promise. Both kinds of data are difficult to obtain—particularly the second. A number of organizations have conducted surveys of enrollments by ethnic status, but despite the number of surveys there are many problems of comparability across surveys and problems of interpretation of the data.

At the undergraduate level, there appears to have been an increase in minority freshman enrollments from about 11 percent in 1967 to about 14 percent in 1976 in four-year institutions. This gain in minority enrollment in four-year institutions, however, has not been matched in two-year institutions.

Despite limitations in available data, it is clear that minority enrollments in graduate and professional schools are somewhat less than in undergraduate four-year institutions. The data in Table 18 are based upon different surveys and are therefore not strictly comparable (for example, the medical school enrollment includes a larger proportion of blacks in traditionally black schools then is the case for law school enrollment). But there is a notable consistency across these types of institutions, both with respect to the extent of minority representation and the increase from 1969 to 1976. For the three minority groups shown, total representation in each institutional setting was about 5 percent in 1969 and some 8 to 9 percent in 1976.

Table 18. Summary comparison of graduate, law, and medical school enrollment representations (in percent) of blacks, Spanish-surnamed persons, and American Indians for 1969 and 1976

Group	Graduate schools[a]	Law schools[b]	Medical schools[c]
		1969	
Blacks	4.0	3.8	4.2
Spanish-surnamed	1.1	1.0	0.5
American Indian	0.3	0.1	0.1
Total	5.4	4.9	4.8
		1976	
Blacks	6.4	5.4	6.7
Spanish-surnamed	1.5	2.3	2.1
American Indian	0.4	0.3	0.3
Total	8.3	8.0	9.1

Note: Total representation of these minorities in 1976 was about 12 percent for undergraduate schools and 5 percent for graduate management schools.

[a] The 1969 figures were estimated from Appendix B-7 as the average of 1968 and 1970 percentages.

[b] Estimated using Appendix C-1 counts for individual groups and Table 6 counts as the base totals.

[c] From Appendix D-2.

There are, however, important differences behind the generally similar increases in different types of institutions. For example, the data for graduate schools include substantial representation of blacks in the field of education where admission is less selective. In law and medicine, on the other hand, admission has become extremely competitive in recent years. The somewhat effective efforts in increasing minority enrollment in these highly prized fields is likely due in part to extensive special aid and recruitment programs organized or facilitated by the national organizations in these professional areas.

Another important trend not revealed by Table 18 is the fact that the recent increases in minority representation occurred largely in the early part of the 1969-1976 time period. The leveling of minority enrollments in the last two or three years may be related to the truly dramatic increase in the numbers and representation of women in higher education. Between 1968 and 1976, the proportion of women in entering medical school classes increased from 9 percent to 25 percent. Between 1971 and 1976, the proportion of women in entering law classes increased from 12 percent to 28 percent. Thus, while minorities have gained some in representation, women have gained much more. Two factors seem to be involved. There are larger numbers of women applicants, and women fare well on traditional academic credentials such as grades and performance on admissions tests.

Data concerning acceptance rates have only recently become available and in only two of the settings investigated. Just this spring (1977) the Law School Admission Council complied extensive data on over 76,000 students who applied to accredited law schools for classes entering in the fall of 1976. Of 4,299 blacks who applied for 1976, 39 percent were offered admission by an accredited law school, while 45 percent of Chicanos, and 59 percent of whites applying were offered admission. The highest acceptance rate for any group was 60 percent for women applicants.

While these gross figures may seem discriminatory on the surface, a closer look at acceptance rates within groups with similar academic credentials tells a different story. Acceptance rates of blacks and Chicanos with average undergraduate grades and average LSAT scores were considerably higher than acceptance rates for other applicants with comparable credentials. From these data it is clear that affirmative action was being practiced by the law schools, but it is also clear that many members of minorities who applied presented academic credentials that were not competitive with those presented by other applicants. Both undergraduate grades and LSAT scores were low on the average for minority applicants to law schools in 1976. Therefore, even if test score considerations were waived for minorities, the problem of low undergraduate grades remained.

Acceptance rate data are also available for medical schools. Of 42,303 applicants to medical schools for 1975-76, 36 percent were accepted. Of 2,288 blacks who applied, 41 percent were accepted; of Chicano applicants, 52 percent were accepted. For other groups, 43 percent of American Indians, 32 percent of Orientals, 42 percent of mainland Puerto Ricans, 36 percent of Commonwealth Puerto Ricans, 32 percent of Cubans, and 37 percent of whites were accepted. Medical school data concerning acceptance rates for students at particular levels of GPA and test scores present a generally similar picture of affirmative action as that of the law school data described above.

This report has also given considerable attention to the strengths and weaknesses of various selection measures, particularly the traditional measures of academic competence: the previous grade record and standardized tests. Both grades and test scores have weaknesses as selection measures, but the strengths of these traditional variables clearly outweigh their weaknesses. Grades give the most direct evidence of capability and motivation for academic achievement, though they incorporate many potential inequities due to wide fluctuations in grading standards. Admissions tests represent a limited type of talent but they reflect very important general abilities and competence developed through the educational process, and evidence indicates that they serve as a useful standard yardstick that offsets some of the weaknesses of grades.

A very substantial amount of research supports the validity and usefulness of tests and grades for selection purposes. The previous grade average tends to be a somewhat better predictor than admissions tests at the undergraduate level and the opposite is true at the graduate level, but in each case both measures make a useful contribution. Though predicting success of students in advanced programs is always uncertain to a degree, the evidence clearly shows the traditional measures to be more accurate than other information available. Even moderately valid measures can be quite useful in more selective programs because predictors are more effective when a small proportion of applicants are selected. Moreover, as long as moderately valid predictors are equally valid for all subpopulations, they make a positive contribution to fair decision-making.

There is little evidence to suggest that validity of tests and grades does not extend to minority groups. In fact, most statistical studies indicate that grades and admission test scores tend to predict that minorities will perform slightly better in subsequent academic work than they actually do perform; that is, the reverse of what one would expect if it were assumed that these measures were biased against minorities.

Because of limitations in predictive accuracy and because there are other important considerations in selecting applicants, experienced admissions officers and measurement specialists have always counseled against undue reliance on the quantified, readily available indicators of scholastic ability. Nevertheless, the traditional measures do receive heavy emphasis in practical use as well as in research on college admissions. This circumstance suggests the need for giving more attention to additional selection measures that represent a broader range of talent and reflect directly the important accomplishments and achievements of students in and out of school that contribute to their educational goals.

It is also evident that many personal qualities and characteristics of students that may be quite relevant in selection cannot be adequately evaluated except through the subjective judgment of experienced faculty and staff of educational institutions. It is important to develop better methods of incorporating such judgment in the admissions process so that significant personal and institutional values are not lost. Some feel that litigation at times has a tendency to force rigid procedures that may create only an illusion of fairness and possibly lead to a mechanistic process that is shortsighted in its social values and effectiveness. It is necessary, however, to guard against inequities which can easily result from ambiguous policy and loose procedure. To maintain an effective and sensible admissions process in the face of legal scrutiny, it would seem especially useful to work toward a more systematic and open process—an educational "due process" that encourages use of all relevant information and subjective judgments that are sound in principle and fair in application.

Appendix A

Undergraduate Admissions

**Appendix A-1. Member Institutions of the
Consortium on Financing Higher Education (COFHE)**

Amherst College
Barnard College
Brown University
Bryn Mawr College
Carleton College
Columbia University
Cornell University
Dartmouth College
Duke University
Harvard University
The Johns Hopkins University
Massachusetts Institute of Technology
Mount Holyoke College
Northwestern University
Pomona College

Princeton University
Radcliffe College
Smith College
Stanford University
Swarthmore College
Trinity College
The University of Chicago
University of Pennsylvania
The University of Rochester
Vanderbilt University
Washington University
Wellesley College
Wesleyan University
Williams College
Yale University

Appendix A-2. Census projections of 18-year-old black and other nonwhites in the United States population by admission years from 1976 through 1994 (in thousands)

Eighteen-year-olds

Admission year	Total number	Black		Other nonwhites	
		Number	Percentage	Number	Percentage
1976	4,253	560	13.2	72	1.7
1977	4,244	573	13.5	76	1.8
1978	4,229	573	13.5	78	1.8
1979	4,292	583	13.6	83	1.9
1980	4,211	581	13.8	85	2.0
1981	4,145	580	14.0	87	2.1
1982	4,087	579	14.2	89	2.2
1983	3,917	569	14.5	92	2.3
1984	3,703	548	14.8	96	2.6
1985	3,604	525	14.6	96	2.7
1986	3,521	519	14.7	97	2.8
1987	3,567	530	14.8	101	2.8
1988	3,653	539	14.8	107	2.9
1989	3,733	566	15.2	117	3.1
1990	3,426	533	15.6	121	3.5
1991	3,240	514	15.9	122	3.8
1992	3,168	496	15.6	125	3.9
1993	3,247	506	15.6	127	3.9
1994	3,199	495	15.5	125	3.9

Source: U.S. Bureau of the Census (1977, pp. 28, 37-54).

Appendix A-3. Percentage of nonwhites in different types of institutions

Institution	1967	1970	1973	1976
Two-year colleges	12.3	17.1	14.2	14.7
Four-year colleges	10.9	9.9	12.7	15.2
Universities	6.4	5.4	5.0	9.7
Total	10.1	11.4	11.5	13.8

Source: ACE/UCLA Freshman National Norms Studies, Astin and others, 1976, p. 47; 1973, p. 39; 1970, p. 37; 1967, p. 32.

Appendix A-4. Fall 1972 postsecondary educational attendance: Percentages by race and ability, and institutional selectivity

Ability quartiles[a]

Type of College	Black				White				Hispanic			
	Low 1	2	3	High 4	Low 1	2	3	High 4	Low 1	2	3	High 4
Four-year	15.5	42.2	54.7	73.8	6.4	15.0	33.7	61.3	9.6	20.2	33.8	52.1
Two-year	10.1	11.3	10.5	4.6	10.7	17.4	18.9	13.2	19.4	30.2	26.4	26.3
Total	25.6	53.5	65.2	78.4	17.1	32.4	52.6	74.5	29.0	50.4	60.2	58.4

Ability

Selectivity levels[b]	Black				White				
	Low	Medium	High	All levels	Low	Medium	High	All levels	
Low 0, 1, 2	77.5	75.0	51.7	70.9	69.0	55.3	43.5	49.2	
Middle 3, 4	18.9	16.0	5.2	17.3	30.7	36.1	32.9	33.5	
High 5, 6, 7	3.6	9.0	43.1	11.8	0.3	8.6	23.6	17.3	
Total	100.0	100.0	100.0	100.0	100.0	100.0	100.0	100.0	

a Student ability based on composite test scores in vocabulary, reading, letter groups, and mathematics.

b Undergraduate institutions are classified on the basis of the average academic ability level of the entering freshman class as follows:

Selectivity levels	Corresponding range of student mean scores		
	NMSQT selection	SAT V + M	ACT composite
7	129 or higher	1,236 or higher	28 or higher
6	121-128	1,154-1,235	26-27
5	113-120	1,075-1,153	25-26
4	105-112	998-1,074	23-24
3	97-104	926- 997	21-22
2	89- 96	855- 925	19-21
1	88 or less	854 or less	18 or less
No estimate available	88	854	19

Source: Adapted from Astin, 1971, Table 2-1, p. 24.

Source: The tables are reprinted by permission from: J. P. Bailey, Jr., and E. F. Collins, "Entry into Postsecondary Education." In J. P. Bailey, Jr. (Chair.), *National Longitudinal Study of the High School Class of 1972 Symposium: Trends in Postsecondary Education.* Symposium presented at the annual meeting of the American Educational Research Association, New York, 1977, p. 17.

Appendix A-5. Percentage distribution of minority baccalaureate recipients among fields of study

Field of study	Total number of recipients[a]	Percentage of minority recipients				
		Subtotal	Black	Spanish surnamed	Asian	American Indian
Arts and humanities	139,900	6.1	3.3	1.8	0.7	0.2
Biological sciences	53,500	6.6	3.6	1.1	1.7	0.1
Business and management	133,300	7.6	4.9	1.2	1.2	0.3
Education	177,800	9.6	7.9	1.1	0.3	0.3
Engineering	62,500	5.1	1.8	1.4	1.5	0.4
Mathematics	24,500	7.2	4.6	0.7	1.7	0.1
Physical sciences	26,400	5.3	2.7	1.3	1.1	0.2
Psychology	52,100	7.4	4.8	1.4	1.0	0.3
Social sciences	158,800	9.7	7.2	1.4	0.8	0.3
All other fields	158,400	7.9	5.2	1.1	1.2	0.4
Total, all fields	989,200	7.8	5.3	1.3	0.9	0.3

Note: The above figures represent population estimates based on a stratified sample of all institutions that confer bachelor's degree. In view of variations in response rates among institutions and other factors that affect the accuracy of the survey findings, caution should be exercised in interpretation of these data. Problems in compiling minority statistics are more fully described in the forthcoming report of the Higher Education Panel of the American Council on Education on bachelor's degrees awarded to minority students, 1973-74.

[a] Includes U.S. citizens and foreign nationals holding permanent visas.

Source: National Board on Graduate Education (1976, p. 236)

Appendix B

Graduate Admissions

Appendix B-1. Graduate enrollment in four-year institutions of higher education by sex, attendance status, and institutional control: United States, fall 1964 to 1984[a] (in thousands)

Year (fall)	Total graduate degree-credit enrollment	Sex		Attendance status		Control	
		Men	Women	Full-time	Part-time	Public	Private
1964[b]	608	410	198	221	387	378	230
1965[b]	697	465	232	256	441	440	257
1966[b]	768	503	265	285	483	489	279
1967[b]	849	547	302	317	532	550	299
1968[b]	885	558	327	337	548	584	301
1969	955	590	366	364	591	666	289
1970	1,031	632	399	379	652	724	307
1971	1,012	615	397	388	624	712	300
1972	1,066	627	439	393	673	757	308
1973	1,123	647	476	409	714	799	324
1974	1,190	663	527	428	762	852	338
			Projected[c]				
1975	1,232	683	549	442	790	885	347
1976	1,268	702	566	455	813	913	355
1977	1,303	716	587	467	836	942	361
1978	1,332	731	601	477	855	966	366
1979	1,347	736	611	482	865	980	367
1980	1,367	745	622	489	878	998	369
1981	1,370	745	625	490	880	1,003	367
1982	1,380	748	632	493	887	1,013	367
1983	1,358	733	625	485	873	1,000	358
1984	1,336	721	615	477	859	986	350

Note: Data are for the 50 states and the District of Columbia for all years. Because of rounding, details may not add to totals. Enrollment data and estimates are based on U.S. Department of Health, Education and Welfare, National Center for Education Statistics publications; *Opening (Fall) Enrollment in Higher Education,* annually, 1964 through 1968, 1971 through 1974; *Fall Enrollment in Higher Education, Supplementary Information,* 1969 and 1970; unpublished data from *Resident and Extension Enrollment in Institutions of Higher Education,* fall 1966 and 1967; and *Residence and Migration of College Students,* fall 1968.

[a] Includes resident and extension graduate degree-credit enrollment. The estimates, 1964-1968, and data, 1969-1972, differ from figures in 1973 and earlier editions of Projections of Educational Statistics because they include extension graduate enrollment, which previously was included in undergraduate and first-professional degree-credit enrollment figures.

[b] The details of estimation procedures are given in Appendix A of the source document.

[c] The projection of graduate enrollment is based primarily on the assumption that, for each sex, full-time graduate enrollment expressed as a percentage of full-time undergraduate and unclassified enrollment will follow the 1968-1974 trend through 1984, and that the percentage that full-time graduate enrollment is of total graduate enrollment will remain constant at the 1974 level through 1984. The projection of total degree-credit enrollment in all institutions of higher education, for each sex, is based primarily on the following assumptions and methodology: (1) The 1974 percentage that full-time undergraduate and unclassified enrollment was of the population aged 18-21 years will remain constant through 1984. (2) The percentage that full-time undergraduate and unclassified enrollment is of total undergraduate and unclassified enrollment will follow the 1968 to 1974 trend through 1984. (3) The percentage of undergraduate and unclassified enrollment in public 2-year institutions will equal 100 percent less the percentage of undergraduate and unclassified enrollment in the three other type and control categories of institutions; the percentage of undergraduate and unclassified enrollment in the three other categories will each follow their 1968 to 1974 trend through 1984. (4) For each type and control category of institutions, the percentage that full-time undergraduate and unclassified enrollment is of total undergraduate and unclassified enrollment will follow the 1968 to 1974 trend through 1984. (5) The number of full-time first-professional enrollments will follow the 1968 to 1974 trend through 1984. (6) The 1974 percentage that full-time first-professional enrollment was of total first-professional enrollment will remain constant through 1984. (7) The 1974 percentage of first-professional enrollment in public institutions will remain constant through 1984. (8) For both public and private four-year institutions, the 1974 percentage that full-time first-professional enrollment was of total first-professional enrollment will remain constant through 1984. (9) The percentage that full-time graduate enrollment is of full-time undergraduate and unclassified enrollment will follow the 1968 to 1974 trend through 1984. (10) The 1974 percentage that full-time graduate enrollment was of total graduate enrollment will remain constant through 1984. (11) The 1974 percentage of graduate enrollment in public institutions will remain constant through 1984. (12) For both public and private four-year institutions, the 1974 percentage that full-time graduate enrollment was of total graduate enrollment will remain constant through 1984.

Source: Simon & Frankel (1976, p. 34). This table appeared as Table 17 in the source document.

Appendix B-2. Earned degrees by level and by sex of student: United States, 1963-64 to 1984-85

Year	Bachelor's degrees[a]			First-professional degrees[b]			Master's degrees[c]			Doctor's degrees (except first-professional)[d]		
	Total	Men	Women	Total	Men	Women	Total	Men	Women	Total	Men	Women
1963-64	466,486	269,861	196,625	27,667	26,815	852	105,551	70,339	35,212	14,490	12,955	1,535
1964-65	501,248	288,538	212,710	28,755	27,748	1,007	117,152	77,544	39,608	16,467	14,692	1,775
1965-66	520,248	299,196	221,052	30,799	29,657	1,142	140,548	93,063	47,485	18,237	16,121	2,116
1966-67	558,075	322,171	235,904	32,472	31,178	1,294	157,707	103,092	54,615	20,617	18,163	2,454
1967-68	631,923	357,270	274,653	34,787	33,237	1,550	176,749	113,519	63,230	23,089	20,183	2,906
1968-69	728,167	409,881	318,286	36,018	34,499	1,519	193,756	121,531	72,225	26,188	22,752	3,436
1969-70	791,510	450,234	341,276	35,724	33,940	1,784	208,291	125,624	82,667	29,866	25,890	3,976
1970-71	839,730	475,594	364,136	37,946	35,544	2,402	230,509	138,146	92,363	32,107	27,530	4,577
1971-72	887,273	500,590	386,683	43,411	40,723	2,688	251,633	149,550	102,083	33,363	28,090	5,273
1972-73[e]	922,130	517,980	404,150	50,100	46,570	3,530	263,340	154,480	108,860	34,630	28,450	6,180
1973-74[e]	945,870	527,390	418,480	53,660	48,390	5,270	277,030	157,840	119,190	33,810	27,360	6,450
1974-75[f]	944,000	522,000	422,000	54,700	47,700	7,000	291,700	160,500	131,200	36,100	28,500	7,600
						Projected[g]						
1975-76	936,000	504,000	432,000	58,200	48,900	9,300	305,300	165,100	140,200	37,600	29,100	8,500
1976-77	952,000	509,000	443,000	59,400	48,800	10,600	315,800	169,700	146,100	39,500	30,300	9,200
1977-78	1,011,000	535,000	476,000	60,600	49,300	11,300	323,800	173,700	150,100	39,700	30,100	9,600
1978-79	1,038,000	548,000	490,000	61,900	50,000	11,900	331,900	176,800	155,100	39,000	29,100	9,900
1979-80	1,052,000	555,000	497,000	62,700	50,200	12,500	337,800	179,800	158,000	39,400	28,600	10,800
1980-81	1,064,000	560,000	504,000	63,800	50,700	13,100	342,400	181,400	161,000	40,200	28,400	11,800
1981-82	1,082,000	570,000	512,000	64,800	51,200	13,600	345,400	182,400	163,000	41,100	28,500	12,600
1982-83	1,089,000	574,000	515,000	65,900	51,700	14,200	346,900	182,900	164,000	41,800	28,700	13,100
1983-84	1,084,000	571,000	513,000	66,400	51,800	14,600	345,400	181,400	164,000	42,600	29,100	13,500
1984-85	1,076,000	568,000	508,000	66,900	51,900	15,000	339,800	177,800	162,000	42,900	28,900	14,000

Note. Data include 50 states and the District of Columbia for all years. Because of rounding, details may not add to totals. Degree and enrollment data and estimates are based on (1) U.S. Department of Health, Education and Welfare, National Center for Education Statistics publications: *Earned Degrees Conferred by Institutions of Higher Education,* 1963-64 through 1973-74; *Opening (Fall) Enrollment in Higher Education,* 1963 through 1968 and 1971 through 1974; *Enrollment for Advanced Degrees,* fall 1961, 1962, and 1963; *Enrollment for Master's and Higher Degrees, Fall 1964; Enrollment for Master's and Higher Degrees, Fall 1965; Summary Report; Students Enrolled for Advanced Degrees,* fall 1966 through 1973; *Fall enrollment in Higher Education, Supplementary Information,* 1969 and 1970; and American Bar Association publication: Millard H. Ruud, "That Burgeoning Law School Enrollment Slows," *American Bar Association Journal,* February 1973, 59, 150-153.

a In the 1971 and prior editions of *Projections of Educational Statistics,* bachelor's degrees were not shown separately but were combined with first-professional degrees.

b The following specified degrees are reported as first-professional: Dentistry (D.D.S. or D.M.D.), law (LL. B. or J.D.), medicine (M.D.), theology, veterinary medicine (D.V.M.), chiropody or podiatry (D.S.C. or D.P.), optometry (O.D.), and osteopathy (D.O.).

c Master's degrees differ from those published in the 1968 and prior editions of *Projections of Educational Statistics* because of adjustments to secure comparability with current reports of these degrees. For estimation details, see appendix A, "Estimation Methods," section I. Master's degrees also differ from those published in the 1969 through 1971 editions because of discrepancies among the reported numbers of degrees.

d Doctor's degrees include the Ph.D. in any field as well as such degrees as doctor of education, doctor of juridical science, and doctor of public health (preceded by a professional degree in medicine or sanitary engineering). They exclude degrees defined as first-professional, such as doctor of veterinary medicine.

e Preliminary data rounded to tens.

f Estimated.

g The estimation and projection of degrees by level and sex of student are based on the following assumptions: (1) The estimates of bachelor's degrees by sex for 1974-75 and the projections of these degrees through 1984-85 assume that the percentage that degrees in these years are of first-time degree-credit enrollment 4 years earlier will follow the 1963-64 to 1973-74 trend through 1984-85; the projections for 1978-79 through 1984-85 are based on projected first-time degree-credit enrollment figures. (2) The estimates of total first-professional degrees for 1974-75 and the projections of these degrees through 1984-85 were obtained by summing the number of degrees in the individual field. (For methods of projecting first-professional degrees in individual fields see footnotes to table 26.) The estimates of first-professional degrees by sex for 1974-75 and the projections of these degrees through 1984-85 assume that the percentage of degrees conferred on women in each field of study would follow the 1963-64 to 1976-77 trend through 1984-85. For 1974-75 through 1976-77, the estimate of the percentage of degrees conferred on women in each field was assumed to be the same as the percentage of women enrolled in the first year of first-professional programs in the same field either 3 or 4 years earlier. For law and "theology and other," a 3-year time lag was used. For medicine, dentistry, and "other health profession," a 4-year time lag was used. (3) The estimates of master's degrees by sex for 1974-75 and projections through 1984-85 assume that the percentage that master's degrees are of the average of first-year enrollment for advanced degrees 1 and 2 years earlier will follow the 1963-64 to 1973-74 trend through 1984-85. The estimates of first-year enrollment for advanced degrees by sex for 1974 and projections through 1984 assume that the 1973 percentage that first-year enrollment for advanced degrees was of graduate enrollment will remain constant through 1984-85 (48.2 percent for men and 52.5 percent for women). (4) The estimates of doctor's degrees by sex for 1974-75 and projections through 1984-85 assume that the percentage that doctor's degrees are of the average of first-year enrollment for advanced degrees 7 and 8 years earlier will follow the 1963-64 to 1973-74 trend through 1984-85. For further methodological details, see Appendix A of the source document.

Source: Simon & Frankel (1976, p. 42). This table appeared as Table 21 in the source document.

Appendix B-3. Total graduate school enrollment by type of institution

Type of institution	Number	Percentage[a]	Year 1975	1976	Percentage change
Master's highest					
Public	65	87	136,309	129,965	−4.7
Private	24	92	19,751	19,610	−0.7
Subtotal	89	83	156,060	149,575	−4.2
Ph.D. highest					
Public	146	94	471,054	459,215	−2.5
Private	77	88	146,298	146,885	+0.4
Subtotal	223	92	617,352	606,100	+1.8
Total institutions					
Public	211	92	607,363	589,180	−3.0
Private	101	89	166,049	166,495	+0.3
Total	312	91[b]	773,412	755,675	−2.3

Note: For purposes of this survey, institutions were asked to include all students considered as registered in the graduate school, including education, engineering, social work, medical, and business programs leading to M.A./M.S. or Ph.D., Ed.D., or other doctorates.

[a] Percentage figures are the number of institutions responding to this question as a percentage of the number available in the total group. For example, 65 public "master's highest degree" institutions responded out of a possible 75 such institutions in the CGS membership for an 87 percent response rate for that group of institutions.

[b] The 312 institutions responding to this question represent 91 percent of the CGS institutions and accounted for approximately 91 percent of the 1975 total student enrollment at CGS institutions.

Source: Somerville (1976, p. 6).

Appendix B-4. First-time graduate enrollment by type of institution

Type of institution	Number	Percentage	Year 1975	1976	Percentage change
Master's highest					
Public	57	76	29,516	29,379	−0.5
Private	22	85	4,827	4,834	+0.1
Subtotal	79	78	34,343	34,213	−0.4
Ph.D. highest					
Public	132	85	112,796	105,333	−6.6
Private	70	80	39,523	39,969	+1.1
Subtotal	202	83	152,319	145,302	−4.6
Total institutions					
Public	189	81	142,312	134,712	−5.3
Private	92	82	44,350	44,803	+1.0
Total	281	82[a]	186,662	179,515	−3.5

[a] The 281 institutions responding to this question represent 82 percent of the CGS institutions and accounted for approximately 81 percent of the 1976 total student enrollment at CGS institutions.

Source: Somerville (1976, p. 7).

Appendix B-5. Number of applications for graduate study

Type of institution	Number	Percentage	Year 1975	Year 1976	Percentage change
Master's highest					
Public	49	65	61,917	59,737	−3.5
Private	19	73	11,798	11,876	+0.7
Subtotal	68	67	73,715	71,613	−2.9
Ph.D. highest					
Public	122	79	358,290	365,763	+2.1
Private	65	74	149,159	151,192	+1.4
Subtotal	187	77	507,449	516,955	+1.9
Total institutions					
Public	171	74	420,207	425,500	+1.3
Private	84	74	160,957	163,068	+1.3
Total	255	74[a]	581,164	588,568	+1.3

[a] The 255 institutions responding to this question represent 74 percent of the CGS institutions and accounted for approximately 74 percent of the 1975 total student enrollment at CGS institutions.

Source: Somerville (1976, p. 8).

Appendix B-6. Number of master's and doctoral degrees granted

Degree offered by institution type	Number	Percentage	School year 1974-75	School year 1975-76	Percentage change
Master's					
Public	208	90	136,955	144,875	+5.8
Private	102	89	41,665	42,053	+0.9
Total	310	90[a]	178,620	186,928	+4.7
Doctoral					
Public	143	82	20,166	19,936	−1.1
Private	78	81	8,631	8,780	+1.7
Total	221	91[b]	28,797	28,716	−0.3

[a] The 310 institutions responding to this question represent 90 percent of the CGS institutions and accounted for approximately 90 percent of the 1975 total student enrollment at CGS institutions.

[b] The 221 institutions responding to this question represent 91 percent of the CGS institutions and accounted for approximately 84 percent of the 1975 total student enrollment at CGS institutions.

Source: Somerville (1976, p. 11).

Appendix B-7. A comparison of reported graduate enrollment by racial or ethnic identity between 1968 and 1976

Racial or ethnic identity	OCR 1968[a] full-time	OCR 1970[b] full-time	Hamilton 1971[c] full- and part-time	OCR 1972[d] full-time	NASULGC 1972[e] full- and part-time	ACE 1973[f] full- and part-time	OCR 1974[g] full-time	CGS 1975[h] full-time	CGS 1976[h]
Total	149,331	392,362[i]	286,755	406,093	495,478	372,964	398,808[j]	433,132	427,703
White or nonminority	141,383 (94.7%)	362,329 (92.3%)	271,356 (94.6%)	368,812 (90.8%)	456,003 (92.0%)	346,472 (92.9%)	362,152 (90.8%)	380,550 (87.8%)	374,435 (87.5%)
Total minority	7,948 (5.3%)	30,033 (7.7%)	15,399 (5.4%)	37,281 (9.2%)	39,475 (8.0%)	26,492 (7.1%)	36,656 (9.2%)	52,582 (12.1%)	53,268 (12.4%)
Black	5,084 (3.4%)	16,334 (4.2%)	9,376 (3.3%)	21,371 (5.3%)	24,257 (4.9%)	16,241 (4.4%)	22,092 (5.5%)	29,128 (6.7%)	27,658 (6.4%)
Spanish surnamed	1,234 (0.8%)	4,820 (1.2%)	2,895 (1.0%)	5,903 (1.5%)	5,536 (1.1%)	3,994 (1.1%)	6,124 (1.5%)	5,993[k] (1.3%)	6,282[k] (1.5%)
American Indian	322 (0.2%)	1,290 (0.3%)	708 (0.2%)	1,664 (0.4%)	1,610 (0.3%)	1,181 (0.3%)	1,397 (0.4%)	1,810 (0.4%)	1,783 (0.4%)
Asian or other minority	1,308 (0.9%)	7,579 (1.9%)	2,420 (0.8%)	8,343 (2.1%)	6,558 (1.3%)	5,076 (1.4%)	7,043 (1.8%)	15,651 (3.6%)	17,545 (4.1%)

a U.S. Department of Health, Education and Welfare (DHEW), Office for Civil Rights, Racial and Ethnic Enrollment Data from Institutions of Higher Education, Fall 1972. Washington, D.C.: U.S. Government Printing Office, 1975, Sect. 9-2, p. 112.

b U.S. DHEW, 1972, p. 177.

c B. I. Hamilton, Graduate School Programs for Minority Disadvantaged Students. Princeton, N.J.: Educational Testing Service, 1973, Table 5.

d U.S. DHEW, 1975, p. 76.

e National Association of State Universities and Land Grant Colleges (NASULGC), Biennial Survey of Minority Enrollments 1972, unpublished data, cited in NBGE, 1976, Table 4, p. 44.

f ... Ph.D.-Granting Institutions, Higher Education Panel Report, No. 19. Washington, D.C.: American Council on Education, 1974.

g "Enrollment of Minority Students, 1974," Chronicle of Higher Education, November 8, 1976, p. 6.

h Unpublished data.

i Includes professional schools other than medicine, dentistry, and law.

j Total enrollment figure calculated from states total enrollment.

k The sum of Chicano and Puerto Rican.

Source: This table is an adaptation and extension of an original table provided by Carlos H. Arce, University of Michigan.

Appendix B-8. Doctorates awarded, by race and ethnic identity, and citizenship status, 1973-74

Racial/ethnic identity	Total	U.S. native	U.S. naturalized	Non-U.S. citizen Permanent visa	Non-U.S. citizen Tempo- rary visa
Black	1,010	833 (82.5%)	13 (1.3%)	42 (4.2%)	122 (12.2%)
American Indian	124	124 (100.0%)	— —	— —	— —
Chicano, Mexican American, Spanish American	214	93 (43.5%)	42 (19.6%)	17 (7.9%)	62 (28.9%)
Puerto Rican	60	59 (98.3%)	1 (1.7%)	— —	— —
Oriental	2,204	142 (6.4%)	151 (6.9%)	858 (38.9%)	1,053 (47.8%)
Total minority	3,612	1,251 (34.6%)	207 (5.7%)	917 (25.4%)	1,237 (34.2%)
White	25,552	22,693 (88.8%)	749 (2.9%)	651 (2.5%)	1,459 (5.7%)
Total	29,241	24,000 (82.1%)	960 (3.3%)	1,571 (5.4%)	2,710 (9.3%)

*Note:*Represents 89 percent sample of 33,000 doctorates awarded in 1973-74. Nonrespondents include persons who did not indicate their racial or ethnic identity or who used an out-of-date questionnaire lacking the racial/ethnic question.

*Source:*National Board on Graduate Education (1976, p. 41). This table appeared as Table 3 in the source document, which should be consulted for details of survey and analysis procedures. Special analysis by NBGE of data from National Research Council, National Academy of Sciences, Doctorate Records File, June 1975.

Appendix B-9. Doctorates awarded showing distribution, within fields of study, by race and ethnic group, 1973-74 (U.S. native-born citizens)

Field	Total	Black	Spanish American[a]	Puerto Rican	American Indian	Oriental	White
Physical sciences and mathematics	3,272	46 (1.4%)	11 (0.3%)	5 (0.2%)	15 (0.5%)	24 (0.7%)	3,171 (96.9%)
Engineering	1,555	16 (1.0%)	4 (0.3%)	7 (0.5%)	7 (0.5%)	18 (1.1%)	1,503 (96.7%)
Life sciences	3,337	69 (2.1%)	16 (0.5%)	6 (0.2%)	15 (0.4%)	33 (1.0%)	3,198 (95.8%)
Social sciences	4,713	104 (2.2%)	20 (0.4%)	12 (0.3%)	18 (0.4%)	22 (0.5%)	4,537 (96.3%)
Arts and humanities	3,950	74 (1.9%)	21 (0.5%)	17 (0.4%)	17 (0.4%)	13 (0.3%)	3,808 (96.4%)
Professional fields	1,038	31 (3.0%)	5 (0.5%)	1 (0.1%)	8 (0.8%)	4 (0.4%)	989 (95.3%)
Education	6,109	493 (8.1%)	72 (1.2%)	11 (0.2%)	44 (0.7%)	28 (0.5%)	5,461 (89.4%)
Other or unspecified fields	26	– –	– –	– –	– –	– –	26 (100.0%)
Total	24,000	833 (3.5%)	149 (0.6%)	59 (0.2%)	124 (0.5%)	142 (0.6%)	22,693 (94.6%)

Note: Represents an 89 percent sample of total doctorates awarded in 1973-74.

[a] Includes Chicano, Mexican American, and Spanish American.

Source: National Board on Graduate Education (1976, p. 47). This table appeared as Table 7 in the source document, which should be consulted for details of survey and analysis procedures. Special analysis by NBGE of data from National Research Council, National Academy of Sciences, Doctorate Records File, May 1975.

Appendix B-10. Doctorates awarded showing distribution among fields of study, by race and ethnic group, 1973-74 (U.S. native-born citizens)

Field	Black	Chicano, Mexican American, Spanish American	Puerto Rican	American Indian	Oriental	White
Physical sciences and mathematics	46 (5.5%)	11 (7.4%)	5 (8.5%)	15 (12.1%)	24 (16.9%)	3,171 (14.0%)
Engineering	16 (1.9%)	4 (2.7%)	7 (11.9%)	7 (5.6%)	18 (12.7%)	1,503 (6.6%)
Life sciences	69 (8.3%)	16 (10.7%)	6 (10.2%)	15 (12.1%)	33 (23.2%)	3,198 (14.1%)
Social sciences	104 (12.5%)	20 (13.4%)	12 (20.3%)	18 (14.5%)	22 (15.5%)	4,537 (20.0%)
Arts and humanities	74 (8.9%)	21 (14.1%)	17 (28.8%)	17 (13.7%)	13 (9.2%)	3,808 (16.8%)
Other professional fields	31 (3.7%)	5 (3.3%)	1 (1.7%)	8 (6.5%)	4 (2.8%)	989 (4.4%)
Education	493 (59.2%)	72 (48.3%)	11 (18.6%)	44 (35.5%)	28 (19.7%)	5,461 (24.1%)
Unspecified fields	— (0.0%)	— (0.0%)	— (0.0%)	— (0.0%)	— (0.0%)	26 (0.1%)
Total	833 (100.0%)	149 (100.0%)	59 (100.0%)	124 (100.0%)	142 (100.0%)	22,693 (100.0%)

Note: Represents an 89 percent sample of total doctorates awarded in 1973-74.

Source: National Board on Graduate Education (1976, p. 49). This table appeared as Table 8 in the source document, which should be consulted for details of survey and analysis procedures. Special analysis by NBGE of data from National Research Council, National Academy of Sciences, Doctorate Records File, May 1975.

Appendix B-11. Intended graduate major area by ethnic group (U.S. citizens only)

Field	American Indian	Black/Afro American	Mexican American	Oriental or Asian	Puerto Rican	Other Hispanic Latin American	White or Caucasian	Other	Total response
Arts	19 (2.21%)	232 (1.77%)	37 (1.38%)	42 (1.66%)	17 (1.38%)	10 (1.04%)	5,103 (2.91%)	116 (2.98%)	5,576 (2.78%)
Other humanities	77 (8.97%)	802 (6.11%)	235 (8.79%)	198 (7.83%)	155 (12.55%)	169 (17.55%)	18,135 (10.34%)	505 (12.97%)	20,276 (10.11%)
Education	149 (17.37%)	2,507 (19.11%)	685 (25.63%)	286 (11.31%)	127 (10.28%)	117 (12.15%)	28,405 (16.20%)	375 (9.63%)	32,651 (16.27%)
Social sciences	89 (10.37%)	1,576 (12.02%)	286 (10.70%)	226 (8.94%)	100 (8.10%)	77 (8.00%)	17,517 (9.99%)	342 (8.78%)	20,213 (10.08%)
Behavorial sciences	248 (28.90%)	4,048 (30.86%)	749 (28.02%)	494 (19.53%)	387 (31.34%)	281 (29.18%)	41,009 (23.39%)	1,059 (27.20%)	48,275 (24.06%)
Biological sciences	51 (5.94%)	788 (6.01%)	115 (4.30%)	342 (13.52%)	119 (9.64%)	73 (7.58%)	16,209 (9.24%)	412 (10.58%)	18,109 (9.03%)
Health	48 (5.59%)	687 (5.24%)	126 (4.71%)	240 (9.49%)	78 (6.32%)	44 (4.57%)	12,171 (6.94%)	208 (5.34%)	13,602 (6.78%)
Applied biology	19 (2.21%)	108 (0.82%)	19 (0.71%)	36 (1.42%)	8 (0.65%)	9 (0.93%)	3,579 (2.04%)	66 (1.69%)	3,844 (1.92%)
Engineering	16 (1.86%)	141 (1.08%)	59 (2.21%)	153 (6.05%)	50 (4.05%)	37 (3.84%)	5,259 (3.00%)	91 (2.34%)	5,806 (2.89%)
Mathematical sciences	8 (0.93%)	215 (1.64%)	28 (1.05%)	122 (4.82%)	35 (2.83%)	22 (2.28%)	3,809 (2.17%)	98 (2.52%)	4,337 (2.16%)
Physical sciences	29 (3.38%)	357 (2.72%)	70 (2.62%)	165 (6.52%)	53 (4.29%)	28 (2.91%)	8,118 (4.63%)	209 (5.37%)	9,029 (4.50%)
Not in above	70 (8.16%)	1,083 (8.26%)	179 (6.70%)	111 (4.39%)	66 (5.34%)	47 (4.88%)	7,218 (4.12%)	207 (5.32%)	8,981 (4.48%)
Undecided	35 (4.08%)	572 (4.36%)	85 (3.18%)	114 (4.51%)	40 (3.24%)	49 (5.09%)	8,825 (5.03%)	206 (5.29%)	9,926 (4.95%)
Total	858 (100.0%)	13,116 (100.0%)	2,673 (100.0%)	2,529 (100.0%)	1,235 (100.0%)	963 (100.0%)	175,357 (100.0%)	3,894 (100.0%)	200,625 (100.0%)

Source: Altman and Holland (1977, p. 32).

Appendix B-12. Summary of Admissions Practices in Graduate Schools

- Some overall admissions policy exists in almost all graduate schools. Only 18 institutions (7 percent of those responding) reported the absence of an overall policy. Although candidates are generally required to meet certain minimum standards such as a specific undergraduate grade-point average, the high Ph.D. group of institutions tends to have a competitive policy, while the master's-only group tends to have more institutions with an open-door policy.

- The use of admissions quotas appears to depend primarily on the type of institution. In the high Ph.D. institutions, 87 percent report the use of admissions quotas for some or all departments; in the master's-only group, only 32 percent have quotas.

- The departments tend to have the major voice in admissions decisions, either through direct decision making (54 percent) or through recommendations (75 percent), although the graduate dean has a veto in 52 percent of the institutions over the decision to admit and in 33 percent over the decision to reject. A separate admissions office has a strong decision-making role in a limited number of institutions.

- The graduate dean's office has a primary role in approximately two-thirds of the schools in: (1) preparing announcements of admissions policy and requirements, (2) setting deadlines, (3) informing students of admissions decisions, (4) informing students of fellowship decisions, and (5) retaining current application files. In 15 percent of the institutions, the graduate dean holds primary responsibility for counseling prospective graduate students and selecting assistantships. At most institutions the departments do not bear a primary responsibility for the administrative functions related to admissions.

- Few institutions conduct validity studies of admissions criteria or follow-up studies of the success of admissions selections; 30 percent of the institutions conducted such studies in some or all departments.

- Most graduate schools make very little use of data processing equipment; 33 percent reported no use at all, although only 2 percent lack such equipment. Of 16 different uses for such equipment listed in the questionnaire, only 26 percent of the schools using data processing equipment checked more than four and only 12 percent checked seven or more. The most common uses related to development of statistics and record keeping. Forty institutions indicated that the use of data processing equipment will be a major need over the next five years.

- Information about admissions policies and procedures is commonly communicated through the catalog, and information about special areas of departmental emphasis most often through departmental publications. Certain kinds of information, which may be of particular interest and importance to students in their thinking and decisions about graduate school, are often not provided or provided only upon special request. Among these kinds of information are the weight given to various factors in selection decisions and profiles of admitted students in terms of undergraduate grades, GRE scores, or other factors.

- In 75 percent of the institutions students do not participate in activities such as establishment of admissions policy, selection of students for admission and/or fellowship, and establishment of admissions procedures. When students are used in these areas it is primarily to give advice. In very few institutions (less than 10 for any activity) does the student have a vote or role equal to that of the faculty. Only in the

area of recruiting and/or counseling and advising of students do students
participate at a number of institutions (46 percent).

- A large majority of graduate schools have some basic minimum requirement that
  applies across all departments. Eighty-nine percent require a bachelor's degree or
  its equivalent and 76 percent require that it be from an accredited institution. Sixty-
  nine percent require a certain undergraduate grade-point average or class rank.
  Less than a fourth of the institutions require an undergraduate major in the field of
  or related to the intended graduate major or a minimum GRE test score.
- Certain requirements or recommendations exist at the graduate school level.
  Ninety-six percent of the institutions require a college transcript, and 92 percent a
  completed application form. Letters of recommendation from undergraduate
  faculty are required by 52 percent of the institutions, GRE Aptitude Test results by
  45 percent, statements of purpose or plans of study by 45 percent, and GRE
  Advanced Test results by 22 percent. Certain criteria, including personality tests,
  photographs, biographical sketches, and academic rating forms, are rarely
  required or recommended and rarely used if available.
- In descending order, the five most important admissions criteria were college
  transcripts, completed application forms, GRE Aptitude Test scores, letters of
  recommendation from undergraduate faculty, and GRE Advanced Test scores.
- The most common use of GRE Aptitude or Advanced Test results is for all
  candidates in relation to other information. Very few departments use either the
  Aptitude or Advanced Test results as the most important or least important single
  factor.
- Regardless of the type of institution, more students are supported by fellowships
  and assistantships in science than in humanities and social science.
- High Ph.D. institutions support a greater percentage of students regardless of field
  than do low Ph.D. and master's-only institutions.
- The relative importance of need versus merit in awarding fellowships varies
  markedly by type of institution. Merit only is the policy in a higher percentage of
  high Ph.D. institutions (65 percent) than in low Ph.D. (49 percent) and master's-
  only (21 percent) institutions. Conversely, "merit, but need to some extent"
  constitutes the policy in fewer of the high Ph.D. institutions (26 percent) than in
  the low Ph.D. (36 percent) and master's-only (31 percent) institutions.
- Current admissions problems cited by the respondents fall into two broad
  categories: admissions procedures (45 percent) and selection problems (51 percent).
  Ninety-one percent of the graduate schools report that they expect their graduate
  enrollment to increase over the next five years. Sixty percent of the institutions
  anticipate an increase of 5 percent or better per year.
- Minority group admissions, policy and procedure development within the
  graduate school, evaluation of various student backgrounds, and pressure for open
  admission versus need to maintain standards are the most frequently cited
  admissions problems in the next five years.

Source: Burns (1970, p. 1-4).

Appendix B-13. Sources of funds for minority students

Graduate and Professional Fellowships and Grants: General

Fellowship Programs for Black Americans, Mexican Americans, Native Americans (American Indians) and Puerto Ricans. The Ford Foundation is sponsoring a limited number of graduate fellowships to members of the groups named above (including Aleuts, Eskimos, native Hawaiians) who wish to pursue a career in higher education. The program is oriented towards persons studying in various fields of the social sciences, natural sciences, and the humanities. However, persons in the professional fields, who plan to complete a doctoral degree in preparation for a career in higher education may apply, providing they hold a first postbaccalaureate degree, such as the M.D., J.D., or the master's degree in architecture, business administration, education, engineering, library science, public administration, public health, or urban affairs and planning. The deadline for filing applications and supporting materials for the 1976-1977 program is January 5, 1976. Black American students should write to Graduate Fellowships for Black Americans, National Fellowships Fund, 795 Peachtree Street, N.E., Suite 484, Atlanta, Georgia 30308. Mexican American students should write to Graduate Fellowships for Mexican Americans, Educational Testing Service, Box 200, Berkeley, California 94704. Native American students (American Indians, and so on) should write to Graduate Fellowships for Native Americans, Educational Testing Service, Box 200, Berkeley, California 94704. Puerto Rican students should write to Graduate Fellowships for Puerto Ricans, Educational Testing Service, Box 2822, Princeton, New Jersey 08540.

The Fulbright-Hayes Program. The Board of Foreign Scholarships makes the final selection for graduate study grants under the Fulbright-Hayes Program which gives U.S. students the opportunity to live and study in a foreign country for one academic year and increases mutual understanding between the people of the United States and other countries through the exchange of persons, knowledge, and skills. Applicants who are enrolled in U.S. colleges and universities should contact their Fulbright Program Advisers for the latest information about awards to the country in which the graduate study is to be undertaken. In many countries preference will be given to advanced graduate students who, in most cases, will be conducting research for the Ph.D. dissertation.

The Southern Fellowships Fund. This fund, acting for the Council of Southern Universities, Inc., offers fellowships for graduate students in colleges and universities now attended primarily by black students and similarly qualified persons in other institutions who can give clear evidence of intent to enter upon a career in institutions attended primarily by black students. Fields included are primarily basic biological and physical sciences, basic social sciences, and humanities. Write to Executive Director, The Southern Fellowships Fund, 795 Peachtree Street, N.E., Atlanta, Georgia 30308.

Source: Educational Testing Service (1975, pp. 6–10).

United Scholarship Service, Inc. This service is a national, American Indian education agency that offers counseling, placement, and limited financial assistance to undergraduate American Indian students. The counseling aspects of the organization's program would be especially beneficial to undergraduate students from this minority group who are contemplating graduate or professional training. Write to United Scholarship Service, Inc., P.O. Box 18285, Capitol Hill Station, 941 East 17 Avenue, Denver, Colorado 80218.

Graduate and Professional Fellowships and Grants: Specific

Accelerated Business Leadership Education (ABLE). This program is designed to identify, recruit, and train minority group members who have the interest, motivation, and potential to pursue the M.B.A. degree. Participating schools are Atlanta University, Howard University, New York University, Syracuse University, the University of Maine, and the University of Massachusetts. Write to the Director, Program ABLE, School of Business Administration, University of Massachusetts, Amherst, Massachusetts 01002.

The American Fund for Dental Education. This fund has established scholarships for needy minority students, including blacks, Mexican Americans, native Americans, and Puerto Ricans. The scholarships begin with the final year of undergraduate work. Application forms may be obtained from the American Fund for Dental Education, 211 East Chicago Avenue, Chicago, Illinois 60611.

American Fund for Dental Health. This fund established its dental teacher training fellowship program in 1958 to help combat the serious shortage of teachers in dental schools. The majority of fellowship recipients use the program to take a two-year course leading to a Master's Degree. All recipients must certify that they will teach a minimum of two-and-a-half days per week for five consecutive years at a dental school accredited by the American Dental Association. Applicants may choose their own course of study and school but are encouraged to pursue their own studies in schools other than those from which they have received their dental degrees. Fellowships are for one year's study at the graduate level. Upon reapplication the fellowship may be renewed, if approved by the Committee, for a second year of study. The maximum award is for $10,000 per year. Fellowships are for study beginning in September. Applicants must be resident citizens of the U.S. They must be graduates of dental schools approved by the American Dental Association and must be eligible for admission to a graduate dental education center in the U.S. Deadline for filing is February 1. Selections will be announced in April by the AFDH Fellowship Awards Committee. For further information write to the American Fund for Dental Health, 211 East Chicago Avenue, Chicago, Illinois 60611, or call (312) 787-6270.

The American Fund for Dental Health's guaranteed loan program was established in 1972 to help meet the urgent needs of undergraduate and graduate dental students for financial assistance. It is intended to supplement all other loan opportunities, including federal, state, and university programs. Any dental student in good standing who is a U.S. citizen is eligible to apply for a loan. A loan may be obtained to meet any expense required to continue or complete the student's education. The maximum loan a graduate or undergraduate dental student may obtain under AFDH sponsorship for any academic year is $5,000. Loan applications are available only from your dental school's financial aid officer. For further information, contact the financial aid officer at your dental school, or the American Fund for Dental Health, 211 East Chicago Avenue, Chicago, Illinois 60611, or call (312) 787-6270.

American Indian Law Center. Native Americans (including Alaska natives) who are interested in attending law school are urged to apply to this federally funded program if they have a degree or if they have completed at least three years of college and are currently working toward a degree. A special summer program is offered at the University of New Mexico School of Law for Native American students who are eligible for admission to law school or who have already been admitted. The summer session is not a mandatory prerequisite for participation in the scholarship program. Write to Sam Deloria, Director, Special Scholarship Program in Law for American Indians, University of New Mexico School of Law, 1117 Stanford, N.E., Albuquerque, New Mexico 87131.

American Indian Scholarships. These scholarships provide financial assistance to American Indian students in graduate programs. Write to American Indian Scholarships, 211 Sierra Drive, S.E., Albuquerque, New Mexico 87108.

American Nurses Association (ANA). For information regarding programs and financial aid, write to Dr. Ruth Gordon, Director, Fellowship Program, ANA, 2420 Pershing Road, Kansas City, Missouri 64108.

American Speech and Hearing Association (ASHA). For information regarding graduate programs and financial aid, write to ASHA, 9030 Old Georgetown Road, Washington, D.C. 20014.

Association of University Programs in Hospital Administration (AUPHA). AUPHA conducts a minority group scholarship and loan program for its member graduate programs. Interested students should write to AUPHA, Mrs. Lynnette Cooper, Director, Office of Educational Opportunity, 1755 Massachusetts Avenue, N.W., Suite 500, Washington, D.C. 20036.

Consortium for Graduate Study in Management. The consortium awards fellowships to minority students to enroll in the regular master of business administration program at one of the following: Indiana University, the University of Rochester, Washington University, the University of Wisconsin, and the University of Southern California. For information, write to: Director, Consortium for Graduate Study in Management, 101 North Skinker Boulevard, Box 1132, St. Louis, Missouri 63130.

Consortium of Metropolitan Law Schools. The member law schools of this consortium —Brooklyn, Fordham, New York, St. John's and Seton Hall—award scholarships to minority students who have good records and real financial need. Each law school has about 10 tuition-free scholarships which can be used for both their evening and day sessions. Applications should be made directly to the particular law school after taking the Law School Admission Test: Brooklyn Law School, 250 Joralemon Street, Brooklyn, New York 11201; Fordham Law School, 140 West 62nd Street, New York, New York 10023; New York Law School, 57 Worth Street, New York, New York 10013;

St. John's Law School, Jamaica, New York 11432; Seton Hall Law School, 1095 Raymond Boulevard, Newark, New Jersey 07102.

Council for Opportunity in Graduate Management Education (COGME). Financial assistance is available to black, Spanish-speaking, and native American students for graduate management programs at the following: Columbia University, University of California, Carnegie-Mellon University, Cornell University, University of Chicago, Dartmouth College, Harvard University, Massachusetts Institute of Technology, The Wharton School (University of Pennsylvania), and Stanford University. Apply directly to Director, Council for Opportunity in Graduate Management Education, Central Plaza, 675 Massachusetts Avenue, Cambridge, Massachusetts 02139.

Council on Legal Education Opportunity (CLEO). The U.S. Department of Health, Education and Welfare (HEW) provides funds for the council to award grants to economically disadvantaged students interested in a legal education. Participation in the program is limited to entering students; former law students or students presently enrolled in law school are ineligible. Write to Council on Legal Education Opportunity, 818 18th Street, N.W., Suite 940, Washington, D.C. 20006.

Earl Warren Legal Training Program, Inc. Scholarship grants are available to minority students. Write to NAACP Scholarship Fund, Earl Warren Legal Training Program, Attention: Butler Henderson, 10 Columbus Circle, New York, New York 10019.

Graduate Fellowships in Atmospheric Sciences. The fellowship program for graduate study in atmospheric sciences and in related fundamental disciplines is sponsored by the University Corporation for Atmospheric Research (UCAR). Fellowships cover a year's study in the broad field of atmospheric sciences at any accredited U.S. graduate school. For information, write to UCAR Fellowship Committee, c/o Peter A. Gilman, National Center for Atmospheric Research, P.O. Box 3000, Boulder, Colorado 80303.

Indian Health Employees Scholarship Fund, Inc. Students of confirmed Indian descent (no certain blood quantum necessary) may apply for scholarships to pursue education in health service fields. For information, write to the Executive Secretary, Indian Health Employees Scholarship Fund, Inc., Federal Building, 115 Fourth Avenue, S.E., Aberdeen, South Dakota 57401.

Martin Luther King, Jr., Fellowships for Graduate and Professional Study. The Woodrow Wilson National Fellowship Foundation offers fellowships to black veterans to pursue graduate or professional school training for careers of service to the nation and to their communities. Fields include business and political organization, community leadership, education, law, library science, communications, journalism, medicine, theology, sociology, and others. The program is designed to augment G.I. Bill education benefits. Write to Director, Martin Luther King, Jr., Fellowship Program, Woodrow Wilson National Fellowship Foundation, Box 642, Princeton, New Jersey 08540.

Mexican-American Legal Defense and Educational Fund (MALDEF). Any Spanish-surnamed law student presently enrolled in a full-time law school program may apply for a MALDEF loan under the Loan Forgiveness Program. Loans are totally or partially forgiven if, upon graduation from law school, the applicant enters the practice of law for a period of one or two consecutive years in such a way as to directly benefit the Chicano community. Inquiries should be addressed to MALDEF, c/o The Educational Programs Department, 145 Ninth Street, San Francisco, California 94103.

National Medical Fellowships, Inc. This company provides financial asistance for students from minority groups currently underrepresented in medicine, specifically American blacks, Mexican Americans, mainland Puerto Ricans, and native Americans, who have been accepted by or are attending a medical school in the United States. Secure an application blank from National Medical Fellowships, Inc., 3935 Elm Street, Downers Grove, Illinois 60615.

National Science Foundation Graduate Fellowships. These fellowships are awarded for study and work leading to master's or doctoral degrees in certain scientific areas. Additional information may be obtained by writing to the Fellowship Office, National Research Council, 2101 Constitution Avenue, N.W., Washington, D.C. 20418.

The Robert Wood Johnson Foundation Student-Aid Program. This program was initiated in 1972 to help provide better access to dental services in areas that lack sufficient numbers of dentists. Students eligible for the program must be U.S. citizens from the following categories: women, students from rural backgrounds, and those from black, Indian, Mexican-American, and mainland Puerto Rican populations. Financial aid to students through this program is available at most dental schools in the U.S. All applications for the aid program must be made through the financial aid officer of your dental school. For further information on the program, contact the American Fund for Dental Health, 211 East Chicago Avenue, Chicago, Illinois 60611, or call (312) 787-6270.

State Loans

Guaranteed Student Loan Program. This program enables you to borrow directly from a bank, credit union, savings and loan association, or other participating lender. The loan is guaranteed by a state or private nonprofit agency or insured by the federal government. A student may borrow up to a maximum of $2,500. (In some states the maximum is lower.) If you qualify for Federal Interest Benefits, the federal government pays the full interest charged on this loan. Mandatory repayment begins 9 to 12 months after the student completes his course of study or leaves school or after completing service in the Armed Forces, the Peace Corps, or VISTA. The maximum repayment period is 10 years. Information and applications are available from schools, lenders, State Guarantee Agencies, and Regional Offices of the U.S. Office of Education.

In addition, each state has a loan program of some type which is usually restricted to residents of the particular state as funds are limited. In most instances, students from other states are discouraged from applying. However, there may be exceptions. For example, the College of Medicine of the University of Arizona, while giving first preference to minority residents of that state, does give second preference to minority applicants from the four western states that do not have medical schools.

In any case, if you want further information about state sources of aid for graduate and professional school training, contact the financial aid office of your school. Early filing of applications is advised.

Federal Loans

The National Direct Student Loan Program (NDSL). This program makes it possible
for a student to borrow up to $10,000 for a full program of graduate or professional
study. (This total *includes* any amount the student may have borrowed under NDSL
for undergraduate study.) Repayment begins nine months after graduation or leaving
school for other reasons and can be over a 10-year period. Interest charges on the
unpaid balance begin at the start of the repayment period. No payments are required
for up to three years while serving in the Armed Forces, Peace Corps, or VISTA.
Applications are made through the financial aid officer at your school.

Other Federal Sources of Funds

The United States government through various agencies provides financial aid to
students engaged in graduate and professional study. Aid is given in the form of
fellowships, traineeships, work-study grants, summer institute grants, and loans.
Funds are available for training persons for public service careers; for mining and
mineral fuel conservation fellowships; for training of persons who are serving or
preparing to serve as teachers, administrators, or educational specialists in colleges or
universities; for fellowships in library science; and for fellowships in special
education.

Other federal aid is available for students in specific disciplines and professional
fields. There are, for instance, grants for study leading to graduate nursing degrees,
Water Pollution Control Research fellowships, and grants for the Training of
Professional Personnel for the Care of Crippled Children.

Information about all federally supported aid programs can be obtained by
writing to the Division of Student Assistance, Bureau of Higher Education, Office of
Education, Washington, D.C. 20202.

Any discussion of federally supported programs is incomplete without
reference to programs limited solely to one important minority, the native American.
Through the Bureau of Indian Affairs (BIA), within the Department of the Interior,
scholarships are provided specifically for native American students. To qualify, a
scholarship recipient must have one quarter or more Indian, Eskimo, or Aleut blood
and membership in a tribal group served by the BIA. (There are nonfederal fellowships
for native Americans only that do not require any specific blood percentage or tribal
membership. See the entry for the Indian Health Employees Scholarship Fund, Inc.)

Application for federal assistance should be made through the Bureau of Indian
Affairs area offices, which maintain tribal memberships. The bureau publishes a
booklet entitled *Scholarships for American Indian Youth*, which contains information on federal, state, and tribal aid, college and university scholarships, and church
and foundation scholarships. Copies are available from the Bureau of Indian Affairs.
Department of the Interior, Washington, D.C. 20242, and the Division of Public
School Relations, 5301 Central Avenue, N.E., Room 201, Albuquerque, New Mexico
87108.

Graduate and Professional School Financial Aid Service

Graduate and Professional School Financial Aid Service (GAPSFAS) is an activity of the Graduate and Professional Financial Aid Council, which includes representatives from the Association of American Medical Colleges, the College Scholarship Service Council, the Admission Council for Graduate Study in Management, the Graduate Record Examinations Board, and the Law School Admission Council, Educational Testing Service operates the program which is designed to collect information about the financial resources and obligations of students, their parents, and their spouses.

For the applicant, GAPSFAS central processing eliminates the duplication of information needed to analyze needed financial data to determine a reasonable contribution from personal, parental, and other sources toward educational costs and transmits the information and analysis to participating schools for their use in allocating grants and loans. Additionally, the Office of Education has authorized the use of GAPSFAS in fulfilling the requirement that financial aid officers determine need of an applicant to obtain federally financed student aid funds. While many graduate and professional schools require candidates applying for financial aid to file the GAPSFAS application form, you are advised to check with the institution to which you are applying to learn if this is a requirement.

The GAPSFAS application forms may be obtained from the undergraduate financial aid officer or from the graduate or professional school to which you are applying. Forms are also available at the first fall administrations of the Graduate Management Admission Test (GMAT), the Graduate Record Examinations (GRE), and the Law School Admission Test (LSAT). Forms and/or information may be secured, as well, from the Graduate and Professional School Financial Aid Service, Box 2614, Princeton, New Jersey 08540.

Appendix C

Law School Admissions

Appendix C-1. Minority students enrolled in approved law schools

Minority group		First year	Second year	Third year	Fourth year	Group not stated	Total
Black, not of Hispanic origin	1976-77	2,128	1,654	1,488	233	0	5,503
	1975-76	2,045	1,511	1,452	119	0	5,127
	1974-75	1,910	1,587	1,329	145	24	4,995
	1973-74	1,943	1,443	1,207	101	123	4,817
	1972-73	1,907	1,324	1,106	74	12	4,423
	1971-72	1,716	1,147	761	55	65	3,744
	1969-70	1,115	574	395	44	—	2,128
Mexican American	1976-77	542	435	446	65	0	1,488
	1975-76	484	421	381	11	0	1,297
	1974-75	559	447	329	17	5	1,357
	1973-74	539	386	271	63	0	1,259
	1972-73	480	337	238	17	0	1,072
	1971-72	403	262	170	11	37	883
	1969-70	245	113	54	0	—	412
Puerto Rican	1976-77	119	94	100	18	0	331
	1975-76	113	121	96	3	0	333
	1974-75	117	87	56	3	0	263
	1973-74	96	47	32	5	0	180
	1972-73	73	40	25	5	0	143
	1971-72	49	25	18	2	0	94
	1969-70	29	14	13	5	—	61
Other Hispanic American	1976-77	255	153	139	9	0	556
	1975-76	217	164	146	16	0	543
	1974-75	182	92	97	11	5	387
	1973-74	94	70	59	4	34	261
	1972-73	96	72	60	3	0	231
	1971-72	74	62	35	3	5	179
	1969-70	35	18	19	3		75

Asian or Pacific Islander	484	439	378	23	0	1,324
1975-76	436	343	287	33	0	1,099
1974-75	429	322	288	21	3	1,063
1973-74	327	297	202	19	5	850
1972-73	298	218	144	20	1	681
1971-72	254	142	72	7	5	480
American Indian or Alaskan native 1976-77	133	87	75	6	0	301
1975-76	118	88	84	5	0	295
1974-75	110	90	65	0	0	265
1973-74	109	65	44	3	1	222
1972-73	79	48	44	2	0	173
1971-72	71	46	18	2	3	140
1969-70	44	17	10	1	—	72
Other 1969-70	84	55	42	4	—	185
Group not stated 1976-77	8	5	5	3	0	21
1975-76	0	0	0	0	9	9
1974-75	1	1	1	0	0	3
1973-74	6	5	1	0	0	12
1972-73	1	2	2	2	0	7
1971-72	0	23	35	0	0	48
Total 1976-77	3,669	2,867	2,631	357	0	9,524
1975-76	3,413	2,648	2,446	187	9	8,703
1974-75	3,308	2,626	2,165	197	37	8,333
1973-74	3,114	2,313	1,816	195	163	7,601
1972-73	2,934	2,041	1,619	123	13	6,730
1971-72	2,567	1,707	1,099	80	115	5,568
1969-70	1,552	791	533	57	—	2,933

Source: American Bar Association (1977, p. 48).

Appendix C-2. Legal education and bar admission statistics, 1963-1975

Year	Total	Enrollment women	First year	LSAT administrations	J.D. or LL.B. awarded	New admissions to the bar
1963	49,552	1,883	20,776	30,528	9,638	10,788
1964	54,265	2,183	22,753	37,598	10,491	12,023
1965	59,744	2,537	24,167	39,406	11,507	13,109
1966	62,556	2,678	24,077	44,905	13,115	14,644
1967	64,406	2,906	24,267	47,110	14,738	16,007
1968	62,779	3,704	23,652	49,756	16,077	17,764
1969	68,386	4,715	29,128	59,050	16,733	19,123
1970	82,499	7,031	34,713	74,092	17,183	17,922
1971	94,468	8,914	36,171	107,479	17,006	20,485
1972	101,707	12,173	35,131	119,694	22,342	25,086
1973	106,102	16,760	37,018	121,262	27,756	30,879
1974	110,713	21,788	38,074	135,397	28,729	30,707
1975	116,991	26,737	39,038	133,546	29,961	34,216[a]

Notes: Enrollment is that in American Bar Association approved schools as of October 1, 1975. The LSAT candidate volume is given for the test year ending in the year stated. Thus, 135,397 administrations of the LSAT occurred in the test year July, 1973, through April, 1974. J.D. or LL.B. degrees are those awarded by approved schools for the academic year ending in the year stated. Thus, 28,729 degrees were awarded in the year beginning with the fall, 1973 term and ending with the summer, 1974 term. Total new admissions to the bar are for the 1974 calendar year and include those admitted by office study, diploma privilege, and examination and study at an unapproved law school; the great bulk of those admitted were graduated from approved schools.

[a] Texas and New Jersey are not included.

Source: American Bar Association (1976, p. 45).

Average Law School Admission Test score

Overall undergraduate GPA	Below 300	300-349	350-399	400-449	450-499	500-549	550-599	600-649	650-699	700-749	750 and over	Total
Above 3.74	2	6	16	52	154	540	889	1,221	1,127	679	179	4,865
	4	14	27	95	251	643	974	1,299	1,165	689	181	5,342
3.50-3.74	1	12	43	126	444	1,121	1,913	2,188	1,586	774	185	8,393
	14	50	119	348	806	1,538	2,203	2,377	1,687	822	187	10,151
3.25-3.49	2	20	58	201	600	1,504	2,390	2,392	1,559	646	143	9,515
	45	115	288	713	1,427	2,462	2,979	2,672	1,688	692	156	13,237
3.00-3.24	3	19	73	264	669	1,507	2,209	2,172	1,236	445	87	8,684
	94	220	466	1,132	1,873	2,901	3,138	2,608	1,407	509	100	14,448
2.75-2.99	2	17	105	226	509	1,097	1,445	1,332	808	288	54	5,883
	166	334	628	1,118	1,803	2,525	2,442	1,814	974	339	62	12,205
2.50-2.74	3	18	52	200	345	660	838	815	451	169	32	3,583
	208	363	674	1,159	1,554	1,904	1,711	1,246	631	222	38	9,710
2.25-2.49	7	13	37	90	177	290	432	420	219	88	19	1,792
	235	351	538	789	1,044	1,164	1,059	760	334	121	24	6,419
2.00-2.24	2	8	17	38	64	108	134	140	78	50	4	643
	167	234	355	470	536	578	492	328	151	71	6	3,388
Below 2.00	0	0	3	5	15	18	38	30	28	12	6	155
	65	94	129	136	180	193	158	111	58	29	8	1,161
Total	22	113	404	1,202	2,977	6,845	10,288	10,710	7,092	3,151	709	43,513
	998	1,775	3,224	5,960	9,474	13,908	15,156	13,215	8,095	3,494	762	76,061

Note: The top number in each cell is an estimate of the number of offers of admission. The bottom number in each cell is the number of candidates.

Source: Evans (1977, p. 20).

Appendix C-4. Number of male candidates and estimated number of male candidates who were offered admission to at least one LSDAS-ABA law school

Average Law School Admission Test score

Overall undergraduate GPA	Below 300	300-349	350-399	400-449	450-499	500-549	550-599	600-649	650-699	700-749	750 and over	Total
Above 3.74	0	3	9	31	87	311	511	711	776	489	148	3,076
	1	7	17	50	131	367	558	758	801	494	149	3,333
3.50-3.74	1	2	25	80	286	671	1,165	1,393	1,071	548	155	5,397
	8	27	63	209	486	906	1,338	1,512	1,145	585	157	6,436
3.25-3.49	2	11	33	121	406	1,016	1,647	1,618	1,102	472	114	6,542
	29	63	174	440	924	1,626	2,005	1,803	1,196	507	125	8,892
3.00-3.24	2	6	38	156	492	1,075	1,565	1,517	868	345	70	6,134
	55	149	301	775	1,323	2,019	2,184	1,817	989	397	83	10,092
2.75-2.99	1	11	69	142	374	848	1,097	1,020	634	226	43	4,465
	104	208	439	802	1,336	1,918	1,822	1,366	758	264	51	9,068
2.50-2.74	3	11	35	146	255	515	665	635	363	132	28	2,788
	142	275	494	875	1,196	1,489	1,365	964	521	172	34	7,527
2.25-2.49	3	8	25	63	144	230	352	342	187	74	17	1,445
	166	255	406	630	873	959	875	638	283	106	22	5,213
2.00-2.24	2	7	13	30	52	85	114	126	65	48	4	546
	124	174	289	392	457	496	429	296	129	68	5	2,859
Below 2.00	0	0	3	3	13	17	33	27	26	10	6	138
	55	84	115	122	160	174	148	106	53	28	8	1,053
Total	14	59	250	772	2,109	4,768	7,149	7,389	5,092	2,344	585	30,531
	684	1,242	2,298	4,295	6,886	9,954	10,724	9,260	5,875	2,621	634	54,473

Note: The top number in each cell is an estimate of the number of offers of admission to male candidates. The bottom number in each cell is the number of male candidates.

Average Law School Admission Test score

Overall undergraduate GPA	Below 300	300-349	350-399	400-449	450-499	500-549	550-599	600-649	650-699	700-749	750 and over	Total
Above 3.74	2	4	7	21	67	229	378	510	352	191	31	1,792
	3	7	10	45	126	276	416	541	364	195	32	2,009
3.50-3.74	0	13	18	46	157	448	747	795	515	226	30	2,995
	6	23	56	139	320	632	865	865	542	237	30	3,715
3.25-3.49	0	8	25	80	194	487	742	774	457	174	29	2,970
	16	52	114	273	503	836	974	869	492	185	31	4,345
3.00-3.24	2	12	34	108	159	431	642	655	368	100	17	2,528
	39	71	165	357	550	882	954	791	418	112	17	4,356
2.75-2.99	0	6	36	84	135	247	347	312	174	62	11	1,414
	62	126	189	316	467	607	620	448	216	75	11	3,137
2.50-2.74	0	7	16	55	90	145	174	180	89	37	4	797
	66	88	180	284	358	415	346	282	110	50	4	2,183
2.25-2.49	4	4	12	29	32	59	80	79	32	14	2	347
	69	96	132	159	171	205	184	122	51	15	2	1,206
2.00-2.24	0	1	3	8	12	23	20	14	13	2	0	96
	43	60	66	78	79	82	63	32	22	3	1	529
Below 2.00	0	0	0	2	1	1	4	3	2	1	0	14
	10	10	14	14	20	19	10	5	5	1	0	108
Total	8	55	151	433	847	2,070	3,134	3,322	2,002	807	124	12,953
	314	533	926	1,665	2,588	3,954	4,432	3,955	2,220	873	128	21,588

Note: The top number in each cell is an estimate of the number of offers of admission to female candidates. The bottom number in each cell is the number of female candidates.

Source: Evans (1977, p. 25).

Appendix C-6. Number of black candidates and estimated number of black candidates who were offered admission to at least one LSDAS-ABA law school

Overall undergraduate GPA	Average Law School Admission Test score											
	Below 300	300-349	350-399	400-449	450-499	500-549	550-599	600-649	650-699	700-749	750 and over	Total
Above 3.74	1	2	8	8	9	8	10	3	2	0	0	51
	1	2	10	10	12	8	10	4	2	0	0	59
3.50-3.74	0	8	24	22	21	31	14	11	3	2	1	137
	4	15	35	33	26	33	14	11	3	2	1	177
3.25-3.49	3	13	26	57	48	36	22	9	5	2	0	221
	22	42	47	72	58	40	23	9	5	2	0	320
3.00-3.24	2	12	38	82	84	66	45	18	10	0	0	357
	41	70	96	128	98	73	47	20	10	0	0	583
2.75-2.99	1	8	64	78	79	73	36	12	6	0	0	357
	85	121	175	152	113	87	37	13	7	0	0	790
2.50-2.74	2	9	26	68	72	80	28	13	3	0	0	301
	110	148	175	171	122	98	35	14	3	0	0	876
2.25-2.49	0	9	18	32	59	39	24	12	3	0	0	196
	13	158	155	135	108	61	28	17	3	0	0	798
2.00-2.24	2	6	4	10	17	15	7	3	1	1	0	66
	86	90	92	91	62	38	17	4	4	1	0	485
Below 2.00	0	0	0	3	4	0	2	2	0	0	0	11
	37	46	37	37	27	15	5	6	0	1	0	211
Total	11	67	208	360	393	348	188	83	33	5	1	1,697
	519	692	822	829	626	453	216	98	37	6	1	4,299

Note: The top number in each cell is an estimate of the number of offers of admission to black candidates. The bottom number in each cell is the number of black candidates.

Source: Evans (1977, p. 31).

Appendix C-7. Number of Chicano candidates and estimated number of Chicano candidates who were offered admission to at least one LSDAS-ABA law school

Overall undergraduate GPA	Average Law School Admission Test score											Total
	Below 300	300-349	350-399	400-449	450-499	500-549	550-599	600-649	650-699	700-749	750 and over	
Above 3.74	0	0	0	2	2	8	3	6	5	0	0	26
	0	0	0	4	2	8	3	7	5	0	0	29
3.50-3.74	0	0	2	4	13	17	16	6	3	2	0	63
	1	1	3	6	16	18	16	8	3	2	0	74
3.25-3.49	0	3	4	11	24	24	18	9	3	1	0	97
	0	11	16	19	30	31	20	9	3	1	0	140
3.00-3.24	0	1	6	20	25	31	18	10	1	0	0	112
	5	13	24	34	40	37	19	10	1	0	0	183
2.75-2.99	0	1	4	13	32	17	19	5	2	0	1	94
	11	17	31	36	44	22	19	6	2	0	1	189
2.50-2.74	1	0	8	10	18	12	7	8	2	1	0	67
	14	19	43	41	33	22	13	11	2	2	0	200
2.25-2.49	2	0	5	7	8	5	8	2	2	0	0	39
	13	18	21	32	29	22	10	3	2	0	0	150
2.00-2.24	0	2	2	1	0	2	0	1	1	0	0	9
	6	22	16	14	10	6	2	1	1	0	0	78
Below 2.00	0	0	1	0	0	2	0	0	0	0	0	3
	3	7	12	10	4	5	1	0	0	0	0	42
Total	3	7	32	68	122	118	89	47	19	4	1	510
	53	108	166	196	208	171	103	55	19	5	1	1,085

Note: The top number in each cell is an estimate of the number of offers of admission to Chicano candidates. The bottom number in each cell is the number of Chicano candidates.

Source: Evans (1977, p. 32).

Appendix C-8. Number of unspecified minority candidates and estimated number of unspecified minority candidates who were offered admission to at least one LSDAS-ABA law school

Overall undergraduate GPA	Average Law School Admission Test score											
	Below 300	300-349	350-399	400-449	450-499	500-549	550-599	600-649	650-699	700-749	750 and over	Total
Above 3.74	0 / 2	2 / 5	2 / 2	5 / 8	6 / 14	27 / 30	35 / 40	32 / 36	31 / 33	10 / 10	5 / 6	155 / 186
3.50-3.74	1 / 5	2 / 9	2 / 8	11 / 29	35 / 48	60 / 87	74 / 88	60 / 66	37 / 40	22 / 24	2 / 2	306 / 406
3.25-3.49	0 / 2	3 / 10	5 / 29	17 / 62	41 / 84	72 / 111	103 / 118	78 / 87	58 / 60	13 / 17	5 / 6	395 / 586
3.00-3.24	1 / 12	2 / 25	10 / 41	26 / 88	54 / 106	93 / 154	89 / 115	75 / 91	39 / 41	12 / 13	3 / 3	404 / 689
2.75-2.99	0 / 15	3 / 43	8 / 59	21 / 73	49 / 129	67 / 120	70 / 105	41 / 61	30 / 36	12 / 14	1 / 1	302 / 656
2.50-2.74	0 / 21	5 / 32	6 / 57	18 / 91	36 / 100	38 / 90	35 / 72	20 / 32	20 / 23	7 / 10	2 / 2	187 / 530
2.25-2.49	4 / 22	0 / 18	3 / 51	11 / 61	22 / 63	15 / 54	23 / 43	14 / 26	12 / 17	6 / 9	0 / 0	110 / 364
2.00-2.24	0 / 23	0 / 19	0 / 41	3 / 34	4 / 36	6 / 29	3 / 14	0 / 5	5 / 10	4 / 4	0 / 0	25 / 215
Below 2.00	0 / 3	0 / 7	0 / 11	0 / 9	4 / 8	3 / 10	0 / 2	1 / 1	0 / 0	0 / 0	0 / 0	8 / 51
Total	6 / 105	17 / 168	36 / 299	112 / 455	251 / 588	381 / 685	432 / 597	321 / 405	232 / 260	86 / 101	18 / 20	1,892 / 3,683

Note: The top number in each cell is an estimate of the number of offers of admission to the unspecified minority candidates. The bottom number in each cell is the number of unspecified minority candidates.

Source: Evans (1977, p. 33).

Appendix C-9. Number of white and unidentified candidates and estimated number of white and unidentified candidates who were offered admission to at least one LSDAS-ABA law school

Average Law School Admission Test score

Overall undergraduate GPA	Below 300	300-349	350-399	400-449	450-499	500-549	550-599	600-649	650-699	700-749	750 and over	Total
Above 3.74	0	2	5	37	137	497	841	1,181	1,090	669	174	4,633
	1	7	15	73	223	597	921	1,252	1,125	679	175	5,068
3.50-3.74	0	2	13	88	372	1,012	1,808	2,111	1,543	748	182	7,879
	4	25	73	280	716	1,400	2,085	2,292	1,641	794	184	9,494
3.25-3.49	0	1	21	109	482	1,371	2,247	2,296	1,494	630	138	8,789
	21	52	196	560	1,255	2,280	2,818	2,567	1,620	672	150	12,191
3.00-3.24	0	2	15	126	497	1,313	2,054	2,070	1,186	433	84	7,780
	36	112	305	882	1,629	2,637	2,957	2,487	1,355	496	97	12,993
2.75-2.99	0	4	24	97	343	932	1,322	1,275	770	276	52	5,095
	55	153	363	857	1,517	2,296	2,281	1,734	929	325	60	10,570
2.50-2.74	0	5	9	95	210	528	767	774	427	161	30	3,006
	63	164	399	856	1,299	1,694	1,591	1,189	603	210	36	8,104
2.25-2.49	0	3	10	36	86	227	377	392	201	81	19	1,432
	67	157	311	561	844	1,027	978	714	312	112	24	5,107
2.00-2.24	0	0	11	24	43	82	124	135	71	45	4	539
	52	103	206	331	428	505	459	318	136	66	6	2,610
Below 2.00	0	0	2	2	6	14	35	27	28	11	6	131
	22	34	69	80	141	163	150	104	58	28	8	857
Total	0	19	110	614	2,176	5,976	9,575	10,261	6,810	3,054	689	39,284
	321	807	1,937	4,480	8,052	12,599	14,240	12,657	7,779	3,382	740	66,994

Note: The top number in each cell is an estimate of the number of offers of admission to white and unidentified candidates. The bottom number in each cell is the number of white and unidentified candidates.

Source: Evans (1977, p. 34).

Appendix C-10. Number and percentage of candidates at or above selected LSAT and UGPA levels and number and percentage who received at least one offer of admission to an LSDAS-ABA law school

Average Law School Admission Test score

	Black					Chicano				
Level	No.	%	Number accepted[a]	%[b]	%[c]	No.	%	Number accepted[a]	%[b]	%[c]
LSAT ≥ 600	142	3	122	86	7	80	7	71	89	14
LSAT ≥ 500	811	19	658	81	39	354	33	278	79	55
LSAT ≥ 450	1,437	33	1,051	73	62	562	52	400	71	78
UGPA ≥ 3.25	556	13	409	74	24	243	22	186	77	36
UGPA ≥ 2.75	1,929	45	1,123	58	66	615	57	392	64	77
UGPA ≥ 2.50	2,805	65	1,424	51	84	815	75	459	56	90
LSAT ≥ 600 and UGPA ≥ 3.25	39	1	38	97	2	38	4	35	92	7
LSAT ≥ 500 and UGPA ≥ 2.75	461	11	425	92	25	251	23	225	90	44
LSAT ≥ 450 and UGPA ≥ 2.50	1,040	24	862	83	51	466	43	369	79	72
Total	4,299	100	1,697	39	100	1,085	100	510	47	100

	Unspecified minority					White and unidentified				
Level	No.	%	Number accepted[a]	%[b]	%[c]	No.	%	Number accepted[a]	%[b]	%[c]
LSAT ≥ 600	786	21	657	84	35	24,468	37	20,814	85	33
LSAT ≥ 500	2,068	56	1,470	71	78	51,307	77	36,365	71	93
LSAT ≥ 450	2,656	72	1,721	65	91	59,359	89	38,541	65	98
UGPA ≥ 3.25	1,178	32	856	73	45	26,753	40	21,301	80	54
UGPA ≥ 2.75	2,523	69	1,562	62	83	50,316	75	34,176	68	87
UGPA ≥ 2.50	3,053	83	1,749	57	92	58,420	87	37,182	64	95
LSAT ≥ 600 and UGPA ≥ 3.25	387	11	353	91	19	13,151	20	12,082	92	31
LSAT ≥ 500 and UGPA ≥ 2.75	1,615	44	1,256	78	66	40,906	61	31,625	77	61
LSAT ≥ 450 and UGPA ≥ 2.50	2,325	63	1,599	69	85	52,868	79	36,353	69	93
Total	3,683	100	1,892	51	100	66,994	100	39,284	59	100

[a] Estimated.

[b] Percentage of the group at that level who were offered admission.

[c] Number at or above the level who were offered admission expressed as a percentage of the total of the ethnically defined group who were offered admission.

Source: Evans (1977, p. 36).

Appendix C-11. University of Virginia Law School Admissions Process

... When an applicant's file is completed, it is reviewed by an administrative assistant to the Director of Admissions. The assistant recommends whether the application should be accepted, rejected or considered further. The Director then reviews the file and takes final action if the applicant clearly appears either qualified or unqualified; he disposes of approximately one-third to one-half of the total applications in this manner. The Director adds his written comments and recommendations next to those previously noted by his assistant on the remaining files and submits them to a faculty committee of five plus the Director.

The entire admissions committee does not review each file, however. Individual decisions are generally made by submitting the file to one or sometimes two members of the committee. If an undergraduate school traditionally sends many applicants, one committee member usually will "specialize" in that institution in order to assess more accurately the significance of its applicants' records. If the committee member agrees with the Director's recommendation, that recommendation is made final. Where there is disagreement, the file is sent to additional committee members for consideration and the final determination is by majority vote. This procedure means that only a small percentage of the applications are considered by the entire committee. Even then the files are seldom considered in committee sessions, though committee members do consult with each other and frequently discuss individual cases. In other words, even the extraordinary or difficult application receives limited attention, and most consume less than half an hour of administrative or committee time; the press of numbers and of finite administrative resources cannot be ignored, despite the fact that skilled administrators can quickly select files deserving further examination.

Once a decision is reached the Director of Admissions informs the applicant that he has been accepted, rejected, or placed on the waiting list. No formal appeal process exists for those rejected or placed on the waiting list, nor is an applicant advised of the specific basis for a decision. But when a question or complaint is registered, the decision is explained or justified informally; that is, the Director will arrange a conference when requested to explain adverse decisions but usually not to change them. In a close case, if new information or the reconsideration at the conference produces a new perspective on an applicant, another committee member will further review the file.

Source: Gellhorn and Hornby (1974, pp. 976, 977).

Appendix C-12. Admissions procedures for Harvard Law School

The large volume of applications for admission makes the admission process highly selective. More than 6,000 applications are expected for approximately 540 places in the first-year class entering in September 1977. We admit between 750 and 800 applicants to fill a class of approximately 540 entering students. The application process is fully described in our application materials, which are available beginning in July. We strongly encourage applicants to apply early (before February 1) and our absolute deadline is March 1.

One basic question that arises in the mind of every prospective applicant is "What are my chances for admission?" Certainly no set of statistics based solely upon objective factors will provide an unambiguous answer to that question. Essentially three factors are considered: the personal qualifications and accomplishments of the applicant; academic skills and performance; and the Law School Admission Test (LSAT) score. In looking at personal accomplishments, the committee considers all the information provided by the applicant including extracurricular and community activities, work experience, personal background, and letters of recommendation. Even the academic record and test scores are not considered solely on a numerical basis. The numbers are weighed as relevant factors along with qualitative evaluations of the academic institutions attended by the candidate, the courses taken, letters of recommendation, and any demonstrated social, economic, or educational disadvantage the candidate has had to overcome.

A person who ranks high on all three factors is likely to be admitted (about 5 percent of our applicant pool) and a person who scores low on more than one is likely to be denied (between 40 and 50 percent of the applicant pool). The committee members spend most of their time carefully reading and comparing the applications of people in the middle group who are characterized as ranking high on at least two of the three criteria.

We urge you to carefully consider how you may compare with other candidates on all three criteria before you apply. The following specifics should be helpful to that comparison:

1. The median LSAT score for more than 6,000 applicants to the 1976 entering class was above 650, and more than half of all applicants presented a GPA from their undergraduate degree school of a strong B+ or better.
2. Applicants whose GPA and LSAT score are below those submitted by a majority of the applicant population stand little chance for admission unless their subjective qualifications, backgrounds, or personal accomplishments are striking.
3. At no point are the chances for admission to Harvard Law School either 0 or 100 percent on an objective scale of qualifications. Some applicants are admitted each year whose GPA or LSAT score is relatively low, and a significant percentage of the 1976 applicants who presented both a GPA from their undergraduate degree school above 3.75 and an LSAT score above 700 were not admitted.

Source: Association of American Law Schools, *Pre-Law Handbook*, 1976–77 (1976, p. 159).

Appendix D

Medical School Admissions

Appendix D-1. Summary of medical school application activity, 1966-67 through 1975-76

First-year class	Number of medical schools	Number of applicants	Number of applications	Applications per individual	Accepted applicants	First-year enrollment[a]	Percentage of total applicants accepted
1966-67	89	18,250	87,627	4.8	9,123	8,991	50.0
1967-68	94	18,724	93,332	5.0	9,702	9,473	51.8
1968-69	99	21,118	112,195	5.3	10,092	9,863	47.9
1969-70	101	24,465	133,822	5.5	10,547	10,422	43.1
1970-71	102	24,987	148,797	6.0	11,500	11,348	46.0
1971-72	108	29,172	210,943	7.2	12,335	12,361	42.3
1972-73	114	36,135	267,306	7.4	13,757	13,677	38.1
1973-74	114	40,506	328,275	8.1	14,335	14,159	35.4
1974-75	114	42,624	362,376	8.5	15,066	14,763	35.3
1975-76	114	42,303	366,040	8.6	15,365	15,295	36.3

[a] Includes students who are repeating first year.

Sources: W. F. Dubé, *Journal of Medical Education,* 1973a, *48,* 1161; 1976, *51,* 867. Data from AAMC annual studies of U.S. medical school applicants; data for first-year enrollments from AAMC annual fall enrollment questionnaire.

Appendix D-2. First-year U.S. medical school enrollments of underrepresented minorities and women

Group	1968-69 No.	1968-69 %	1969-70 No.	1969-70 %	1970-71 No.	1970-71 %	1971-72 No.	1971-72 %	1972-73 No.	1972-73 %	1973-74 No.	1973-74 %	1974-75 No.	1974-75 %	1975-76 No.	1975-76 %	1976-77 No.	1976-77 %
Selected U.S. minorities																		
Black American	266	2.7	440	4.2	697	6.1	882	7.1	957	7.1	1,027	7.2	1,106	7.5	1,036	6.8	1,040	6.7
American Indian	3	*	7	0.1	11	0.1	23	0.2	34	0.3	44	0.3	71	0.5	60	0.4	43	0.3
Mexican American	20	0.2	44	0.4	73	0.6	118	1.0	137	1.0	174	1.2	227	1.5	224	1.5	245	1.6
Mainland Puerto Rican	3	*	10	0.1	27	0.2	40	0.3	44	0.3	56	0.4	69	0.5	71	0.5	72	0.5
Total	292	2.9	501	4.8	808	7.0	1,063	8.6	1,172	8.6	1,301	9.2	1,473	10.0	1,391	9.1	1,400	9.0
Women	887	9.0	948	9.1	1,256	11.1	1,693	13.7	2,284	16.8	2,790	19.7	3,275	22.2	3,647	23.8	3,858	24.7

* Less than 0.1.

Sources: W. F. Dubé, *Journal of Medical Education*, 1973b, 48, 294; 1977, 52, 165.

Appendix D-3. MCAT scores and undergraduate college grades of medical school applicants by acceptance status and by self-description, 1975-76 first-year class

Self-description	Number with MCATs	Percentage with MCATs	Mean MCAT scores				Number with GPAs	Percentage with GPAs	Mean UG GPAs			Total number	Total Percentage
			VA	QA	Gen	Sci			BCPM	AO	Total		
Black/Afro-American													
Accepted	941	41.8	479	515	466	500	872	44.7	2.77	3.06	2.89	945	41.3
Nonaccepted	1,306	58.1	411	429	419	391	1,077	55.2	2.35	2.78	2.55	1,343	58.7
Total	2,247	5.4	440	465	439	436	1,949	5.2	2.54	2.90	2.70	2,288	5.4
American Indian													
Accepted	57	43.1	510	550	499	527	55	47.8	3.10	3.22	3.16	57	43.1
Nonaccepted	75	56.8	491	497	496	485	60	52.1	2.70	2.98	2.81	75	56.8
Total	132	0.3	499	520	498	503	115	0.3	2.89	3.10	2.98	132	0.3
White/Caucasian													
Accepted	12,956	37.3	584	629	559	627	12,135	37.5	3.52	3.52	3.52	12,985	37.2
Nonaccepted	21,716	62.6	533	573	523	552	20,168	62.4	3.06	3.21	3.13	21,883	62.7
Total	34,672	83.4	552	594	537	580	32,303	86.3	3.23	3.33	3.28	34,868	82.4
Mexican/American or Chicano													
Accepted	219	51.7	508	554	493	542	202	53.5	3.00	3.23	3.10	220	51.5
Nonaccepted	204	48.2	458	482	467	455	175	46.4	2.54	2.88	2.69	207	48.4
Total	423	1.0	484	519	480	500	377	1.0	2.79	3.07	2.91	427	1.0
Oriental/Asian American													
Accepted	386	31.8	573	654	536	631	365	32.4	3.52	3.52	3.53	387	31.7
Nonaccepted	826	68.1	496	603	481	549	761	67.5	3.13	3.24	3.19	833	68.2
Total	1,212	2.9	520	619	498	575	1,126	3.0	3.26	3.33	3.30	1,220	2.8
Puerto Rican (mainland)													
Accepted	86	42.7	522	548	511	531	74	56.0	3.05	3.30	3.17	86	42.5
Nonaccepted	115	57.2	452	456	448	415	58	43.9	2.58	2.98	2.77	116	57.4
Total	201	0.4	482	495	475	465	132	0.3	2.85	3.16	3.00	202	0.4

Puerto Rican (Commonwealth)												
Accepted	104	36.4	496	531	471	492	35	40.7	3.42	3.48	3.45	104	36.2
Nonaccepted	181	63.5	451	455	442	408	51	59.3	2.76	3.09	2.90	183	63.7
Total	285	0.6	468	482	453	439	86	0.2	3.04	3.25	3.13	287	0.6
Cuban												
Accepted	60	31.7	532	583	527	571	51	32.6	3.33	3.50	3.43	60	31.7
Nonaccepted	129	68.2	467	521	476	495	105	67.3	2.82	3.23	3.00	129	68.2
Total	189	0.4	488	541	492	519	156	0.4	3.00	3.33	3.14	189	0.4
Other												
Accepted	264	23.4	564	605	542	594	226	24.2	3.38	3.46	3.41	265	22.8
Nonaccepted	863	76.5	492	548	490	511	706	75.7	2.99	3.19	3.08	893	77.1
Total	1,127	2.7	509	561	502	530	932	2.4	3.08	3.25	3.16	1,158	2.7
No response												
Accepted	119	11.4	583	636	562	605	44	19.5	3.38	3.40	3.38	256	16.7
Nonaccepted	922	88.5	516	542	508	517	181	80.4	3.02	3.15	3.09	1,276	83.2
Total	1,041	2.5	524	553	514	527	225	0.6	3.09	3.21	3.15	1,532	3.6
Total												
Accepted	15,192	36.5	575	620	550	615	14,059	37.5	3.46	3.48	3.47	15,365	36.3
Nonaccepted	26,337	63.4	522	562	513	539	23,342	62.4	3.02	3.19	3.10	26,938	63.6
Total	41,529	100.0	541	583	527	567	37,401	100.0	3.18	3.30	3.24	42,303	100.0

Source: Gordon (1977, pp. 70-71).

Appendix D-4. Percentage of 1970 and 1971 medical school matriculants by race who were in various categories of academic status at end of first year of medical school[a]

Status of medical student	Caucasians		Black Americans		American Indians		Mexican Americans	Puerto Ricans[b]	All individuals[c]	
	1970 (5,799)	1971 (8,943)	1970 (388)	1971 (546)	1970 (20)	1971 (39)	1971 (82)	1971 (108)	1970 (10,187)	1971 (11,904)
Attrition										
Dismissal, academic	0.3	0.5	2.6	4.4	5.0	0.0	0.0	0.0	0.6	0.8
Left, other reasons	1.2	1.5	1.5	2.4	5.0	0.0	1.2	1.9	1.3	1.6
Total	1.5	2.0	4.1	6.8	10.0	0.0	1.2	1.9	1.9	2.4
Retention										
Leave of absence	0.2	0.5	0.8	0.9	0.0	0.0	1.2	0.0	0.3	0.6
Repeating all or part of year	0.6	0.6	16.5	9.7	0.0	5.1	4.9	1.9	1.5	1.5
Promoted with class	97.3	95.8	77.8	80.8	90.0	94.9	92.7	96.3	95.8	94.5
Total	98.1	96.9	96.1	91.5	90.0	100.0	98.8	98.2	97.6	96.6
Other	0.4	1.1	0.8	1.8	0.0	0.0	0.0	0.0	1.5	1.0

Note: Figures in parentheses are the total number of individuals about whom retention and promotion information was available at the time study was conducted.

[a] No data available for Mexican Americans or Puerto Ricans for the 1970 entering class.

[b] Includes both mainland and island Puerto Ricans.

[c] Includes "unknown" and "other" racial designations.

Source: Johnson, Smith, and Tarnoff (1975, p. 754).

Appendix D-5. University of California at Davis, School of Medicine

Dr. C. John Tupper, Dean
Dr. George H. Lowrey, Associate Dean, Student Affairs

General Information

The School of Medicine of the University of California, Davis, admitted its eighth class for the fall quarter of 1975. The school provides its students with a foundation of medical knowledge upon which they may proceed to careers in family practice, specialty practice, research, public health, or administration.

Curriculum

The curriculum is designed around a core program of instruction in basic, behavioral, and clinical sciences during the first three years, with the fourth year consisting of elective courses under faculty guidance. Multidisciplinary teaching is achieved by means of integration of the basic and clinical science facilities. The curriculum is designed to provide an opportunity for the student to learn significant facts and principles, to develop habits of inquiry and self-discipline of continuing education, and to provide the setting for the refinement of skills and judgment necessary to apply scientific knowledge toward solving the problems of health and disease. Beginning with the first year, the student is encouraged and given the opportunity to take elective courses to broaden his knowledge of the health sciences.

The Davis campus affords an exceptional environment for the School of Medicine. There are opportunities for interaction with other schools, colleges, departments, and laboratories of the university. Research, service, and teaching are interrelated at Davis, with strength in the biological and allied sciences. Close relationships are enjoyed with the School of Veterinary Medicine, the California Primate Research Center, the Radiobiology Laboratory, and the Food Protection and Toxicology Center. The opportunities for exchange between the School of Veterinary Medicine and the School of Medicine deserve emphasis.

First-and second-year students will occupy new permanent facilities housing the basic sciences for the first time in 1976; these include classrooms, laboratories, and a health science library shared with the School of Veterinary Medicine. Very early in the student's training, use is made of the clinical facilities of the nearby 650-bed Sacramento Medical Center.

A combined program for both the M.D. and Ph.D. degrees is available to qualified students.

Requirements for Entrance

The MCAT and three years (90 semester hours or 135 quarter hours) in an approved college or univesity in the United States or Canada are required. A course of study leading to a bachelor's degree is recommended.

The school believes a medical student should have a sound background in the humanities and behavioral and social sciences as well as in the physical and biological sciences. Although most premedical students elect to major in one of the biological or

Source: Association of American Medical Colleges (1977).

physical sciences, they are strongly advised to make every effort to broaden their education through a variety of electives in other disciplines. The following college level courses are required:

	Years
Biological science	1
General chemistry	1
Organic chemistry	1

If two or more undergraduate courses are offered, the more rigorous option is recommended.

Physics	1
English	1

Mathematics through integral calculus

Not required but recommended is a course in introductory biochemistry or cell biology.

Selection Factors

Selection of applicants is based on those intellectual and personal characteristics that would lead the Admissions Committee to believe there is a likelihood of completion of the requirements of the medical curriculum and subsequent discharge of the demands of the profession. The school recognizes that society has looked to the physician for wisdom as well as scientific learning. Factors that will be considered are the applicant's scholastic record, MCAT performance, and reports of teachers and advisers with regard to intellectual capacity, motivation, and emotional stability. No distinction will be made between applicants who have majored in sciences or in the nonsciences in their undergraduate courses. A minimum overall and science GPA of 2.5 is required.

A personal interview will normally be required of each applicant who is accepted. Out-of-state interviews may be arranged in those instances in which travel to Davis would constitute an undue hardship. Primary consideration for admission will be given to students who are legal residents of California. No age limitations have been specified.

A program for selection from disadvantaged social and educational backgrounds was begun in 1969. A special introductory three-week course is offered to these students. The purpose of this course is to introduce these students to the faculty through small group meetings, to familiarize the students with medical terminology, and to improve their learning techniques.

Financial Aid

Inasmuch as the course of study involves 15 consecutive quarters, relatively little part-time work by the student is feasible. For those applicants eligible by virtue of financial need and scholastic ability, scholarship awards and loans are available. Applications for financial aid and other information will be forwarded to accepted students who request them.

Timetable of application and acceptance for 1977–78 first year class

Filing of AMCAS application
  Earliest date: July 1, 1976
  Latest date: Nov. 1, 1976

School application fee to all applicants: $20
Acceptance of regular applicants
  Earliest date: December 15, 1976
  Latest date: varies
Does not have early decision plan
Applicant response to acceptance offer
  Maximum time: 3 weeks
Deposit to hold place in class: none
Estimated size of class: 100
Starting date: October 1, 1977

Estimated expenses per year for 1977–78 first-year class

Tuition
  Resident: $670
  Nonresident: $2,170
Room and board (minimum): $2,200
Books and supplies: $400
Microscope provided by school

Information on 1975–76 first-year class

Number of	Instate	Out-of-state	Foreign	Total
Applicants [a].................	3,209	437	149	3,795
New Entrants [b]	98	1	1	100

[a] 13 percent were interviewed

[b] 100 percent were interviewed, took the MCAT, and had four years of college.

Appendix D-6. Meharry Medical College School of Medicine

Dr. Ralph J. Cazort, Dean
Dr. Philip A. Nicholas, Assistant Dean-Admissions
Dr. Eugene P. Caruthers, Director of Admissions and Records

General Information

The school of Medicine of Meharry Medical College was organized in 1876.

The George W. Hubbard Hospital owned by the college is the main teaching hospital, and the current 200-bed capacity is presently being expanded to 600 beds in keeping with the general growth of the Medical Center.

Meharry places considerable emphasis upon keeping a meaningful partnership with the community in delivery of health care, education, and research. It is possible to obtain the M.S. and M.D. degrees.

Curriculum

The curriculum, which is constantly under revision, consists essentially of two parts: the preclinical and the clinical years. The preclinical years commence with

Source: Association of American Medical Colleges (1977).

an integrated introduction to cell biology followed by an organ system approach to the teaching of anatomy, biochemistry, and physiology. The second year contains the traditional disciplines of microbiology, pathology, clinical pathology, pharmacology, and physical diagnosis; formal lectures in the behavioral sciences; and family, and community health.

The clinical years are treated as a single unit with initiation of a block system. In five 12-week blocks, the third- and fourth-year students rotate through the major clinical departments (that is, internal medicine, surgery, pediatrics, obstetrics-gynecology, and psychiatry-family and community medicine). The sixth block is used for a guided elective. In each block students' sole responsibilities are to the department to which they are assigned, except for grand rounds on Wednesday mornings.

An uncommon feature of the clinical years is the emphasis on special types of health care delivery through several outreach programs and facilities.

Requirements for Entrance

The MCAT is required. The baccalaureate degree is desirable; however, three years of college work is acceptable. Premedical work must include:

	Sem/Qtr. hrs.
General biology or zoology (with lab)	8/12
Inorganic chemistry (with lab)	8/12
Organic chemistry (with lab)	8/12
General physics (with lab)	8/12
English	6/9

Applicants are urged to take the MCAT in the spring of the year of application. This will enhance earlier consideration of the application.

Selection Factors

Applicants are selected on a competitive basis from a standpoint of scholarship, character, personality, and general fitness to study medicine. This is done by careful evaluation of the material of every applicant—GPA, MCAT scores, and professional committee recommendations. Of special interest are the grades in the following courses: English, general biology, general chemistry, organic chemistry, and general physics. Interviews are extended to applicants whose credentials are accepted by the Committee on Admissions. Although there are no strict geographical limitations, preferential consideration is given to qualified applicants from states that contract to subsidize the education of their citizens at Meharry. Special empathy is held for minority groups and disadvantaged applicants of all origins.

Early decision applicants must have their complete application on file by September 1 for consideration.

Of the 1975 entering class 23 percent were women and 90 percent were minority students.

Financial Aid

The college has loan funds from which financial aid may be given; loans secured bear a small amount of interest. The element of need must be demonstrated and these funds can be applied to tuition and fees. The college is also a participant in the federal scholarship and loan programs.

The spouses of students may frequently find employment within the college. Teaching positions are available in the neighboring colleges and in the city schools for those with the proper qualifications.

A limited number of scholarships will be awarded each year to outstanding students who are in need of financial assistance.

Information for Minorities

For over 90 years, Meharry has produced a large percentage of the minority health professionals in the United States.

Timetable of Application and Acceptance for 1977-78 First-Year Class

Filing of application
    Earliest date: March 15, 1976
    Latest date: Jan. 2, 1977
School application fee to all applicants: $10
Acceptance of regular applicants
    Earliest date: Nov. 15, 1976
    Latest date: May 30, 1977
Does have early decision plan (EDP)
    EDP application deadline: Aug. 15, 1976
    School notification date: Oct. 1, 1976
Applicant response to acceptance offer
    Maximum time: 14 days
Deposit to hold place in class (applies on tuition):
    $100, due with acceptance
Deposit refundable prior to: March 1, 1977
Estimated size of class: 124
Starting date: August 29, 1977

Estimated expenses per year for 1977-78 first-year class

Tuition
    Resident: $2,500
    Nonresident: $2,500
Student fees: $731
Room and board (minimum): $1,200
Books and supplies: $350
Microscope rental available: $150

Information on 1975-76 first-year class

Number of	Instate	Out-of-state	Foreign	Total
Applicants[a]	385	2,798	317	3,500
New entrants[b]	16	90	7	113

[a] 6 percent were interviewed.

[b] 100 percent were interviewed and took the MCAT; 88 percent had four years of college.

Appendix D-7. Acceptance to medical school by undergraduate major
for 1975-76 entering class

Undergraduate major	Total applicants		Accepted applicants	
	Number	Percentage	Number	Percentage
Biology	15,522	36.7	5,297	34.1
Chemistry	4,717	11.2	2,032	43.1
Zoology	3,161	7.5	1,046	33.1
Psychology	2,646	6.3	880	33.3
Premedicine	2,497	5.9	905	36.2
Biochemistry	1,178	2.8	541	45.9
Microbiology	850	2.0	270	31.8
Chemistry and biology	742	1.8	311	41.9
Mathematics	687	1.6	273	39.7
Pharmacy	558	1.3	100	17.9
English	510	1.2	210	41.2
Natural sciences	504	1.2	195	38.7
Physics	411	1.0	178	43.3

Note: Includes only those majors taken by more than 1 percent of entering class.

Source: Gordon (1977, p. 37).

Appendix D-8. Mean MCAT scores of accepted, nonaccepted, and total medical school applicants, 1966-67 through 1975-76

First-year class	*Mean MCAT scores*				Number taking MCAT	Percentage of total applicants
	Verbal ability	*Quantitative ability*	*General information*	*Science*		
Accepted applicants						
1966-67	549	584	566	550	9,109	99.8
1967-68	554	596	566	565	9,676	99.7
1968-69	556	600	570	577	10,010	99.2
1969-70	562	603	569	577	10,493	99.5
1970-71	559	606	560	558	11,434	99.4
1971-72	560	606	556	565	12,324	99.9
1972-73	562	614	555	575	13,633	99.1
1973-74	567	609	563	592	14,062	98.1
1974-75	563	611	559	603	14,943	99.2
1975-76	575	620	550	615	15,192	98.9
Nonaccepted applicants[a]						
1966-67	488	510	516	578	8,781	96.2
1967-68	496	514	514	485	8,580	95.1
1968-69	497	526	519	495	10,433	94.6
1969-70	506	536	524	507	13,139	94.4
1970-71	506	539	518	499	12,783	94.7
1971-72	519	549	517	510	15,941	94.7
1972-73	512	551	514	510	21,080	94.2
1973-74	518	550	521	524	25,217	96.4
1974-75	518	555	518	532	26,921	97.7
1975-76	522	562	513	539	26,337	97.8
Total applicants						
1966-67	519	548	541	515	17,890	98.0
1967-68	527	558	542	527	18,256	97.5
1968-69	526	562	544	535	20,443	96.8
1969-70	531	566	544	538	23,632	96.6
1970-71	531	571	538	527	24,217	96.9
1971-72	537	574	534	534	28,265	96.9
1972-73	531	575	530	536	34,713	96.1
1973-74	535	571	536	548	39,279	97.0
1974-75	534	575	532	558	41,864	98.2
1975-76	541	583	527	567	41,529	98.2

[a] Includes those who withdrew before any action was taken on any of their applications.

Sources: Dubé (1973a, *48*, 1162.

Appendix D-9. Percent of first-year medical students with premedical grade point
average of A (3.6 to 4.0 on a four-point scale), B (2.6 to 3.5), C (less than 2.6),
1966-1975; and U (unknown), 1972-1975.

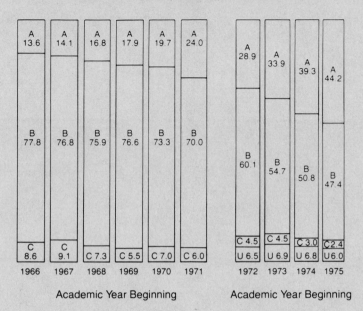

Academic Year Beginning   Academic Year Beginning

Source: American Medical Association (1976, *236*, p. 2962).

Appendix E

Admissions to Graduate Schools of Management

Appendix E-1. Enrollment for advanced business and management degrees during the fall of 1973

Group	First-year students[a]	Students beyond first-year[b]	Total
Men			
Full-time	22,938	13,557	36,495
Part-time	39,540	21,220	60,750
Women			
Full-time	2,748	1,322	4,070
Part-time	4,412	2,137	6,549
Total	69,638	38,236	107,874

[a] Students with less than 1 full year of required study for an advanced degree or its equivalent in part-time study.

[b] Students with 1 or more years of required study for an advanced degree.

Source: Grant and Lind (1976, p. 85). Original source: U.S. Department of Health, Education and Welfare, National Center for Education Statistics, *Students Enrolled for Advanced Degrees, Fall 1973.*

Appendix E-2. Master's and doctor's degrees in business and management by field of study, 1971-72

Field	Master's degrees			Doctoral degrees		
	Total	Men	Women	Total	Men	Women
Business and management	30,433	29,232	1,201	902	882	20
Business and commerce general	9,612	9,172	440	131	129	2
Accounting	1,377	1,269	108	51	51	—
Business statistics	73	69	4	10	10	—
Banking and finance	1,783	1,733	50	49	49	—
Investments and securities	52	49	3	1	1	—
Business management and administration	12,114	11,718	396	399	387	12
Operations research	339	321	18	37	36	1
Hotel and restaurant management	26	24	2	2	2	—
Marketing and purchasing	1,492	1,443	49	46	44	2
Transportation and public utilities	66	66	—	6	6	—
Real Estate	61	60	1	1	1	—
Insurance	31	29	2	3	3	—
International business	693	674	19	14	14	—
Secretarial studies	—	—	—	—	—	—
Personnel management	297	284	13	18	18	—
Labor and industrial relations	300	273	27	18	18	—
Business economics	269	244	25	78	76	2
Other	1,848	1,804	44	38	37	1

Source: Grant and Lind (1976, p. 103). Original source: U.S. Department of Health, Education and Welfare, National Center for Education Statistics, *Earned Degrees Conferred: 1971-72.*

**Appendix E-3. Master's and doctor's degrees in business and management
by field of study, 1972-73**

Field	Master's degrees			Doctoral degrees		
	Total	Men	Women	Total	Men	Women
Business and management	31,166	29,638	1,528	932	879	53
Business and commerce general	9,053	8,595	458	190	182	8
Accounting	1,621	1,480	141	83	82	1
Business statistics	99	85	14	13	13	—
Banking and finance	1,741	1,683	58	33	32	1
Investments and securities	61	58	3	—	—	—
Business management and administration	12,488	11,965	523	323	313	10
Operations research	369	353	16	21	21	—
Hotel and restaurant management	22	22	—	—	—	—
Marketing and purchasing	1,078	1,022	56	75	51	24
Transportation and public utilities	159	157	2	9	8	1
Real Estate	75	73	2	—	—	—
Insurance	22	21	1	2	2	—
International business	745	714	31	5	4	1
Secretarial studies	36	18	18	1	1	—
Personnel management	352	327	25	12	12	—
Labor and industrial relations	325	299	26	21	21	—
Business economics	242	214	28	74	70	4
Other	2,678	2,552	126	70	67	3

Source: Grant and Lind (1976, p. 109). Original source: U.S. Department of Health, Education, and Welfare, National Center for Education Statistics, *Earned Degrees Conferred: 1972-73.*

**Appendix E-4. Number and percentage of minority students enrolled in
graduate business study in 37 schools during 1971-72**

Group	Number	Percentage
Blacks	236	2.18
Indian or Native American	30	0.28
Puerto Rican, Chicano, or Spanish American	84	0.77
Oriental American	99	0.91
Total minority	449	4.14
Total nonminority	10,384	95.86
Grand total	10,833	100.00

Source: Hamilton (1973, p. 17).

Appendix E-5. Master's level students enrollment in AACSB member schools for 1973-74 broken down according to area of concentration and minority grouping

Area of concentration	Total enrollment	American Caucasians	American Indians	American Negroes	American Orientals	Spanish Americans	Foreign students
Accounting	2,560 (100%)	2,228 (87%)	1 (0%)	63 (2.5%)	59 (2.3%)	27 (1.1%)	182 (7.1%)
Business education	519 (100%)	413 (79%)	2 (0.4%)	76 (14.6%)	6 (1.2%)	13 (2.5%)	9 (1.7%)
Economics	726 (100%)	607 (83.6%)	–	11 (1.5%)	13 (1.8%)	6 (0.8%)	89 (12.3%)
Finance	2,349 (100%)	1,982 (84.4%)	3 (0.1%)	85 (3.6%)	30 (1.3%)	20 (0.8%)	230 (9.8%)
General business	4,941 (100%)	4,191 (84.8%)	5 (0.1%)	254 (5.1%)	34 (0.7%)	40 (0.8%)	417 (8.4%)
Hospital and health care administration	204 (100%)	187 (91.7%)	–	6 (2.9%)	–	5 (2.5%)	6 (2.9%)
Hotel and restaurant management	65 (100%)	44 (67.7%)	–	1 (1.5%)	–	–	20 (30.8%)
Industrial and labor relations	311 (100%)	269 (86.5%)	–	15 (4.8%)	4 (1.3%)	–	23 (7.4%)
Information systems	401 (100%)	351 (87.5%)	–	12 (3%)	5 (1.3%)	2 (0.5%)	31 (7.7%)
Insurance	21 (100%)	15 (71.4%)	–	–	1 (4.8%)	2 (9.5%)	3 (14.3%)
International business	207 (100%)	167 (80.6%)	–	4 (2%)	5 (2.4%)	4 (2%)	27 (13%)
Management	3,324 (100%)	3,041 (91.5%)	29 (0.9%)	47 (1.4%)	30 (0.9%)	16 (0.5%)	160 (4.8%)
Marketing	1,250 (100%)	1,014 (81.1%)	–	47 (3.8%)	14 (1.1%)	16 (1.3%)	159 (12.7%)
Office administration and secretarial science	5 (100%)	1 (20%)	–	1 (20%)	1 (20%)	2 (40%)	–
Personnel and organizational behavior	725 (100%)	614 (84.7%)	–	46 (6.3%)	7 (1%)	3 (0.4%)	55 (7.6%)

Private policy and administration	4	4	—	—	—	—	—
	(100%)	(100%)					
Production management	167	119	—	—	2	5	41
	(100%)	(71.2%)			(1.2%)	(3%)	(24.6%)
Public administration	432	350	—	35	1	14	32
	(100%)	(81%)		(8.1%)	(0.2%)	(3.2%)	(7.4%)
Real estate and urban economics	145	125	—	6	1	—	13
	(100%)	(86.2%)		(4.1%)	(0.7%)		(9%)
Transportation	80	76	—	2	—	—	2
	(100%)	(95%)		(2.5%)			(2.5%)
Other business fields	1,149	1,084	—	20	1	5	39
	(100%)	(94.3%)		(1.7%)	(0.1%)	(0.4%)	(3.4%)
No formal concentration	11,705	10,373	42	346	131	160	653
	(100%)	(88.6%)	(0.4%)	(2.9%)	(1.1%)	(1.4%)	(5.6%)
Grand total	31,290	27,255	82	1,077	345	340	2,191
	(100%)	(87.1%)	(0.3%)	(3.4%)	(1.1%)	(1.1%)	(7%)

Source: AACSB (1975, p. IV). This table appeared as Table II in the source document.

Appendix E-6. Doctoral level student enrollment in AACSB member schools for 1973-74 broken down according to area of concentration, and minority grouping

Area of concentration	Total enrollment	American Caucasians	American Indians	American Negroes	American Orientals	Spanish Americans	Foreign students
Accounting	395 (100%)	327 (82.8%)	—	3 (0.8%)	1 (0.2%)	1 (0.2%)	63 (16%)
Business education	119 (100%)	21 (17.6%)	—	98 (82.4%)	—	—	—
Economics	566 (100%)	450 (79.5%)	—	2 (0.4%)	11 (1.9%)	—	103 (18.2%)
Finance	331 (100%)	239 (72.2%)	—	4 (1.2%)	3 (0.9%)	—	85 (25.7%)
General business	22 (100%)	22 (100%)	—	—	—	—	—
Hospital and health care administration	—	—	—	—	—	—	—
Hotel and restaurant management	—	—	—	—	—	—	—
Industrial and labor relations	51 (100%)	40 (78.4%)	—	—	—	—	11 (21.6%)
Information systems	87 (100%)	63 (72.4%)	—	1 (1.2%)	—	—	23 (26.4%)
Insurance	26 (100%)	22 (84.6%)	—	—	—	—	4 (15.4%)
International business	55 (100%)	21 (38.2%)	—	—	—	—	34 (61.8%)
Management	411 (100%)	329 (80%)	1 (0.2%)	7 (1.7%)	—	1 (0.2%)	73 (17.8%)
Marketing	384 (100%)	302 (78.6%)	—	10 (2.6%)	2 (0.5%)	—	70 (18.2%)
Office administration and secretarial science	50 (100%)	—	—	40 (80%)	—	1 (2%)	9 (18%)
Personnel and organizational behavior	268 (100%)	207 (77.2%)	—	12 (4.5%)	1 (0.4%)	—	48 (17.9%)

Private policy and administration	29 (100%)	20 (69%)	—	2 (6.9%)	—	—	7 (24.1%)
Production management	81 (100%)	53 (65.4%)	—	1 (1.2%)	—	—	27 (33.3%)
Public administration	14 (100%)	12 (85.7%)	—	1 (7.1%)	—	—	1 (7.1%)
Real estate and urban economics	14 (100%)	12 (85.7%)	—	—	—	—	2 (14.3%)
Transportation	42 (100%)	27 (64.3%)	—	—	1 (2.4%)	—	14 (33.3%)
Other business fields	311 (100%)	210 (67.5%)	—	6 (1.9%)	—	3 (1%)	92 (29.6%)
No formal concentration	57 (100%)	25 (43.9%)	—	1 (1.7%)	—	—	31 (54.4%)
Grand total	3,313 (100%)	2,402 (72.5%)	1 (0%)	188 (5.7%)	19 (0.6%)	6 (0.2%)	697 (21%)

Source: AACSB (1975, p. V). This table appeared as Table III in the source document.

Appendix E-7. Graduates and enrollment, all AACSB member schools

Number of 1975-76 master business school/unit graduates, estimated head count

Area of concentration	White Male	White Female	Black Male	Black Female	American Indian Male	American Indian Female	Oriental Male	Oriental Female	Spanish origin Male	Spanish origin Female	Foreign Male	Foreign Female
Accounting	1,883	397	57	45	4	1	40	25	14	4	97	29
Economics	265	56	13	6	1		19	6	5	2	69	14
Finance	1,643	234	70	23	2		23	7	15	2	178	23
Management	2,694	288	106	27	7	3	41	7	40	5	228	40
Marketing	828	166	45	24			12	2	10	2	73	8
Quantitative methods	362	57	7	2	1		6	2	10		44	5
Other	1,597	397	48	30	3	1	16	6	22	6	132	13
No formal concentration	7,809	1,067	173	48	8		185	36	92	13	589	75
Total	17,081	2,662	519	205	26	5	342	91	208	34	1,410	207
Ethnic total	19,743		724		31		433		242		1,617	

Grand total 22,790

Number of students enrolled in fall 1976 master business school/unit programs, estimated head count

Area of concentration	White Male	White Female	Black Male	Black Female	American Indian Male	American Indian Female	Oriental Male	Oriental Female	Spanish origin Male	Spanish origin Female	Foreign Male	Foreign Female
Accounting	6,203	1,585	156	101	6	2	96	55	59	24	310	130
Economics	830	197	27	16	4		20	13	8	4	133	39
Finance	3,904	668	209	62	8		79	20	40	10	347	59
Management	10,417	1,985	575	188	28	4	165	37	125	31	700	115
Marketing	2,432	621	137	62	2	1	44	13	20	6	192	30
Quantitative methods	988	229	25	7	1	1	30	5	14	2	149	20
Other	4,909	1,222	155	108	12	5	47	23	74	30	398	81
No formal concentration	24,885	5,440	692	312	31	7	494	132	304	77	1,598	262
Total	54,568	11,947	1,976	856	92	20	975	298	644	184	3,827	736
Ethnic total	66,515		2,832		112		1,273		828		4,563	

Grand total 76,123

Projected number of 1976-77 master business school/unit graduates, estimated head count

Accounting	2,288	526	65	47	2	2	46	32	22	9	110	54
Economics	428	112	14	11	3		18	7	9	2	101	29
Finance	1,725	296	71	30	1		27	5	15		154	40
Management	3,501	571	163	54	7	3	77	12	41	8	311	55
Marketing	1,008	243	48	24	1		11	7	10	1	88	8
Quantitative methods	465	76	13	2			6	4	4		48	8
Other	1,980	456	62	26	2		14	7	21	4	170	17
No formal concentration	8,664	1,599	215	85	19	1	178	57	98	23	685	104
Total	20,059	3,879	651	279	35	6	377	131	220	47	1,667	315
Ethnic total	23,938		930		41		508		267		1,982	
Grand total	27,666											

Source: AACSB (1977, p. 13).

Appendix E-8. Enrollment data in business and management from institutions of higher education, fall 1974, state and regional summaries, by major fields

	American Indian		Black		Asian American		Spanish surnamed American		Total minority		All other students		Grand total	
	No.	%	No.	%	No.	%	No.	%	No.	%	No.	%	No.	%
Undergraduate														
Full-time	2,669	0.5	57,642	10.1	6,617	1.2	13,462	2.4	80,390	14.2	487,615	85.8	568,005	100.0
Female	837	0.6	23,857	17.2	2,379	1.7	3,905	2.8	30,978	22.4	107,351	77.6	138,329	100.0
Male	1,832	0.4	33,785	7.9	4,238	1.0	9,557	2.2	49,412	11.5	380,264	88.5	429,676	100.0
Part-time	1,257	0.5	23,008	10.0	3,649	1.6	9,323	4.0	37,237	16.2	193,321	83.8	230,558	100.0
Female	477	0.6	10,566	14.3	1,513	2.1	3,247	4.4	15,803	21.4	57,924	78.6	73,727	100.0
Male	780	0.5	12,442	7.9	2,136	1.4	6,076	3.9	21,434	13.7	135,397	86.3	156,831	100.0
Total	3,926	0.5	80,650	10.1	10,266	1.3	22,785	2.9	117,627	14.7	680,936	85.3	798,563	100.0
Female	1,314	0.6	34,423	16.2	3,892	1.8	7,152	3.4	46,781	22.1	165,275	77.9	212,056	100.0
Male	2,612	0.4	46,227	7.9	6,374	1.1	15,633	2.7	70,846	12.1	515,661	87.9	586,507	100.0
Graduate														
Full-time	99	0.2	1,760	4.4	921	2.3	368	0.9	3,148	7.9	36,852	92.1	40,000	100.0
Female	13	0.2	499	8.9	163	2.9	59	1.1	734	13.1	4,866	86.9	5,600	100.0
Male	86	0.2	1,261	3.7	758	2.2	309	0.9	2,414	7.0	31,986	93.0	34,400	100.0
Part-time	160	0.2	2,685	3.7	1,156	1.6	835	1.2	4,836	6.7	67,481	93.3	72,317	100.0
Female	22	0.2	663	6.4	234	2.3	107	1.0	1,026	9.9	9,359	90.1	10,385	100.0
Male	138	0.2	2,022	3.3	922	1.5	728	1.2	3,810	6.2	58,122	93.8	61,932	100.0
Total	259	0.2	4,445	4.0	2,077	1.8	1,203	1.1	7,984	7.1	104,333	92.9	112,317	100.0
Female	35	0.2	1,162	7.3	397	2.5	166	1.0	1,760	11.0	14,225	89.0	15,985	100.0
Male	224	0.2	3,283	3.4	1,680	1.7	1,037	1.1	6,224	6.5	90,108	93.5	96,332	100.0

Category	N	%	N	%	N	%	N	%	N	%	N	%	Total	%
Professional														
Full-time	6	0.4	68	5.0	39	2.9	38	2.8	151	11.2	1,200	88.8	1,351	100.0
Female	1	0.4	30	10.5	8	2.8	3	1.1	42	14.7	243	85.3	285	100.0
Male	5	0.5	38	3.6	31	2.9	35	3.3	109	10.2	957	89.8	1,066	100.0
Part-time	11	0.5	58	2.8	11	0.5	52	2.5	132	6.3	1,974	93.7	2,106	100.0
Female	2	0.4	13	2.7	3	0.6	17	3.5	35	7.2	451	92.8	486	100.0
Male	9	0.6	45	2.8	8	0.5	35	2.2	97	6.0	1,523	94.0	1,620	100.0
Total	17	0.5	126	3.6	50	1.4	90	2.6	283	8.2	3,174	91.8	3,457	100.0
Female	3	0.4	43	5.6	11	1.4	20	2.6	77	10.0	694	90.0	771	100.0
Male	14	0.5	83	3.1	39	1.5	70	2.6	206	7.7	2,480	92.3	2,686	100.0
Und. + Grad. + Prof.														
Full-time	2,774	0.5	59,470	9.8	7,577	1.2	13,868	2.3	83,689	13.7	525,667	86.3	609,356	100.0
Female	851	0.6	24,386	16.9	2,550	1.8	3,967	2.8	31,754	22.0	112,460	78.0	144,214	100.0
Male	1,923	0.4	35,084	7.5	5,027	1.1	9,901	2.1	51,935	11.2	413,207	88.8	465,142	100.0
Part-time	1,428	0.5	25,751	8.4	4,816	1.6	10,210	3.3	42,205	13.8	262,776	86.2	304,981	100.0
Female	501	0.6	11,242	13.3	1,750	2.1	3,371	4.0	16,864	19.9	67,734	80.1	84,598	100.0
Male	927	0.4	14,509	6.6	3,066	1.4	6,839	3.1	25,341	11.5	195,042	88.5	220,383	100.0
Total	4,202	0.5	85,221	9.3	12,393	1.4	24,078	2.6	125,894	13.8	788,443	86.2	914,337	100.0
Female	1,352	0.6	35,628	15.6	4,300	1.9	7,338	3.2	48,618	21.2	180,194	78.8	228,812	100.0
Male	2,850	0.4	49,593	7.2	8,093	1.2	16,740	2.4	77,276	11.3	608,249	88.7	685,525	100.0
Unclassified														
Total	99	0.7	1,398	10.3	251	1.9	693	5.1	2,441	18.0	11,094	82.0	13,535	100.0
Female	45	1.1	602	14.2	104	2.5	244	5.8	995	23.5	3,236	76.5	4,231	100.0
Male	54	0.6	796	8.6	147	1.6	449	4.8	1,446	15.5	7,858	84.5	9,304	100.0
Total enrollment	4,301	0.5	86,619	9.3	12,644	1.4	24,771	2.7	128,335	13.8	799,537	86.2	927,872	100.0
Female	1,397	0.6	36,230	15.5	4,404	1.9	7,582	3.3	49,613	21.3	183,430	78.7	233,043	100.0
Male	2,904	0.4	50,389	7.3	8,240	1.2	17,189	2.5	78,722	11.3	616,107	88.7	694,829	100.0

Source: U.S. Department of Health, Education and Welfare, Office of Civil Rights (1976, p. 370).

Appendix E-9. Master's degrees awarded by AACSB member schools during 1973-74 identified by area of concentration, and minority grouping

Area of Concentration	Total degrees awarded	American Caucasians	American Indians	American Negroes	American Orientals	Spanish Americans	Foreign students
Accounting	1,252 (100%)	1,132 (90.4%)	1 (0.1%)	36 (3%)	13 (1%)	8 (0.6%)	62 (4.9%)
Business education	302 (100%)	257 (85.1%)	–	35 (11.6%)	–	1 (0.3%)	9 (3%)
Economics	252 (100%)	222 (88.1%)	1 (0.4%)	6 (2.4%)	2 (0.8%)	3 (1.2%)	18 (7.1%)
Finance	1,384 (100%)	1,234 (89.1%)	5 (0.4%)	33 (2.4%)	19 (1.4%)	8 (0.6%)	85 (6.1%)
General business	1,282 (100%)	1,009 (78.7%)	12 (0.9%)	124 (9.7%)	3 (0.2%)	4 (0.3%)	130 (10.1%)
Hospital and health care administration	87 (100%)	83 (95.4%)	–	4 (4.6%)	–	–	–
Hotel and restaurant management	21 (100%)	21 (100%)	–	–	–	–	–
Industrial and labor relations	124 (100%)	112 (90.3%)	–	5 (4%)	1 (0.8%)	1 (0.8%)	5 (4%)
Information systems	111 (100%)	93 (83.8%)	–	4 (3.6%)	3 (2.7%)	–	11 (9.9%)
Insurance	17 (100%)	17 (100%)	–	–	–	–	–
International business	86 (100%)	71 (82.6%)	–	3 (3.5%)	1 (1.1%)	–	11 (12.8%)
Management	1,314 (100%)	1,211 (92.2%)	3 (0.2%)	25 (1.9%)	13 (1%)	14 (1%)	48 (3.7%)
Marketing	786 (100%)	683 (86.9%)	1 (0.1%)	27 (3.4%)	3 (0.4%)	10 (1.3%)	62 (7.9%)
Office administration and secretarial science	40 (100%)	36 (90%)	–	3 (7.5%)	–	–	1 (2.5%)
Personnel and organizational behavior	287 (100%)	230 (80.1%)	1 (0.3%)	28 (9.8%)	2 (0.7%)	3 (1%)	23 (8%)

Private policy and administration	2 (100%)	2 (100%)	—	—	—	—	—
Production management	66 (100%)	51 (77.3%)	—	—	—	4 (6.1%)	11 (16.6%)
Public administration	143 (100%)	125 (87.4%)	—	14 (9.8%)	—	1 (0.7%)	3 (2.1%)
Quantitative methods	15 (100%)	11 (73.3%)	1 (6.7%)	1 (6.7%)	—	—	2 (13.3%)
Real estate and urban economics	40 (100%)	33 (82.5%)	—	2 (5%)	2 (5%)	1 (2.5%)	2 (5%)
Transportation	78 (100%)	76 (97.4%)	—	1 (1.3%)	—	—	1 (1.3%)
Other business fields	606 (100%)	579 (95.5%)	1 (0.2%)	4 (0.7%)	3 (0.5%)	3 (0.5%)	16 (2.6%)
No formal concentration	5,860 (100%)	4,878 (83.2%)	27 (0.5%)	178 (3%)	36 (0.6%)	150 (2.6%)	591 (10.1%)
Grand total	14,155 (100%)	12,166 (85.9%)	53 (0.4%)	533 (3.8%)	101 (0.7%)	211 (1.5%)	1,091 (7.7%)

Source: AACSB (1975, p. VIII). This table appeared as Table V in the source document.

Appendix F

Use and Limitations of Selective Measures

Appendix F-1. Illustrative test items

A. Directions and sample questions for related cases sets from
description of the Law School Admission Test, 1976-77[1]

Directions: This part consists of several groups of fictional law cases. Each case includes a set of facts and a legal holding handed down by the court. Four legal principles follow each case. You are to choose the narrowest principle that reasonably explains the decision and is not inconsistent with the ruling given in any of the earlier cases in the group.

A principle that reasonably explains a decision gives a good reason for the decision and must fit both the set of facts and the resulting court decision. For the first case in a group, compare those principles that reasonably explain the decision and choose the narrowest. The narrowest principle is not the principle with the fewest restrictions, such as, "Law books must be bound in red," but the principle covering the smallest relevant group of cases, such as, "A casebook that is assigned by a professor in a torts course must be bound in red."

In the remaining cases in the group, however, the answer chosen must also be consistent with the rulings given in the earlier cases in that group. The rulings include both the decisions and the principles chosen to explain the decisions. Therefore, for these cases, find the principles that reasonably explain the decision, eliminate those that contradict preceding rulings, and choose the narrowest.

You may make marginal notes in your test book if you wish. However, be sure to record all of your answers on the answer sheet.

These questions do not presuppose any specific legal knowledge on your part. You are to arrive at your answers entirely by the ordinary processes of logical reasoning and common sense.

[1] *Description of the Law School Admission Test 1976-77.* Copyright © 1975, (1976 p. 25, 26) by the Law School Admission Council. All rights reserved. Certain sample questions are reprinted by permission of Educational Testing Service, the copyright owner.

Group I

1.   While waiting for a plane in the airport, Peter was approached by Frank, a stranger. Frank asked Peter if he could take out an insurance policy on him at his own expense. Peter replied, "It's no skin off my nose," whereupon Frank purchased a policy on Peter's life for $100,000 and paid the premium of $3.00 to All Risk Insurance Company. Three hours later, the plane on which Peter was riding crashed under mysterious circumstances and Peter was killed. All Risk declined to pay Frank the $100,000 and Frank sued. Held, for All Risk.

The narrowest principle that reasonably explains this result is:

(A)   An insurance policy is not valid unless the beneficiary had an insurable interest in the life of the insured at the policy's inception.

(B)   An insurance company does not have to pay a beneficiary when the death of the insured takes place under mysterious circumstances.

(C)   An insurance policy that has not been accepted by the company at the home office may be canceled at the company's option.

(D)   An insurance policy only becomes incontestable after a period of two years from the date the policy was issued.

All the choices present principles that would support the decision in favor of All Risk. (D) is quite broad; it covers all insurance policies and makes it impossible for any insurance policy to be challenged after two years. (C) is narrower than (D), but it would apply to most airline flight insurance policies. It allows the company to cancel for any reason. Both (A) and (B) restrict the class of insurance policies to which they apply according to beneficiaries and so are narrower than (C) and (D). (B) seems narrower than (A), since only a few people die in mysterious circumstances, but the way in which (B) restricts the class of valid insurance policies does not seem so reasonable as the way in which (A) does. Under (B), no payment would be made on a policy that had as beneficiary the spouse of anyone on Peter's plane or the child of someone whose last illness was undiagnosed. (A) is the best choice. It explains the case most clearly by requiring some relationship stronger than chance encounter to exist between the beneficiary and the person insured.

2.   David owed a debt to Myrna of $5,000. Since David was in serious financial difficulty, on June 15, 1971, with his consent, Myrna obtained a $5,000 life insurance policy on David from the Expert Insurance Company, payable to her upon his death. On September 1, 1972, David paid his debt in full to Myrna. However, she continued to pay the premiums on the policy until David died. At David's death, Myrna requested payment of the policy. Expert refused and Myrna sued Expert. Held, for Myrna.

The narrowest principle that reasonably explains this result, and is not inconsistent with the ruling given in the preceding case, is:

(A)   A policy that is obtained on the life of the insured with his consent is an enforceable policy.

(B)   A beneficiary who has paid all of the premiums on a life insurance policy is entitled to collect the proceeds.

(C)   An insured's obligation to the beneficiary at inception is sufficient interest to sustain the policy.

(D)   An insurance company must pay all policies that are fully paid and cannot question the right of the beneficiary.

(A), (B), and (D) are inconsistent with the ruling on Question 1 of this set, since each would have required All Risk to pay Frank in that case. (C) is consistent with both cases, since Peter had no obligation to Frank, but David did have an obligation to Myrna. It is also a reasonable explanation; following along the line of thought suggested by (A) in Question 1 of this set, it specifies one kind of relation between beneficiary and insured that counts as an "insurable interest." (C) is therefore correct.

3.   On January 1, the Slick Insurance Company issued a $10,000 paid-up policy on the life of Sam, at his request and expense. The person Sam designated as the beneficiary was Mary, to whom he was not married but who lived with him as his mistress. Three months later, after Sam had been convicted on a charge of embezzlement, Mary left him and went to another city. Sam died five years later. Mary requested payment under the policy but Slick refused. Mary sued Slick. Held, for Mary.

The narrowest principle that reasonably explains this result, and is not inconsistent with the rulings given in the preceding case, is:

(A)   The right of the beneficiary is incontestable in the case of a paid-up life insurance policy.

(B)   The relationship of a man and his mistress is recognized as sufficient for one to be a beneficiary under an insurance policy on the life of the other.

(C)   It is not necessary for a beneficiary to have an insurable interest in the insured if the policy is over two years old.

(D)   A beneficiary may recover under a policy of life insurance as long as the beneficiary did not pay the premium.

(A) is inconsistent with the decision given in Question 1 of this set, since it would have required All Risk to pay Frank in that case. (C) is inconsistent with the principle that supports the decision in Question 1 of this set; there, principle (A) requires an insurable interest to exist at the start of the policy. It is also not clear what reason might be given for a two-year limit on the requirement of insurable interest. (D) at first seems inconsistent with the ruling in Question 2 of this set, since Myrna paid the premium and recovered, but the principle in (D) does not cover Myrna's case; it says what would happen if the beneficiary did not pay the premium. Myrna may have had another independent ground for recovering from Expert, such as (C) of Question 2 of this set. So (B) and (D) may be viewed as consistent with the rulings in Questions 1 and 2. (D), however, covers a very wide class of insurance policies. (B), the correct answer, is narrower and is a reasonable explanation. It gives another instance of a relationship between beneficiary and insured that counts as insurable. Questions 1 through 3 are of moderate difficulty.

4.   Harold, a well-known news commentator, signed a one-year contract with RTC, a television network. RTC insured Harold's life for $1,000,000. RTC was named as beneficiary and paid the premiums when due. When his contract with RTC expired, Harold moved to ABS, which also took out a $1,000,000 policy on Harold from the same insurance company, with ABS as beneficiary. After Harold's contract with ABS expired, he returned to work for RTC. Both television networks continued to pay the premiums on the policies. Harold was still employed by RTC on the date of his death. The insurance company refused to pay either RTC or ABS. Both RTC and ABS sued the insurance company. Held, for RTC and ABS.

The narrowest principle that reasonably explains this result, and is not inconsistent with the rulings given in the preceding cases, is:

(A)   An employer is sufficiently concerned with the welfare of irreplaceable employees so that he is deemed to have an insurable interest in their lives.

(B)   An insurance policy is incontestable after two years have passed from the date the policy was issued.

(C)   An insurance company cannot refuse to pay a policy after it has accepted premiums from the beneficiary continuously throughout the life of the policy.

(D)   A company may not refuse payment of a policy if the beneficiary had an insurable interest when the policy was issued and throughout the life of the policy.

If "continuously" is taken to mean repeatedly, (C) appears consistent with the ruling in Question 1 of this set. But Frank did make the one payment that was required in the short life of his policy, so probably (C) should be viewed as inconsistent with the situation presented in Question 1. In any case, (B), (C), and (D) all cover large classes of insurance policies, including those in which there may be grounds for canceling the policy, such as fraud against the insurance company. (A) is much more modest and can be taken as narrowest. It is also reasonable, since it provides another example of an insurable interest. (A) is the best choice. This question is quite difficult.

B. Mathematics Aptitude[2]

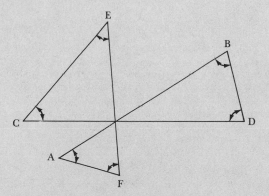

In the triangles above, if AB, CD, and EF are line segments, what is the sum of the measures of the marked angles?

(A) 180°   (B) 360°   (C) 540°   (D) 720°   (E) It cannot be determined from the information given.

This is an example of a moderately difficult question. The ability to reason insightfully in a nonroutine manner is almost essential to solving the problem within a reasonable period of time. One such solution requires discovering that the sum of the measures of the unmarked angles in the three triangles is 180°. Since the sum of the measures of all the angles in the three triangles is 540°, it follows that the sum of the

[2] *About the SAT*. Copyright © 1971 by College Entrance Examination Board (1976, p. 9). All rights reserved. The sample questions are reprinted by permission of Educational Testing Service, the copyright owner.

marked angles is 540°–180°, or 360°. Answer: (B)

A line segment is drawn from the point (0, 0) to the point (6, 4). What are the coordinates of the midpoint?

    (A) (2, 3)   (B) (3, 2)   (C) (3, 4)   (D) (6, 2)   (E) (12, 8)

Answer: (B)

C. Analytical ability from *Graduate Record Examinations Information Bulletin, 1977–1978*[3]

Analysis of Explanations

Directions: For each set of questions, a fact situation and a result are presented. Several numbered statements follow the result. Each statement is to be evaluated in relation to the fact situation and result.

Consider each statement separately from the other statements. For each one, examine the following sequence of decisions, in the order A, B, C, D, E. Each decision results in selecting or eliminating a choice. *The first choice that cannot be eliminated is the correct answer.*

A   Is the statement *inconsistent* with, or contradictory to, something in the fact situation, the result, or both together? If so, choose A. If not,

B   Does the statement present a *possible adequate explanation* of the result? If so, choose B. If not,

C   Does the statement have to be true if the fact situation and result are as stated? If so, the statement is deducible from something in the fact situation, the result, or both together; choose C. If not,

D   Does the statement either support or weaken a possible explanation of the result? If so, the statement is *relevant* to an explanation; choose D.

E   If not, the statement is *irrelevant* to an explanation of the result; choose E.

Use common sense to decide whether explanations are adequate and whether statements are inconsistent or deducible. No formal system of logic is presupposed. Do not consider extremely unlikely or remote possibilities.

Sample Set

Situation: In an attempt to end the theft of books from Parkman University Library, Elnora Johnson, the chief librarian, initiated a stringent inspection program at the beginning of the fall term. At the library entrance, Johnson posted inspectors to check that each library book leaving the building had a checkout slip bearing the call number of the book, its due date, and the borrower's identification number. The library retained a carbon copy of this slip as its only record that the book had been checked out. Johnson ordered the inspectors to search for concealed library books in attache cases, bookbags, and all other containers large enough to hold a book. Since no

---

[3] *Graduate Record Examinations Information Bulletin, 1977–1978* Copyright © 1970 by Educational Testing Service, (1977, pp. 18, 19). All rights reserved. Sample questions reprinted by permission.

new personnel could be hired, all library personnel took turns serving as inspectors, though many complained of their embarrassment in conducting the searches.

Result: During that term Margaret Zimmer stole twenty-five library books.

29. Zimmer stole the books before the inspection system began.

The answer to this question of average difficulty is A, because the statement is inconsistent with the information given in the result, which states that Zimmer stole the books during the term in which the inspection system was initiated.

30. Zimmer dropped the books out of a second-story window into a clump of bushes and retrieved them after she left the building.

Since the statement could be true given the information in the situation and the result, this statement is consistent with the information given, so the correct answer is not A. The next option to be considered is B. The statement is a possible explanation of the result, since Zimmer could have avoided the inspection system in this way. This question is an easy one.

31. During that term, if Zimmer carried a bookbag out of the library entrance door during regular hours, an inspector was supposed to check it.

This statement is not inconsistent with the information given, so the correct answer cannot be A. Although the statement brings to mind two possible explanations of the result (that Zimmer removed the books after regular hours or that a negligent inspector failed to check her bag), it does not actually state either of these possibiliteis. Therefore, the correct answer cannot be B. At this point, in fact, one might be tempted to conclude that the statement weakens a possible explanation of the result (an explanation stating that Zimmer stole the books by hiding them in her bookbag) and might therefore decide that D is the correct answer. However, according to the directions, the next option to be considered is C. The statement can be deduced from the information given, since it is stated that inspectors had been ordered to search for concealed library books in bookbags. The correct answer to this question is therefore C.

32. The library had at one time kept two carbon copies of each checkout slip.

This statement is not inconsistent with the information given, is not a possible explanation of the result, cannot be deduced from the information given, and does not support or weaken a possible explanation of the result. Information about the system used in the past is not relevant to any explanation of the result, so the correct answer is E.

33. The doors to the library fire escapes are equipped with alarm bells set off by opening the doors.

This statement is not inconsistent with the information given, and it is not a possible explanation of the result. It cannot be deduced since it is not necessarily true given the information in the situation and the result. The correct answer is D because the statement weakens a possible explanation of the result. For instance, an explanation stating that Zimmer dropped the books from a fire escape to a confederate below would be unlikely if it were known that the fire escape doors could not be opened without setting off an alarm.

D. Science Problems from New *MCAT* Student Manual[4]

Directions: Questions 15 through 23 are related to science problems. The questions are in groups of three, with each group preceded by descriptive material. First study the material; then select the one best answer to each question in the group. Indicate your selection by marking the corresponding oval on your Practice Test Answer Form.

It is known that drug resistance may be acquired by a fungal cell in one of several ways: (1) mutation at a single gene locus, (2) infection by an RNA virus, with viral control of cell metabolism, (3) conjugation, in which one cell donates genetic material to another through an interconnecting tube, and (4) transformation, occurring only during certain phases of growth, in which free DNA released from one cell is taken up without physical contact by another cell and incorporated into its DNA.

A unicellular fungus causing a particular skin infection is usually arrested by treatment with neomycin. However, a recent outbreak proved to be resistant. Samples of the normal sensitive (S) and the new resistant (R) strains were cultured and studied to determine the basis for the resistance. The fungus was found to be normally haploid, but able to mate, with each resulting diploid zygote producing 4 spores.

15. Sensitive and resistant fungal strains were crossed. If resistance is due to a simple mutation at a single locus, the result of this cross would be that

   A   all zygotes would produce 2 R and 2 S spores.

   B   all zygotes would produce 4 R spores or all would produce 4 S spores.

   C   half of the zygotes would produce 4 R and half would produce 4 S spores.

   D   half of the zygotes would produce 4 R and half would produce 2 R and 2 S spores.

   E   the proportion of R and S spores could not be definitely predicted.

            Answer: A

16. If resistance to neomycin was acquired by a fungus cell from infection by an RNA virus, which of the following would be found in resistant (R) *BUT NOT* in sensitive (S) strains?

   A   An enzyme that converts thymine to uracil

   B   An enzyme that catalyzes synthesis of new DNA using a DNA template

   C   An enzyme that catalyzes synthesis of new nucleic acids using an RNA template

   D   A ribosomal protein that requires neomycin for normal functioning

   E   A defect in the enzyme that is required for the synthesis of cell wall proteins

            Answer: C

[4] *New MCAT Student Manual*. Copyright © 1976 (pp. 23, 24), Association of American Medical Colleges. All rights reserved. Sample items reprinted by permission.

17. After a period of extremely rapid growth in fresh medium, about 90% of a resistant cell sample lost resistance and became sensitive to neomycin. When a sample of these newly sensitive cells were then grown in a medium with free DNA from resistant cells, resistance to neomycin was regained. This indicates that neomycin-resistance was most likely acquired

A   by conjugation.

B   by transformation.

C   by infection with an RNA virus.

D   by mutation at a single gene locus.

E   through a normal variation of its genetic makeup.

        Answer: B

Appendix F-2. College Board Admissions Testing
Program Score Report

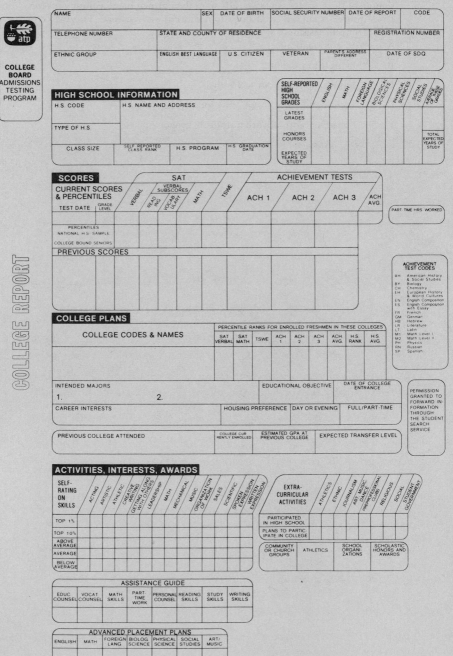

Appendix G

Student Performance on Selective Measures

Appendix G-1. Notes on figures and tables

Note 1. The Figure in G-2 is a plot of the freshman average grade and the average admission test score entering freshmen at all of the public higher institutions in the state of Georgia. While the figure demonstrates that students of widely differing scholastic ability earn similar grades in different institutions, the fact of such differences in grade scales is certainly no secret. In fact, just because of such differences, considerable effort was directed in the 1960s to the development of "expectancy tables" and similar guidance information to help students anticipate what grades they might expect in different colleges.

Note 2. The tables and figures in G-3 through G-9 show collections of representative validity data for five types of institutional settings. Appendix G-3 indicates the range of validity coefficients for men and women at undergraduate institutions that use the Scholastic Aptitude Test. These data come from the College Board's Validity Study Service that is provided for use by member colleges. American College Testing Program also offers such a service and the validity information is generally similar. The tables in G-4 and G-5 provide a summary of all validity data concerning the Graduate Record Examination and other selection measures that were used in the same studies. These two tables are based on the same data sorted differently to show differential predictability by criterion (G-4) and by field (G-5). Law schools place high priority on current information and careful prediction research. Thus, the data is G-6 represent validity studies for the majority of accredited law schools. Medical schools tend not to place as much emphasis on multiple prediction equations but considerable data are available (G-7 and G-8) concerning the relationship of individual MCAT scores and different criteria. The figure in G-9 includes results of validity studies for a large proportion of the member institutions of the Graduate Management Admission Council. Median values for validity of tests and GPA in four institutional settings are shown in Table 15 in the text. Those values come from G-3 (Undergraduate), G-4 (Graduate), G-6 (Law) and G-9 (Management). Validity of the total SAT score shown in Table 15 is based upon the validity of the two subscores shown in G-3 using an estimated intercorrelation of .65 between the two.

Note 3. The figure in G-10 illustrates the fact that reductions in the typical size of validity coefficients at successive educational levels are to be expected when the range of scores becomes progressively smaller at the higher levels. The table in G-11 shows that the validity of selection measures also varies from college to college depending upon the range of scores at the college.

Note 4. The tables in G-12 and G-13 are both concerned with the relationship of standardized test scores and long-range life success. In both cases the researcher identified a "success group" (Ph.D.'s or individuals listed in *Who's Who*), located their test scores, and compared the incidence of achieving such success at different test score levels.

Note 5. The tables in G-12 and the figures in G-15 and G-16 show different types of information concerning test bias. The table in G-12 contains Linn's (1973) summary of 22 studies of black-white predictive bias at undergraduate institutions reported by three previous authors. For each of the sets of data Linn shows what grade would be predicted for a black student if his or her grades were predicted on the basis of the majority (close to the regular) equation as opposed to a special equation based only upon blacks. Such a comparison was made at three different levels of black students: above average, average, and below average. If the admission tests were biased against black students, higher predicted grades would be expected when the black equation was used. The opposite finding occurred in the majority of studies. The figures in G-15 and G-16 address a different type of bias issue; that is, whether there is bias in the selection of items. The figure shows typical results concerning the relative consistency of difficulties of individual test items in different populations. The items have very nearly the same difficulties in two white samples (G-15). There is somewhat less consistency when item difficulties are compared in black and white samples (G-16) but both groups tend to find the same items difficult or easy. If the test construction process resulted in the inclusion of some racially biased items, one would expect some items to stray noticeably away from the swarm toward the lower right (that is, uncharacteristically difficult for blacks). Instead, it appears that the whole test is uniformly more difficult for blacks and does not show evidence of item bias.

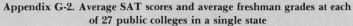

Appendix G-2. **Average SAT scores and average freshman grades at each of 27 public colleges in a single state**

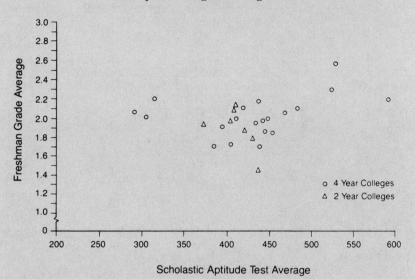

Source: Adapted from Pounds and others (1970), in Willingham, 1973.

Appendix G-3. Validity coefficients of SAT and high school record:
Selected percentiles of validity coefficients based on students in liberal arts
and general programs classified by sex

	SAT-verbal	SAT-math	High school record	Three predictors combined
		Men		
Percentile				
90	0.48	0.47	0.62	0.68
75	0.42	0.40	0.56	0.62
50	0.33	0.30	0.47	0.55
25	0.24	0.24	0.39	0.48
10	0.17	0.16	0.31	0.40
Number of groups	116	116	116	116
		Women		
Percentile				
90	0.55	0.52	0.68	0.74
75	0.48	0.45	0.61	0.68
50	0.41	0.36	0.54	0.62
25	0.32	0.27	0.44	0.52
10	0.23	0.21	0.35	0.43
Number of groups	143	143	143	143
		Men and women		
Percentile				
90	0.54	0.48	0.67	0.73
75	0.48	0.41	0.62	0.68
50	0.39	0.33	0.55	0.62
25	0.35	0.24	0.44	0.54
10	0.26	0.20	0.33	0.46
Number of groups	51	51	51	51

Source: Schrader (1971).

**Appendix G-4. Median validity coefficients for various predictors
and criteria of success in graduate school**

The number of coefficients upon which each median is based is given in parentheses. Coefficients
involving dichotomized criteria were sometimes reported as biserials and sometimes as point-biserials.)

			Criteria of success		
Predictors	*Graduate GPA*	*Overall faculty rating*	*Departmental examination*	*Attain Ph.D.*	*Time to Ph.D.*
GRE-verbal	.24 (46)	.31 (27)	.42 (5)	.18 (47)	.16 (18)
GRE-quantitative	.23 (43)	.27 (25)	.27 (5)	.26 (47)	.25 (18)
GRE-advanced	.30 (25)	.30 (8)	.48 (2)	.35 (40)	.34 (18)
GRE-composite	.33 (30)	.41 (8)	a	.31 (33)	.35 (18)
Undergraduate GPA	.31 (26)	.37 (15)	a	.14 (30)	.23 (9)
Recommendations	a	a	a	.18 (15)	.23 (9)
GRE-GPA composite	.45 (24)	a	a	.40 (16)	.40 (9)

[a] No data available.

Source: Willingham (1974, p. 127).

Appendix G-5. Median validity coefficients for five predictors of success in graduate school in nine fields

(The number of coefficients upon which each median is based is given in parentheses. Coefficients involving dichotomized criteria were sometimes reported as biserials and sometimes as point-biserials. In those sets of data where two criteria were included, one was selected in the following order of priority: GPA, attain Ph.D., departmental examination, and faculty rating.)

Predictors	Biological science	Chemistry	Education	Engineering and applied science	English	Mathematics	Physics	Psychology	Social science
GRE-verbal	.18 (7)	.22 (14)	.36 (15)	.29 (11)	.21 (6)	.30 (6)	.02 (6)	.19 (23)	.32 (11)
GRE-quantitative	.27 (8)	.28 (13)	.28 (14)	.31 (10)	.06 (6)	.27 (6)	.21 (6)	.23 (22)	.32 (10)
Undergraduate GPA	.13 (2)	.27 (7)	.30 (5)	.18 (4)	.22 (4)	.19 (4)	.31 (4)	.16 (15)	.37 (6)
GRE-GPA composite (weighted)	.35 (3)	.42 (6)	.42 (7)	.47 (4)	.56 (2)	.41 (3)	.45 (2)	.32 (4)	.40 (5)

Source: Willingham (1974, p. 274).

Appendix G-6. Validity coefficients of undergraduate average alone, LSAT scores, alone, and undergraduate average combined with LSAT scores[a]

Correlation with first-year average grades in law school	*Number of schools with indicated coefficient*		
	UGPA alone	*LSAT alone*	*UGPA and LSAT*
.65—.69	–	–	4
.60—.64	–	1	2
.55—.59	–	3	15
.50—.54	1	7	16
.45—.49	4	15	24
.40—.44	3	22	20
.35—.39	11	11	11
.30—.34	16	22	16
.25—.29	23	17	4
.20—.24	23	9	3
.15—.19	12	6	1
.10—.14	9	0	–
.05—.09	11	2	–
.00—.04	2	1	–
-0.5—-.01	1	–	–
Median coefficient	.25	.36	.45

[a] *Note.* Based on studies in 116 law schools for which data for 1973—74 and 1974—75 entering classes could be combined.

Source: Pitcher, Schrader, and Winterbottom (1976, p. 9).

Appendix G-7. Probability of being dismissed or repeating the first year of medical school by four MCAT Scores for 9,614 students entering Canadian and United States medical schools in 1970

MCAT score range	*Proportion dismissed or repeating*			
	Verbal	*Quantitative*	*General information*	*Science*
Less than 350	0.19	0.26	0.23	0.26
350—399	0.09	0.18	0.15	0.17
400—449	0.07	0.13	0.08	0.10
450—499	0.04	0.08	0.05	0.06
500—549	0.03	0.05	0.03	0.04
550—599	0.03	0.03	0.03	0.02
600—649	0.02	0.03	0.02	0.02
650—699	0.02	0.02	0.02	0.02
700—799	0.02	0.02	0.02	0.02

Source: Association of American Medical Colleges (1973, p. 6).

Appendix G-8. Median validity coefficients for MCAT scores against four criteria

		Median validity coefficients			
Criterion	No. of Schools	Verbal	Quantitative	General information	Science
First-year grades	71	.10	.16	.07	.26
Fourth-year grades	66	.12	.11	.10	.14
National Board Exam, Part I	50	.19	.28	.16	.42
National Board Exam, Part II	29	.32	.30	.31	.35

Source: Sedlacek (1967, pp. 33, 34).

Appendix G-9. Distribution of validity coefficients for Admission Test for Graduate Study of Business (ATGSB) and Undergraduate Record (UGR) for 67 schools

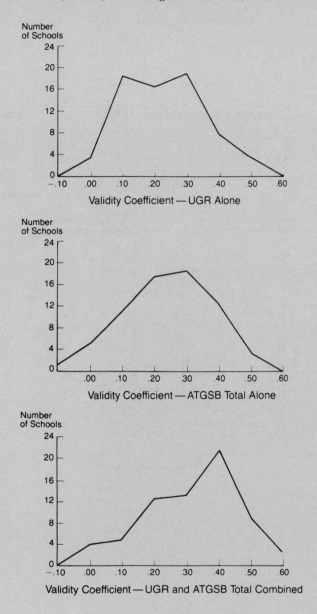

Source: Pitcher (1971, p. 3).

Appendix G-10. Hypothetical example showing effect of restriction in range of talent on the size of the validity coefficient

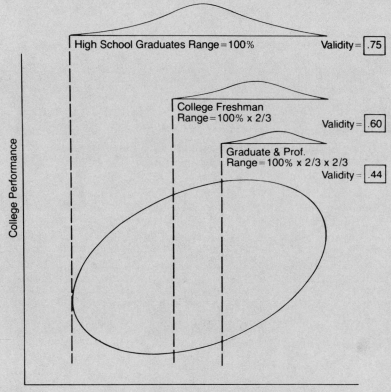

Appendix G-11. Median validity coefficients for groups with varying degrees of restriction in range as indicated by the standard deviation of SAT verbal scores

Standard deviation of SAT-V

	85 or more		75—85		Less than 75	
	Men	Women	Men	Women	Men	Women
SAT-V	.41	.48	.32	.43	.29	.32
SAT-M	.40	.46	.28	.37	.26	.28
High school record	.55	.59	.47	.58	.41	.46
Multiple correlation	.61	.67	.54	.64	.50	.54
Number of groups	43	43	36	42	37	58

Source: Schroader (1971, p. 129).

Appendix G-12. Distribution of intelligence test scores for total doctorate population

IQ interval (AGCT units)	Approx. general population at age 32 in 1958	Observed number of Ph.Ds in all fields	Number of Ph.Ds per 1000[a]
170 and higher	530	46	189
160—169	2,670	101	83
150—159	12,150	337	61
140—149	39,250	530	30
130—139	108,000	826	17
120—129	218,200	806	8
110—119	361,800	520	3
100—109	457,400	298	1
Below 100	1,200,000	103	0.2

[a]Adjusted to include estimated number of Ph. D.s at each level among missing cases.
Source: Harmon (1961). Cited by Chauncey and Hilton (1965, pp. 7—15).

Appendix G-13. SAT scores of individual listed in Who's Who—Observed and expected proportions at different score levels

SAT score level	(E) Percent expected at each level[a]	(O) Percent in Who's Who group (N=232)	O/E
Over 695	2.6	10	3.8
629—695	7.3	15	2.1
563—628	18.9	25	1.3
500—562	21.2	25	1.2
450—499	19.1	15	0.8
Below 450	30.9	10	0.3

[a] Assuming the *Who's Who* group was evenly distributed through the SAT score distribution and that the distribution of scores was normal.
Source: Kallop, 1951; cited by Chauncey and Hilton (1965, p. 116).

Appendix G-14. Predicted GPA for black students using weights for black students and weights for white students

(1) College[a]	(2) SD of GPA for blacks	Test scores one SD below the mean for black students			Test scores at the mean for black students			Test scores one SD above the mean for black students		
		(3) White weights	(4) Black weights	(5) Col (3) −col. (4)	(6) White weights	(7) Black weights[b]	(8) Col (6) −col (7)	(9) White weights	(10) Black weights	(11) Col (9) −col. (10)
C1	0.65	1.68	1.53	0.15	1.98	1.82	0.16	2.28	2.11	0.17
C2	0.69	1.45	1.42	0.03	1.81	1.83	−0.02	2.17	2.24	−0.07
C3	0.56	1.68	1.46	0.22	1.94	1.81	0.13	2.20	2.16	0.04
D1	0.77	2.03	1.55	0.48	2.19	1.76	0.43	2.35	1.96	0.39
D2	0.73	1.71	1.64	0.07	1.99	1.92	0.07	2.27	2.20	0.07
D3	0.84	1.61	1.28	0.33	1.89	1.52	0.37	2.17	1.76	0.41
D4	0.69	1.46	1.73	−0.27	1.75	1.89	−0.14	2.04	2.05	−0.01
D5	0.67	1.36	1.39	−0.03	1.76	1.77	−0.01	2.16	2.15	0.01
D6	0.67	1.68	1.11	0.57	1.87	1.66	0.21	2.05	2.21	−0.16
T1	0.48	2.54	2.48	0.06	2.77	2.58	0.19	3.00	2.68	0.32
T2	0.58	2.61	2.21	0.40	2.74	2.30	0.44	2.87	2.39	0.48
T3	0.58	2.25	2.07	0.18	2.53	2.26	0.27	2.81	2.45	0.36
T4	0.57	2.13	2.04	0.09	2.35	2.14	0.21	2.57	2.24	0.33
T5	0.66	2.11	1.70	0.41	2.43	2.06	0.37	2.75	2.42	0.33
T6	0.65	2.02	2.00	0.02	2.33	2.17	0.16	2.64	2.34	0.30
T7	0.66	2.48	2.07	0.41	2.60	2.15	0.45	2.72	2.23	0.49
T8	0.73	2.08	2.23	−0.15	2.47	2.45	0.02	2.86	2.67	0.19
T9	0.64	2.02	2.09	−0.07	2.31	2.11	0.20	2.60	2.13	0.47
T10	0.65	2.24	1.72	0.52	2.43	1.96	0.47	2.62	2.20	0.42
T11	0.55	2.09	2.24	−0.15	2.35	2.30	0.05	2.61	2.36	0.25
T12	0.51	1.87	1.86	0.01	2.10	2.11	−0.01	2.33	2.36	−0.03
T13	1.30	3.72	3.79	−0.07	4.29	4.05	0.24	4.86	4.31	0.55
Median	—	—	—	0.08	—	—	0.20	—	—	0.31

[a] Colleges are coded as follows: C from Cleary (1968), D from Davis and Kerner-Hoeg (1971), and T from Temp (1971).

[b] Equals the actual mean GPA for black students.

Source: Linn (1973, p. 144).

Appendix G-15. Cross-plot of item difficulties for two samples—North Central whites and Southeastern whites

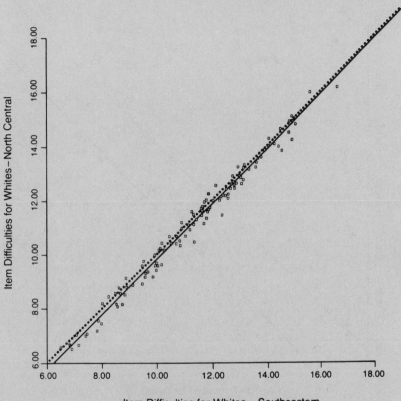

Source: Breland, Stocking, Pinchack, and Abrams (1974), p. 20.

Appendix G-16. Cross-plot of item difficulties for two samples—North Central whites and blacks

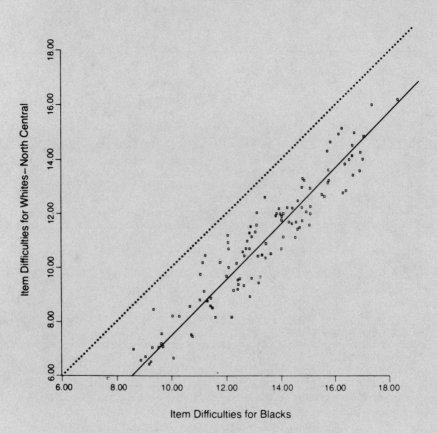

Source: Breland, Stocking, Pinchack, and Abrams (1974), p. 32.

References

Abramowitz, E. *Equal Educational Opportunity for Blacks in U.S. Higher Education: An Assessment.* Report No. 1. Washington, D.C.: Institute for the Study of Educational Policy, Howard University, 1975.

Aiken, L. R., Jr. "The Grading Behavior of a College Faculty." *Educational and Psychological Measurement,* 1963, *23,* 319–322.

Altman, R. A. and Holland, P. W. *A Summary of Data Collected from Graduate Record Examinations Test-Takers During 1975–76.* GRE Data Summary Report No. 1. Princeton, N.J.: Educational Testing Service, 1977.

American Assembly of Collegiate Schools of Business. *Enrollment Trends Survey with Minority Data.* St. Louis, Mo.: 1977.

American Assembly of Collegiate Schools of Business, Statistical Service. *1974 Report on Minority Student Enrollments and Faculty Distribution.* Creve Coeur, Mo.: 1975.

American Bar Association. Law School and Bar Admission Requirements: *A Review of Legal Education in the United States—Fall 1975.* Chicago: 1976.

American Bar Association. *Law School and Bar Admission Requirements: A Review of Legal Education in the United States—Fall 1976.* Chicago: 1977.

American College Testing Program. *Assessing Students on the Way to College.* Iowa City, Iowa: 1973.

American Medical Association. "Medical Education in the U.S. 1975–76." *Journal of American Medical Association,* 1976, *236,* 2964.

American Medical College Application Service. *AMCAS Instruction Booklet.* Washington, D.C.: *Association of American Medical Colleges, 1977.*

Anastasi, A., Meade, M. J., and Schneiders, A. A. *The Validation of a Biographical Inventory as a Predictor of College Success.* Research Monograph No. 1. New York: College Entrance Examination Board, 1960.

Angoff, W. H., and Ford, S. F. "Item-Race Interaction on a Test of Scholastic Aptitude." *Journal of Educational Measurement,* 1973, *10,* 95–106.

Arce, C. H. "Historical, Institutional, and Contextual Determinants of Black Enrollment in Predominately White Colleges, 1946 to 1974." Unpublished doctoral dissertation, University of Michigan, 1976.

Association of American Law Schools. *Proceedings of the 1970 Annual Meeting, Part One, Section II: The Law Schools and the Minority Group Law Students, a Survey for the A.A.L.S. Committee on Minority Groups.* Washington, D.C.: 1970.

Association of American Law Schools and Law School Admission Council. *Pre-Law Handbook: Annual Official Guide to ABA-Approved Law Schools* (1972–73 edition). Washington, D.C., and Princeton, N.J.: 1972.

Association of American Law Schools and Law School Admission Council. *Pre-Law Handbook: Annual Official Guide to ABA-Approved Law Schools* (1976-77 edition). Washington, D.C., and Princeton, N.J.: 1976.

Association of American Medical Colleges. "Proceedings for 1968." *Journal of Medical Education,* 1970, *44,* 731-736.

Association of American Medical Colleges. "Proceedings for 1972." *Journal of Medical Education,* 1973, *48,* 497-530.

Association of American Medical Colleges. "Report of a Study, the MCAT and Success in Medical School." *The MCAAP Report,* 1973, *1* (2), 5-8.

Association of American Medical Colleges. *Minority Student Opportunties in United States Medical Schools 1975-76.* Washington, D.C.: 1975.

Association of American Medical Colleges. *New MCAT Student Manual.* Washington, D.C.: 1976.

Association of American Medical Colleges. *Medical School Admission Requirements 1978-1979.* Washington, D.C.: 1977.

Astin, A. W. "Folklore of Selectivity." *Saturday Review,* 1969, *52* (51), 57.

Astin, A. W. *Predicting Academic Performance in College.* New York: Free Press, 1971.

Astin, A. W., King, M. R., and Richardson, G. T. *The American Freshman: National Norms for Fall 1976.* Los Angeles: University of California and American Council on Education, 1976 (also see previous editions, particularly for 1967, 1970, 1973).

Bailey, J. P., Jr., and Collins, E. F. "Entry into Postsecondary Education." Paper presented at the annual meeting of the American Educational Research Association, New York City, April 1977.

Baird, L. L. *Using Self-Reports to Predict Student Performance.* Research Monograph No. 7. New York: College Entrance Examination Board, 1976a.

Baird, L. L. "Development of an Inventory of Documented Accomplishments: Report on Phase I and Proposal for Phase II." Princeton, N.J.: Educational Testing Service, December 1976b (unpublished paper and proposal for Graduate Record Examinations Board).

Bowles, F. "The Democratization of Education—A World-Wide Revolution." *College Board Review,* Fall 1969, *73,* 11-13.

Breland, H. M., Stocking, M., Pinchack, B. M. and Abrams, N. *The Cross-Cultural Stability of Mental Test Items: An Investigation of Response Patterns for Ten Socio-Cultural Groups.* Project Report 74-2. Princeton, N.J.: Educational Testing Service, 1974.

Brown Daily Herald. "Study Shows Blacks Shunning Top Schools." March 30, 1977, p. 12.

Burns, R. L. *Graduate Admissions and Fellowship Selection Policies and Procedures, Parts I and II.* Princeton, N.J.: Educational Testing Service and Graduate Record Examinations Board, 1970.

Carnegie Commission on Higher Education. *Continuity and Discontinuity: Higher Education and the Schools.* New York: McGraw-Hill, 1973a.

Carnegie Commission on Higher Education. *A Classification of Institutions of Higher Education.* Berkeley, Calif.: 1973b.

Carnegie Council on Policy Studies in Higher Education. *Making Affirmative Action Work in Higher Education.* San Francisco: Jossey-Bass, 1975.

Chauncey, H. and Hilton, T. L. "Are Aptitude Tests Valid for the Highly Able?" *Science,* June 4, 1965, *148,* 1297-1304.

College Entrance Examination Board. "A Statement on Personality Testing," *College Board Review*, Fall 1963, no. 51, 11–13.

College Entrance Examination Board. *A Chance to Go to College: A Directory of 800 Colleges that Have Special Help for Students from Minorities and Low Income Families*. New York: 1971.

College Entrance Examination Board. *About the SAT*. Princeton, N.J. 1976.

College Entrance Examination Board. *A Role for Marketing in College Admissions*. New York: 1976.

Cleary, T. A. "Test Bias: Prediction of Grades of Negro and White Students in Integrated Colleges." *Journal of Educational Measurement*, 1968, *5*, 115–124.

Cleary, T. A., and Hilton, T. L. "An Investigation of Item Bias." *Education and Psychological Measurement*, 1968, *28*, 61–75.

Consortium on Financing Higher Education. *Enrolling the Class of 1979: Second Annual Report on the Student Market at Twenty-Three Institutions*. Hanover, N.H.: October 1976.

Creager, J. A. *Predicting Doctorate Attainment with GRE and Other Variables*. Technical Report No. 25. Washington, D.C.: Office of Scientific Personnel, National Academy of Sciences-National Research Council, 1965.

Cuca, J. M., Sakakeeny, L. A., and Johnson, D. G. *The Medical School Admissions Process: A Review of the Literature 1955–1976*. Washington, D.C.: Association of American Medical Colleges, 1976.

Davis, J. A., and Kerner-Hoeg, S. *Validity of Pre-Admissions Indices for Blacks and Whites in Six Traditionally White Public Universities in North Carolina*. Project Report PR-71-15. Princeton, N.J.: Educational Testing Service, 1971.

D'Costa, A., Bashook, P., Elliott, P., Jarecky, R., Leavell, W., Prieto, D., and Sedlacek, W. *Simulated Minority Admissions Exercise*. Washington, D.C.: Association of American Medical Colleges, 1974.

Doermann, H. "The Future Market for College Education." In *A Role for Marketing in College Admissions*. New York: College Entrance Examination Board, 1976.

Dubé, W. F. "Datagram: Applicants for the 1972–73 Medical School Entering Class." *Journal of Medical Education*, 1973a, *48*, 1161–1163.

Dubé, W. F. "Datagram: U.S. Medical Student Enrollments 1968–1969 through 1972–73." *Journal of Medical Education*, 1973b, *48*, 293–297.

Dubé, W. F. and Gordon, T. L. "Datagram: Applicants for 1975–76 First-Year Medical School Class." *Journal of Medical Education*, 1976, *51*, 867–869.

Dubé, W. F. "Datagram: Medical Student Enrollment, 1972–73 through 1976–77." *Journal of Medical Education*, 1977, *52*, 164–166.

Duncan, D. D., Featherman, D. L., and Duncan, B. *Socioeconomic Background and Achievement*. New York: Seminar Press, 1972.

Dyer, H. S. "Admissions—College and University." In R. L. Ebel (Ed.), *Encyclopedia of Educational Research*. (4th ed.) New York: Macmillan, 1969.

Educational Testing Service. *Graduate and Professional School Opportunities for Minority Students*. (6th ed.) Princeton, N.J.: 1975.

Educational Testing Service. *1976-77 Minority Graduate Student Locater Service*. Princeton, N.J.: 1976.

Educational Testing Service *Graduate Record Examination Information Bulletin, 1977-78*, 1977.

El-Khawas, E. H., and Kinzer, J. L. *Enrollment of Minority Graduate Students at*

Ph.D-Granting Institutions. Higher Education Panel Report No. 19. Washington, D.C.: American Council on Education, 1974.

"Enrollment of Minority Students, 1974." *Chronicle of Higher Education,* Nov. 8, 1976, p. 6.

Erdmann, J. B., Mattsonm, D. E., Hutton, J. G., and Wallace, W.L. "Medical College Admission Test: Past, Present, Future." *Journal of Medical Education,* 1971, *46,* 937–946.

Evans, F. R. *Applications and Admissions to ABA Accredited Law Schools: Fall 1966.* Princeton, N.J.: Law School Admission Council, May 1977.

Freeburg, N. E. "The Biographical Information Blank as a Predictor of Student Achievement: A Review." *Psychological Reports,* 1967, *20,* 911–925.

French, J.W. *The Description of Aptitude and Achievement Tests in Terms of Rotated Factors.* Psychometric Monograph No. 5. Chicago: University of Chicago Press, 1951.

Fuess, C. M. *The College Board: Its First Fifty Years.* New York: College Entrance Examination Board, 1950.

Gellhorn, E., and Hornby, D. B. "Constitutional Limitations on Admissions Procedures and Standards—Beyond Affirmative Action." *Virginia Law Review,* 1974, *60,* 975–1101.

Glazer, N. "Are Academic Standards Obsolete?" *Change,* 1970, *2* (6), 38–44.

Goldman, R. D., and Slaughter, R. E. "Why College Grade Point Average Is Difficult to Predict." *Journal of Educational Psychology,* 1976, *66,* 9–14.

Gordon, E. W. "Transition from School to College: A Review of the Literature." *Review of Educational Research,* 1970, *40,* 151–179.

Gordon, T. L. *Descriptive Study of Medical School Applicants, 1975–76.* Washington, D.C.: Association of American Medical Colleges, 1977.

Graduate Business Admission Council. *Survey of the Admissions Offices of Graduate Schools of Business.* Princeton, N.J.: 1972.

Graduate Management Admission Council. *Graduate Study in Management: A Guide for Prospective Students.* Princeton, N.J.: 1976.

Graduate Management Admission Council. *Memorandum for Graduate Management School Admission Officers,* Princeton, N.J.: Jan. 31, 1977.

Graduate Record Examinations Board. *Graduate Programs and Admissions Manual.* Princeton, N.J.: Educational Testing Service, 1976.

Grant, W. V., and Lind, C. G. *Digest of Educational Statistics: 1975 Edition.* National Center for Education Statistics 76-211. Washington, D.C.: U.S. Government Printing Office, 1976.

Greene, H., and Minton, R. *Scaling the Ivy Wall: Getting into the Selective Colleges.* New York: Abelard-Schuman, 1975.

Hamilton, I. B. *Graduate School Programs for Minority/Disadvantaged Students.* Princeton, N.J.: Educational Testing Service, 1973.

Harbison, F., and Myers, C. A. *Education, Manpower and Economic Growth.* New York: McGraw-Hill, 1964.

Harmon, L. R. "High School Backgrounds of Science Doctorates." *Science,* 1961, *133,* 679–688.

Henderson, A. D., and Gumas, N. B. *Admitting Black Students to Medical and Dental Schools.* Berkeley: Center for Research and Development in Higher Education, University of California, 1971.

Hoyt, D. P. *The Relationship between College Grades and Adult Achievement: A Review of the Literature.* ACT Research Report No. 7. Iowa City, Iowa: American College Testing Program, 1965.

Hughes, E. C., Thorne, B., DeBaggis, A. M., Gurin, A., and Williams, D. *Education for the Professions of Medicine, Law, Theology, and Social Welfare.* New York: McGraw-Hill, 1973.

Johnson, D. G., Smith, V. C., and Tarnoff, S. L. "Recruitment and Progress of Minority Medical School Entrants 1970-1972." *Journal of Medical Education,* 1975, *50,* 713-755.

Kallop, J. W. "A Study of Scholastic Aptitude Test and Eminence." Unpublished manuscript, Princeton University, 1951.

Kinkead, K. T. *How an Ivy League College Decides on Admissions.* New York: W. W. Norton, 1961.

Knapp, J. *Assessing Prior Learning—A CAEL Handbook.* Princeton, N.J.: Educational Testing Service, 1977.

Law School Admission Council. *Description of the Law School Admission Test 1976-77.* Princeton, N.J.: 1976.

Levine, D. M., Weisman, C. S., and Seidel, H. M. *Career Decisions of Unaccepted Applicants to Medical School: A Case Study in Reactions to a Blocked Career Pathway.* Baltimore: Johns Hopkins University, 1974.

Linn, R. L. "Grade Adjustments for Prediction of Academic Performance: A Review." *Journal of Educational Measurement,* 1966, *3,* 313-329.

Linn, R. L. "Fair Test Use in Selection." *Review of Educational Research,* 1973, *43,* 139-161.

Linn, R. L. *Test Bias and the Prediction of Grades in Law School.* LSAC-75-1. Princeton, N.J.: Law School Admission Council, 1974.

Littlemeyer, M. H. (Ed.) *New MCAT Student Manual.* Washington, D.C.: Association of Medical Colleges, 1976.

López, R. W., Madrid-Barela, A., and Macías, R. F. *Chicanos in Higher Education: Status and Issues.* Monograph No. 7. Los Angeles: Chicano Studies Center, University of California, 1976.

Manning, W. H. "Educational Research, Test Validity and Court Decisions." Paper presented at the meeting of the American Educational Research Association, New York, April 1977.

Messick, S. "Personality Measurement and College Performance in Educational Testing Service." *Proceedings of the 1963 Invitational Conference on Testing Programs.* Princeton, N.J.: Educational Testing Service, 1964, 110-129.

National Board on Graduate Education. *Outlook and Opportunities for Graduate Education.* Washington, D.C.: 1975.

National Board on Graduate Education. *Minority Group Participation in Graduate Education.* Washington, D.C.: National Board on Graduate Education and National Academy of Sciences, 1976.

New York Times. "Job Prospects for Young Lawyers Dim as Field Grows Overcrowded." May 17, 1977, pp. 1, 55.

New York Times. "Medical Schools Urged to Intensify Recruitment of Minority Students." May 10, 1977, p. 12.

Novick, M. R., and Ellis, D. D. "Equal Opportunity in Educational and Employment Selection." *American Psychologist,* May 1977, *32,* 306-320.

Odegaard, C. E. *Minorities in Medicine: From Receptive Passivity to Positive Action 1966-1976.* New York: Josiah Macy, Jr., Foundation, 1977.

Oden, M. H. "The Fulfillment of Promise: 40-Year Follow-Up of the Terman Gifted Group." *Genetic Psychology Monographs,* 1968, 77, 3-93.

Pitcher, B. *Summary Report of Validity Studies Carried Out by ETS for Graduate Schools of Business 1954-1970.* Princeton, N. J.: Educational Testing Service, 1971.

Pitcher, B., Schrader, W. B., and Winterbottom, J. A. *Law School Validity Study Service.* Princeton, N.J.: Educational Testing Service, 1976.

Pounds, H. R., Brown, S. L., and Astin, S. *Normative Data for the 1969-1970 Freshman Class, University of Georgia.* Atlanta: Regents of the University System of Georgia, 1970.

Pre-Law Handbook. See full citation under Association of American Law Schools and Law School Admission Council (1972 and 1976).

Reilly, R. R., and Powers, D. E. "Extended Study of the Relationship of Selected Transcript Information to Law School Performance." LSAC-73-4. In Law School Admission Council, *Reports of LSAC Sponsored Research: Volume II, 1970-74.* Princeton, N.J.: Law School Admission Council, 1976.

Rice, L. D. (Ed.) *Student Loans: Problems and Policy Alternatives.* New York: College Entrance Examination Board, 1977.

Richards, J. M., Jr., Holland, J. L., and Lutz, S. W. "Prediction of Student Accomplishment in College." *Journal of Educational Psychology,* 1967, 58, 343-355.

Schein, E. H. *Professional Education: Some New Directions.* New York: McGraw-Hill, 1972.

Schrader, W. B. *Test Data as Social Indicators.* ETS SR-68-77. Princeton, N.J.: Educational Testing Service, 1968.

Schrader, W. B. "The Predictive Validity of College Board Admission Tests." In W. H. Angoff (Ed.), *The College Board Admissions Testing Program: A Technical Report on Research and Development Activities Relating to the Scholastic Aptitude Test and Achievment Tests.* New York: College Entrance Examination Board, 1971.

Schrader, W. B., and Pitcher, B. *Predicting Law School Grades for Black American Law Students.* LSAC-73-6. Princeton, N.J.: Law School Admission Council, 1973.

Schrader, W. B., and Pitcher, B. *Prediction of Law School Grades for Mexican American and Black American Students.* LSAC-74-8. Princeton, N.J.: Law School Admission Council, 1974.

Sedlacek, W. E. (Ed.). *Medical College Admission Test: Handbook for Admissions Committees.* (2nd ed.). Evanston, Ill.: Association of American Medical Colleges, 1967.

Simon, K. A., and Frankel, M. M. *Projections of Education Statistics to 1984-85.* National Center for Education Statistics 76-210. Washington, D.C.: U.S. Government Printing Office, 1976.

Somerville, J. I. *Report on the Council of Graduate Schools—Graduate Record Examinations Board 1976-77 Survey of Graduate Enrollment, Part I.* CGS Communicator Special Report No. 8. Princeton, N.J.: Educational Testing Service, December 1976.

Somerville, J. I. *Report on the Council of Graduate Schools—Graduate Record Examinations Board 1976-77 Survey of Graduate Enrollment, Part II.* CGS

Communicator Special Report No. 10, May 1977. Princeton, N.J.: Educational Testing Service, December 1977.

Suslow, S. "Grade Inflation: End of a Trend?" *Change,* March 1977, *9* (3), 44-45.

Temp, G. "Test Bias: Validity of the SAT for Blacks and Whites in Thirteen Integrated Institutions." *Journal of Educational Measurement,* 1971, *8,* 245-251.

Terman, L. M. *Genetic Studies of Genius: I. Mental and Physical Traits of a Thousand Gifted Children.* Stanford, Calif.: Stanford University Press, 1925.

Thorndike, R. L. "Concepts of Culture-Fairness." *Journal of Educational Measurement,* 1971, *8,* 63-70.

Thresher, B. A. *College Admissions and the Public Interest.* New York: College Entrance Examination Board, 1966.

Tiffin, J., and McCormick, E. J. *Industrial Psychology* (6th ed.) Englewood Cliffs, N.J.: Prentice-Hall, 1974.

Turnbull, A. R., Mckee, W. S., and Galloway, L. T. "Law School Admissions: A Descriptive Study." Report no. LSAC-72-7. In Law School Admission Council, *Reports of LSAC Sponsored Research: Volume II, 1970-74.* Princeton, N.J.: Law School Admission Council, 1976, 276-332.

Turner, R. C. "Enrollment Prospects in Graduate Schools of Business: The Next Ten Years." Keynote address at the annual meeting of the Graduate Management Admission Council, San Francisco, May 1977.

U.S. Bureau of the Census. *Statistical Abstract of the United States.* Washington, D.C.: U.S. Government Printing Office, 1968.

U.S. Bureau of the Census. "Projections of the Population of the United States: 1977-2050." *Current Population Reports,* series P-25, no. 704. Washington, D.C.: U.S. Government Printing Office, 1977.

U.S. Department of Health, Education, and Welfare, Office for Civil Rights. *Racial and Ethnic Enrollment Data from Institutions of Higher Education, Fall 1968.* Washington, D.C.: U.S. Government Printing Office, 1970.

U.S. Department of Health, Education, and Welfare, Office for Civil Rights. *Racial and Ethnic Enrollment Data from Institutions of Higher Education, Fall 1970.* Washington, D.C.: U.S. Government Printing Office, 1972.

U.S. Department of Health, Education, and Welfare, Office for Civil Rights. *Racial and Ethnic Enrollment Data from Institutions of Higher Education, Fall 1972.* Washington, D.C.: U.S. Government Printing Office, 1975.

U.S. Department of Health, Education, and Welfare, Office for Civil Rights. *Racial and Ethnic Enrollment Data from Institutions of Higher Education, Fall 1974.* Washington, D.C.: U.S. Government Printing Office, 1976.

University of California, Berkeley. *Developing Opportunities for Minorities in Graduate Education.* Proceedings of a conference on minority graduate education. Berkeley, Calif.: Graduate Minority Program, Graduate Division, 1973.

Waldman, B. *Economic and Racial Disadvantage as Reflected in Traditional Medical School Selection Factors: A Study of 1976 Applicants to U.S. Medical Schools.* Washington, D.C.: Association of American Medical Colleges, 1977.

Wallach, M. A. "Psychology of Talent and Graduate Education." In S. Messick and associates, *Individuality in Learning.* San Francisco: Jossey-Bass, 1976.

Wallach, M. A., and Wing, C. W., Jr. *The Talented Student: A Validation of the Creativity-Intelligence Distinction.* New York: Holt, Rinehart and Winston, 1969.

Ward, L. B. "The Interview as an Assessment Technique." In College Entrance

Examination Board, *College Admissions 2.* New York: College Entrance Examination Board, 1955, 62-710.

Washington, W. E., et al. (Petitioners) vs. Davis, A. E. et al. (Respondents). *Motion for Leave to File Brief as Amicus Curiae and Brief Amicus Curiae for Educational Testing Service* (on Writ of Certiorari to the United States Court of Appeals for the District of Columbia Circuit). Supreme Court of the United States, October term, 1975.

Webb, S. C. "Changes in Student Personal Qualities Associated with Change in Intellectual Abilities." *College and University,* 1966, *41,* (3), 280-289.

Willingham, W. W. "Erroneous Assumptions in Predicting College Grades." *Journal of Counseling Psychology,* 1963, *10,* 389-394.

Willingham, W. W. *The Source Book for Higher Education.* New York: College Entrance Examination Board, 1973a.

Willingham, W. W. "Transfer Standards and the Public Interest." Paper presented at the Airlie House Conference on College Transfer, December 1973b.

Willingham, W. W. "Predicting Success in Graduate Education," *Science,* Jan. 25, 1974, *183,* 273-278.

Wing, C. W., Jr., and Wallach, M. A. *College Admissions and the Psychology of Talent.* New York: Holt, Rinehart and Winston, 1971.

Wright, O. R., Jr. "Summary of Research on the Selection Interview Since 1964." *Personnel Psychology,* 1969, *22,* 391-413.

Index